BEYOND THE GLOBAL CAPITALIST CRISIS

T0300527

Globalization, Crises, and Change

Series Editor

Professor Berch Berberoglu
University of Nevada, Reno, USA

Careful sociological analysis of the dynamics and contradictions of neoliberal globalization is sorely needed in order to assess the social consequences of this process on affected populations and develop appropriate responses to overcome the current global economic, political, and social crises.

Volumes in the series will focus on three interrelated processes that are the product of the latest phase of global capitalist development at the end of the twentieth and the beginning of the twenty-first century:

1. The nature and dynamics of neoliberal globalization;
2. the worldwide contradictions and crises of neoliberal globalization;
3. the responses to neoliberal globalization with focus on social change and transformation including popular social movements based on grassroots people's organizations, mass protests, rebellions, and revolution.

Taken together, these provide a comprehensive analysis of the nature, contradictions, and transformation of globalization through its inner logic that ultimately leads to the changes wrought by this process on a global scale. The significance of this series is that it provides the opportunity to examine this multifaceted phenomenon that has had (and continues to have) a major impact on society and societal development in our time.

Beyond the Global Capitalist Crisis
The World Economy in Transition

Edited by

BERCH BERBEROGLU
University of Nevada, Reno, USA

LONDON AND NEW YORK

First published 2012 by Ashgate Publishing

2 Park Square, Milton Park, Abingdon, Oxon OX14 4RN
711 Third Avenue, New York, NY 10017, USA

Routledge is an imprint of the Taylor & Francis Group, an informa business

First issued in paperback 2017

Copyright © 2012 Berch Berberoglu

Berch Berberoglu has asserted his right under the Copyright, Designs and Patents Act, 1988, to be identified as the editor of this work.

All rights reserved. No part of this book may be reprinted or reproduced or utilised in any form or by any electronic, mechanical, or other means, now known or hereafter invented, including photocopying and recording, or in any information storage or retrieval system, without permission in writing from the publishers.

Notice:
Product or corporate names may be trademarks or registered trademarks, and are used only for identification and explanation without intent to infringe.

British Library Cataloguing in Publication Data
Beyond the global capitalist crisis : the world economy in
    transition.--(Globalization, crises, and change)
    1. Economic history--21st century. 2. Capitalism--
    History--21st century. 3. Globalization--Economic
    aspects. 4. International economic relations--History--
    21st century. 5. Global Financial Crisis, 2008-2009.
    I. Series II. Berberoglu, Berch.
    337-dc22

Library of Congress Cataloging-in-Publication Data
Beyond the global capitalist crisis : the world economy in transition / by
Berch Berberoglu.
       p. cm. -- (Globalization, crises, and change)
    Includes bibliographical references and index.
    ISBN 978-1-4094-1239-7 (hardback)
    1. Capitalism--History. 2. Income distribution--History. 3.
Recessions--History. 4. Financial crises--History. 5.
Globalization--History. I. Berberoglu, Berch.
    HB501.B487 2011
    330.9'0511--dc23

                                                                                  2011018596

ISBN 978-1-4094-1239-7 (hbk)
ISBN 978-1-138-11734-1 (pbk)

Contents

List of Figures

List of Tables

Notes on Contributors

Berch Berberoglu is Professor and Director of Graduate Studies in Sociology at the University of Nevada, Reno, where he has taught for 34 years. He received his Ph.D. in sociology from the University of Oregon in 1977. His areas of specialization include globalization, class analysis, political economy of development, and comparative-historical sociology. He is the author and editor of 28 books and many articles, including *Labor and Capital in the Age of Globalization, Globalization of Capital and the Nation-State, Globalization and Change, Class and Class Conflict in the Age of Globalization* and *Globalization in the 21st century.*

Mike-Frank G. Epitropoulos is a Lecturer in Sociology and the Faculty Director of the University of Pittsburgh's *Pitt in Greece Program.* He received his Ph.D. in sociology from the University of Pittsburgh in 1999. His interests are grounded in teaching sociology and practicing public sociology, and he has taught in both Greece and the United States. His areas of specialization include development, political economy, state theory, social movements and Greece. He is a regular contributor to *Znet* and the editor (with Victor Roudometof) of *American Culture in Europe: Interdisciplinary Perspectives.*

Walda Katz-Fishman is Professor of Sociology at Howard University in Washington, D.C., where she has taught for 40 years. She received her Ph.D. from Wayne State University in 1978. She is a public sociologist and scholar activist who combines theory and practice through her scholarship and teaching on social theory, political economy, inequality, race, class, gender, and social change, and her participation in grassroots organizations and transformative social movements. She has published numerous articles and books, and is an editor and contributor to *The United States Social Forum: Perspectives of a Movement.*

Martin Orr is Associate Professor of Sociology at Boise State University. He received his Ph.D. in Sociology from the University of Oregon in 1992. His research and teaching interests include social inequality, social movements, the environment, political sociology, and global political economy. He has published numerous articles on these and related issues focused on the crisis of global capitalism and its transformation.

James Petras is Emeritus Professor of Sociology, State University of New York at Binghamton and Adjunct Professor at St. Mary's University in Halifax,

Nova Scotia, Canada. He received his Ph.D. from the University of California at Berkeley in political science in 1967. His areas of specialization include the political economy of the U.S. Empire, social movements, and Latin America. He has published 65 books in 29 languages and over 500 articles. He is the author of *Global Depression and Regional Wars* and co-author (with Henry Veltmeyer) of *Globalization Unmasked: Imperialism in the 21st Century, System in Crisis, Multinationals on Trial,* and other books.

Jerome Scott is a labor and community organizer and educator in Atlanta, Georgia for over 30 years. He is a founder and former director of Project South: Institute for the Elimination of Poverty & Genocide, and a founding member of the League of Revolutionary Black Workers in Detroit in the late 1960s. He serves on the U.S. Social Forum National Planning Committee and is active in transformative social movement organizations. He has published numerous articles on race, class, movement building and the revolutionary process, and is an editor and contributor to *The United States Social Forum: Perspectives of a Movement.*

Howard J. Sherman is Professor Emeritus of Economics, University of California, Riverside, and Visiting Scholar in Political Science at the University of California at Los Angeles. He received his Ph.D. in Economics from the University of California at Berkeley in 1964. He has published numerous books and many articles on the political economy of capitalism, including *The Business Cycle: Growth and Crisis Under Capitalism, How Society Makes Itself: The Evolution of Political and Economic Institutions,* and *The Roller Coaster Economy: Financial Crisis, Great Recession, and the Public Option.*

Alvin Y. So is Professor in the Division of Social Science at Hong Kong University of Science and Technology. He received his Ph.D. in sociology from the University of California at Los Angeles in 1982. His research interests include social classes and the development of China and East Asia. He is the author of *The South China Silk District; Social Change and Development;* and *East Asia and the World Economy.* He is the editor or co-editor of several volumes, including *China's Developmental Miracle: Origins, Transformations, and Challenges.*

Alan J. Spector is Professor of Sociology at Purdue University Calumet in Hammond, Indiana. He received his Ph.D. in sociology from Northwestern University in Evanston, Illinois in 1980. His areas of teaching and research interests include political economy, globalization, capitalist crises, and social change. He is currently on the editorial board of the journal *Critical Sociology* and is the co-author (with Peter Knapp) of *Crisis and Change Today: Basic Questions of Marxist Sociology.*

Henry Veltmeyer is Professor of Sociology and Development Studies at Saint Mary's University, Halifax, Nova Scotia, Canada and the Universidad Autónoma de Zacatecas in Mexico. He is author, co-author, and editor of over 40 books on issues of Latin American and world development, including *Transcending Neoliberalism: Community-Based Development in Latin America* and *Dynamics of Social Change in Latin America,* and with James Petras, *Globalization Unmasked, System in Crisis, Social Movements and the State, Multinationals on Trial, What's Left in Latin America*, and, most recently, *Social Movements in Latin America: Neoliberalism and Popular Resistance.*

This book is dedicated to
my uncle "Koko"
for his friendship, intellectual curiosity,
and political wisdom.

Preface and Acknowledgements

As the first decade of the twenty-first century comes to a close and a new decade begins to unfold, the global capitalist system continues to be in deep crisis. And this latest crisis of the system which began in late 2007 and continued through late 2009, labeled "the Great Recession" in the United States—for being the deepest and most severe economic crisis since the Great Depression of the 1930s—has rapidly spread around the world, first in Europe, East and West, then to the less-developed and countries across the globe, including Latin America, Asia, Africa and the Middle East, is now threatening to become a full blown crisis of depression proportions. While the U.S. treasury has already collapsed and depends on heavy debt-financing and printing of dollars to see its way out of total collapse, other countries, especially in Europe—from Hungary to Ukraine and from Iceland to Ireland and Greece and the rest of the PIIGS in between, including Portugal, Spain and Italy—have come face to face with bankruptcy and default in the unfolding sovereign debt crisis that only powerful international financial institutions, such as the IMF and the World Bank, have been able to bail them out for the time being to secure them another day amidst mass protests, demonstrations, and the emergence of a revolutionary situation that governments across Europe are forced to extinguish by moving against their people in revolt—and this includes nominally Socialist states, such as Greece, where the people are up in arms against the Socialist government of Papandreou.

Neoliberal capitalist globalization and "free market"/"free trade" policies of puppet states in the less-developed countries that promote privatization, foreign investment, and foreign control of resources allowed by these collaborator pro-imperialist regimes, such as those in Latin America during the 1980s and 1990s, have been replaced during the 2000s, as many countries in this region—such as Venezuela, Brazil, Argentina, Uruguay, Chile, Bolivia, Ecuador, Nicaragua, El Salvador, and others—have moved to the left, adopting policies away from neoliberalism. Likewise, many countries across North Africa and the Middle East that have followed a similar neoliberal path reliant on imperialism and ruled by puppet dictators for decades, such as in Tunisia, Egypt, Yemen, Bahrain, and elsewhere in the region, have collapsed and are in the process of being replaced through the protracted struggles of the laboring masses who have suffered long from extreme poverty and destitution inflicted upon them by the global capitalist system and its internal collaborator agents that have been kept in power by the United States and other imperialist states that are now themselves in trouble and face at once collapse and resistance as the era of Empire comes to an end, and as we move beyond the global capitalist crisis and towards a more just and egalitarian system in the early decades of this new, twenty-first century.

Clearly, we now live in challenging times, and as the global capitalist crisis leads to the collapse of Empire and disintegration of the imperialist states, the process of transition and transformation of the world economy and society will usher in a new configuration of forces that will lead us into the twenty-first century. The chapters included in this book provide us a superb analysis of the origins, development, and unfolding of this drama on the global scene and chart the course of this process that is evolving and will—of necessity—culminate in the great transformations that are yet to come in this what promises to become a tumultuous and turbulent century.

A project of this nature involves the contributions of many people—above all, the contributors of this book: my mentors Jim Petras and Howard Sherman, my colleagues and friends Henry Veltmeyer, Alan Spector, Martin Orr, Walda Katz-Fishman, Jerome Scott, Alvin So, and Mike-Frank Epitropoulos. Others, who have contributed to discussions on many of the issues examined in the pages of this book, include Jan Nederveen Pieterse, David Elliott, Johnson W. Makoba, David Lott, and many others. Most of the chapters included in this book are original works that were commissioned specifically for this book. The chapters by James Petras, Howard Sherman, and Henry Veltmeyer are revised and edited versions of sections of their recently published books or articles that are reprinted here with the permission of the authors and the publishers, with full acknowledgement and credit given in a footnote on the first page of their respective chapters. This book was funded in part by the Scholarly and Creative Activities Grant Program of the College of Liberal Arts at the University of Nevada, Reno. I would like to thank Dean Heather Hardy and members of the grant committee for providing me with financial assistance to complete this project. Finally, I would like to thank my wife Suzan for her unwavering intellectual support and encouragement to undertake this project and bring it to fruition. This book is dedicated to my 84-year-young uncle "Koko" for his keen understanding of the dynamics of the global political economy and for the many hours we have spent discussing issues surrounding the global economic crisis while traveling together through several countries as I delivered numerous lectures on globalization and the global economic crisis at universities in the United States, the Czech Republic, Austria, Greece, Cyprus, and Turkey over the course of the past several years. I am grateful for his friendship, intellectual curiosity, and political wisdom in contributing to the untangling of complex issues that we face in the world today.

Berch Berberoglu

Chapter 1

Introduction: The Global Capitalist Crisis and its Aftermath

Berch Berberoglu

Global capitalism is in serious crisis, and the current continuing severe global recession is the worst economic downturn since the Great Depression of the early twentieth century. As neoliberal capitalist globalization comes under mounting criticism and attack across the world, and as the global economic crisis takes on depression-era characteristics, neoliberalism and neoliberal economic policies have now become thoroughly discredited in many countries around the world. As millions of unemployed working people look for a job to pay for their basic necessities, capitalist states throughout the world have spent hundreds of billions of tax dollars to bail out failed commercial and financial institutions, with more than a trillion dollars of economic stimulus program by the United States government alone and several hundreds of billions of dollars by other governments in Europe, China, and elsewhere, to save the global capitalist system from total collapse.

Despite the active role of the imperial state in intervening in the global capitalist economy to reverse its decline and fall, corporations and banks, ranging from mainstays of capitalist economies, such as General Motors and Chrysler, to some of the biggest commercial banks, such as Citigroup and Bank of America, to financial and brokerage firms, insurance companies, and real estate underwriters, such as Lehman Brothers, American Insurance Group (AIG), Fannie Mae and Freddie Mack, have come to a halt with some having declared bankruptcy, and by so doing have threatened to take down with them the entire global capitalist system. As a result, and with a ripple effect across the U.S. economy over a period of less than a year, the U.S. stock market plunged more than 50 percent from its highs of 14,000 in late 2007 to 6,500 in early 2009, with more than a trillion dollars of value lost in the stock market—a development that has shaken markets across the globe and resulted in similar losses in stock markets throughout the capitalist world. Clearly, from late 2007 to early 2009 capitalism has gone through its biggest worldwide economic decline since the Great Depression of 1929, and this has come to signal the end of global capitalism as we have come to know it.

Although the U.S. stock market has recovered from its February 2009 low of around 6,500 to above 12,000 in February 2011, with hundreds of billions of dollars in profits recovered by the owners of capital, such recovery has not touched millions of workers who have lost their jobs and millions more who have lost their homes to foreclosures, while the living conditions of tens of millions of employed workers have deteriorated to the point of a drastic decline in their standard of living, shouldering massive personal and family debt, compounded by a national debt that they have been forced to bare for the bailout of failed banks and financial institutions, as well as costly wars from which only a small segment of the population (the capitalist class) benefits at the cost of the working people and the nation as a whole. Hence we have the irony of Wall Street recovery (amassing of enormous profits) and Main Street decline and demise (and increasing destitution) of the working class now facing continued high levels of unemployment, loss of benefits, and a precarious existence near the boundaries of poverty and mass deprivation, which is threatening the very fabric of life under advanced capitalism.

Given the failure of neoliberalism and neoliberal capitalist policies around the world, capitalist globalization—as an extension of the capitalist system in general on a global scale—has led to such a crisis across the world that many are now asking what is in store for the future of the global economy and which direction it will take in the period ahead. This was the main topic of discussion among the leaders of the world's leading economies at the G-20 meetings in London in April 2009, which resulted in guarded optimism that through substantial reforms in global financial institutions and an active interventionist state that monitors the situation with greater regulation of the economy, the evolving economic situation might provide the basis of a new global economic order. What that order will look like and what role the United States will play in it are questions that remain open and contingent on the solutions adopted at the national and global levels, especially in Europe, East and South Asia, and other emergent centers of global economic power in the aftermath of the current global capitalist crisis.

Contradictions and Crises of Global Capitalism and the Capitalist State

The development of capitalism over the past one-hundred years has formed and transformed capitalism in a crucial way, one that is characterized by periodic crises resulting from the capitalist business cycle that now unfolds at the global level. The current crisis of global capitalism is an outcome of the consolidation of monopoly power that the globalization of capital has secured for the transnational monopolies (Sassen 2009). This has led to a string of problems associated with the contradiction between the expanded forces of production and existing exploitative social relations of production (i.e., class relations), which manifests itself in a number of ways, including:

1. The problem of overproduction, resulting from the imbalance created between wages and prices of commodities fueled by low purchasing power;
2. Sub-prime mortgage and credit card debt and rising foreclosures and bankruptcies as the unemployed become unable to pay off their debts;
3. Increasing unemployment and underemployment resulting from outsourcing of jobs to low-wage sweatshops in export processing zones abroad,

compounded by the continued application of high technology in production (i.e., automation);

4. Intensification of the exploitation of labor through expanded production and reproduction of surplus value and profits by further accumulation of capital and the reproduction of capitalist relations of production on a world scale;

5. Increased polarization of wealth and income at the national and global level between the capitalist and working classes and growth in numbers of the poor and marginalized segments of the population throughout the world.

These and other related contradictions and crises of global capitalism define the parameters of modern capitalist imperialism and provide us the framework of discussion on the nature and dynamics of imperialism, capitalist globalization, and the global capitalist crisis today.

Given the logic of global capital accumulation in late capitalist society, it is no accident that the decline of the domestic economy of advanced capitalist countries over the past three decades corresponds to the accelerated export of capital abroad in search of cheap labor, access to raw materials, new markets, and higher rates of profit. The resulting deindustrialization of the domestic economy has had a serious impact on workers and other affected segments of the laboring population and has brought about a major dislocation of the national economy (Bluestone and Harrison 1982; Phillips 1998; Berberoglu 2003).[1] This has necessitated increased state intervention on behalf of the monopolies and has heightened the contradictions that led to the crisis of advanced capitalist society in the early twenty-first century.

The widening gap between the accumulated wealth of the capitalist class and the declining incomes of workers (within a deteriorating national economy and the state's budgetary crisis) has led to the ensuing political crisis within the state apparatus and has sharpened the class struggle in a new political direction. As the crisis of the capitalist economy has brought the advanced capitalist/imperial state to the center stage of economic life and revealed its direct ties to the monopolies, thus exacerbating the state's legitimization crisis, the struggles of the working class and the masses in general are becoming directed not only against capital, but against the state itself.

The crisis of the capitalist state on the global scene is a manifestation of the contradictions of the world economy, which in the early twenty-first century has reached a critical stage in its development. The massive flow of U.S. transnational investment throughout the world, especially in Western Europe, Japan, and other advanced capitalist regions, has led to the post-World War II reemergence of inter-imperialist rivalry between the major capitalist powers, while fostering

---

1   This paradox of growth and expansion of capital on a world scale, simultaneously with the decline and contraction of the domestic economy, is a central feature of globalization and imperialism at its highest and most intense stage of worldwide capitalist expansion. For further elaboration on this point see Berberoglu (2003, 2005, and 2010).

antagonisms between them in the scramble for the peripheral regions of the global capitalist economy through the imposition of neoliberal policies across Latin America, Asia, Africa, and the Middle East (Hart 1992; Falk 1999; Halliday 2001).

With the integration of the economies of Western Europe into the European Union (EU) and the emergence of China as a powerful economic force in the late twentieth and early twenty-first century, the position of the United States in the global economy has declined relative to both its own postwar supremacy in the 1940s and 1950s and to other advanced capitalist economies since that time. Despite the fact that U.S. capital continues to control the biggest share of overseas markets and accounts for the largest volume of international investments, its hold on the global economy has recently begun slipping in a manner similar to Britain's in the early twentieth century. This has, in turn, led the U.S. state to play a more aggressive role in foreign policy to protect U.S. transnational interests abroad. Its massive deployment in the Middle East in the early 1990s, which led to the Persian Gulf War of 1991, and subsequently its intervention in Afghanistan in 2001 and war against Iraq in 2003 (both of which are still continuing as of 2011) has resulted in great military expenditures that has translated into an enormous burden on working people of the United States, who have come to shoulder the colossal cost of maintaining a global empire whose vast military machine encompasses the world (Berberoglu 1999, 2003, 2005).

In the current phase of the crisis of U.S. capitalism and the capitalist state the problems the state faces are of such magnitude that they threaten the supremacy of the United States in the global political economy and by extension the global capitalist system itself. Internal economic and budgetary problems have been compounded by ever-growing military spending propped up by armed intervention abroad, while a declining economic base at home manifested in the housing and banking crisis, deindustrialization, and a recessionary economy is further complicated by the global rivalry between the major capitalist powers plus China that is not always restricted to the economic field, but has political (and even military) implications that are global in magnitude (Harvey 2003; see also Panitch and Leys 2003).

The growing prospects of inter-imperialist rivalry between the major economic powers, backed up by their states, are effecting changes in their relations that render the global political economy an increasingly unstable character. Competition between the United States, Japan, and Europe, and the emergence of China, Russia, and other rival states, are leading them on a collision course for world supremacy, manifested in struggles for markets, raw materials, and spheres of influence in geopolitical—as well as economic—terms, which may in fact lead to a new balance of forces, and, consequently, alliances that will have serious political implications in global power politics. As the continuing economic ascendance of the major economic rivals of the United States take their prominent position in the global economy, pressures will build toward the politicization and militarization of these states from within, where the forces of the leading class bent on dominating the world economy will press forward with the necessary political and military corollary of their growing economic power in the global capitalist system (Hart 1992; Falk 1999), as has been the case with the German, French, Russian, and Chinese opposition to war against Iraq in the United Nations Security Council in 2003.

These developments in global economic and geopolitical shifts in the balance of forces among the major powers will bring to the fore new and yet untested international alliances for world supremacy and domination in the post—cold war era. Such alliances will bring key powers such as Russia and China into play in a new and complicated relationship that holds the key for the success or failure of the newly rising economic centers that will emerge as the decisive forces in the global economic, political, and military equation in the early decades of the twenty-first century (Halliday 2001; Guthrie 2006; Stephens 2009).

The contradictions and conflicts imbedded in relations between the rival states of the world will again surface as an important component of international relations in the years ahead. And these are part and parcel of the restructuring of the international division of labor and the transfer of production to overseas territories in line with the globalization of capital on a worldwide basis—a process that has serious consequences for the economies of both the advanced capitalist and less-developed capitalist countries. Economic decline in the imperial centers (manifested in plant closings, unemployment, and recession) and super-exploitation of workers around the world (maintained by repressive military regimes) yield the same combined result that has a singular global logic: the accumulation of transnational profits for the capitalist class of the advanced capitalist countries—above all, that of the United States, the current center of global capitalism. It is in this context of the changes that are taking place on a world scale that the imperial state is beginning to confront the current crisis of global capitalism.

Impact of Capitalist Globalization on the Current Global Economic Crisis

The global expansion of capital (i.e., capitalist globalization) has had a great impact on the current global economic crisis. This impact is the result of the globalization process which has destroyed national economies in the interests of transnational capital that profits from its global operations on a worldwide basis. This has brought about contradictions at a dual level. At the global level, it has meant first and foremost the ever-growing exploitation of workers through the use of cheap labor. In addition, it has caused a depletion of resources that could be used for national development, as well as environmental pollution, and other health hazards, a growing national debt, tying many countries to the World Bank, the International Monetary Fund, and other global financial institutions, and a growing militarization of society through the institution of brutal military and civilian dictatorships that violate basic human rights. The domination and control of less-developed countries for transnational profits through the instrumentality of the imperial state has at the same time created various forms of dependence on the center that has become a defining characteristic of globalization in the age of imperialism (Amaladoss 1999; Sklair 2002).

Domestically, the globalization of capital and imperialist expansion has had immense dislocations in the national economies of imperialist states. Expansion of manufacturing industry abroad has meant a decline in local industry, as plant closings in the United States and other advanced capitalist countries have worsened the unemployment situation. The massive expansion of capital abroad has resulted in hundreds of factory shutdowns with millions of workers losing their jobs, hence the surge in unemployment in the United States and other imperialist states (Wagner 2000). This has led to a decline in wages of workers in the advanced capitalist centers, as low wages abroad have played a competitive role in keeping wages down in the imperialist heartlands. The drop in incomes among a growing section of the U.S. working class has thus lowered the standard of living in general and led to a further polarization between labor and capital (Berberoglu 1992a, 2002).

The globalization of capital and the integration of national capitalist economies into the global capitalist system, a process that has been developing over the past several decades, and its intensification under neoliberal policies over the past twenty years, has had a direct impact on the extent and depth of the current global economic crisis. Previously nationally-based economies, now under the control of transnational corporations and international financial institutions, have become appendages of the global economy that operates under the logic of global capital accumulation for the benefit of the transnationals and their owners, while at a great cost to those who become victims of this process.

A major global economic crisis, such as the one we are experiencing today, greatly affects the economies of those nations that have become part of the global capitalist system. Thus, all the known consequences of such economic downturn (growing consumer debt, rising unemployment and underemployment, declining purchasing power, home mortgage foreclosures, bankruptcies, and a host of other economic problems) are the very ingredients of a system-wide crisis that has affected not only the advanced capitalist countries (where the current crisis originated), but all others integrated into the global capitalist system. And more so is the case with the latter, as they are more vulnerable to the forces of the global economy and its periodic crises.

The contradictions of global capitalist expansion, which has caused so much exploitation, oppression, and misery for the peoples of the world, both in the less-developed and in the imperialist countries themselves, has in turn created the conditions for its own downfall. Economically, it has afflicted the system with recessions, depressions, and associated realization crises; politically, it has set into motion an imperial interventionist state that through its presence in every corner of the world has incurred an enormous military expenditure to maintain an empire, while gaining the resentment of millions of people across the globe who are engaged in active struggle against it.[2]

The imperial capitalist state, acting as the repressive arm of global capital and extending its rule across vast territories, has dwarfed the militaristic adventures of past empires many times over. The global capitalist state, through its political and military supremacy, has come to exert its control over many countries and has thus facilitated the exploitation of labor on a world scale. As a result, it has reinforced the domination of capital over labor and its rule on behalf of capital. This, in turn, has greatly politicized the struggle between labor and capital and called for the recognition of the importance of political organization that many find necessary to effect change in order to transform the global capitalist system.

The greatest voices are being heard in this regard in countries most affected by the global capitalist crisis, in particular the southern European countries of Greece, Portugal, Spain, and Italy, as well as Ireland and Iceland further north. But, while there has developed a mass movement against neoliberalism across Latin America over the past several decades, the center of attention has quickly turned to the Middle East, as rebellion and revolution have spread across North Africa, from Tunisia to Egypt and the rest of the Middle East, including Yemen, Bahrain, Jordan, Lebanon, and Iran.

The contradictions of the unfolding process of global expansion and accumulation have brought to the fore new political realities: renewed repression at home and abroad to control an increasingly frustrated working class in the imperial heartland, and a militant and revolutionary mass of workers and peasants in the Third World poised to resist capitalist globalization (Houtart and Polet 2001; Petras and Veltmeyer 2001; Polet 2007). It is these inherent contradictions of modern global capitalism that are making it increasingly difficult for the imperial state to control and manage the global political economy, while at the same time preparing the conditions for international solidarity of workers in confronting global capital throughout the world.

---

2 While one consequence of imperialism and globalization has been economic contraction and an associated class polarization, a more costly and dangerous outcome of this process has been increased militarization and intervention abroad, such that the defense of an expanding capitalist empire worldwide has come to require an increasing military presence and a permanent interventionist foreign policy to keep the global economy clear of obstructions to safeguard the interests of the transnational monopolies. However, such aggressive military posture has had (and continues to create) major problems for the imperialist state and is increasingly threatening its effectiveness and, in the long run, its very existence (see Petras 2009).

Outline of the Book

This book has been conceived as a long-term project exploring the evolution, development, crises, and transformation of global capitalism and its impact around the world through the current global capitalist crisis and beyond. While it is important to understand the origins and sources of the global economic crisis that has spread to every corner of the world, it is equally important to focus on the future course of development of the world economy beyond the current global capitalist crisis. And it is in this spirit that the problems associated with this crisis are explored, while its inherent internal contradictions are *exposed*.

Following this introductory chapter, Alan J. Spector provides in Chapter 2 a survey of the evolution of the capitalist economy from its early beginnings through its many crises over the course of its development from the nineteenth to the early twenty-first century. Spector argues that the global capitalist crisis that intensified in 2008 was not simply the result of unethical or irresponsible investments by a few rogue financial institutions. Rather, it was the culmination of the basic dynamics and contradictions that are internal to capitalist economies—the contradiction between the extraordinary productive capacity of capitalist industry and the profit system that ultimately chokes off production, as the goods that are produced cannot be sold at a sustainable level of profit. These contradictions, Spector adds, evolved into major periodic crises, as Marx and others predicted, but as financial institutions attained supremacy in the economy and economic and political power became more tightly intertwined around the globe, it was possible, for a time, to sustain profitability by using cheap labor and securing markets for goods in other countries. By the early 1900s, Spector reminds us, capitalist "boom and bust" cycles were engulfing major parts of the world, and economic rivalry among the powerful capitalist states became political conflicts that developed into military confrontation resulting in World War I.

The twentieth century was characterized by periods of conflict and collaboration driven by the needs of various capitalist powers to maintain stability of the capitalist system. The period that followed was a period of major worldwide economic collapse and political tension, leading to World War II. For two decades after the war, Spector points out, the "boom and bust" cycles of capitalism continued, but were somewhat softened because (1) the devastation of the war created a new "market" for goods as Europe and Japan had to be rebuilt and reindustrialized and (2) the United States had emerged from the war much stronger than the other capitalist powers and was therefore able to negotiate the terms for international commerce that favored U.S. interests. However, as the other capitalist powers rebuilt their industrial engines, intense rivalry reemerged. By the 1970s, Western Europe and Japan were again crowding the marketplace and secondary powers, including OPEC, were also impinging on the profits of the major powers. International financial arrangements were renegotiated. The decline of resistance in the "less-developed countries" and the development of neoliberal policies enforced by the World Bank and International Monetary Fund resulted in intensified exploitation of those areas leading to more profitability. But even this flow of profits could not stop the inherent contradictions from reemerging. As the twentieth century drew to a close, Spector concludes, economic conditions were in place that set the stage for the widespread financial speculation that first alleviated and then greatly intensified the contradictions within global capitalism. The fundamental contradictions of capitalism have taken many forms and evolved into global processes, but the core contradictions of this exploitative system have emerged again and again, as in the latest round of global capitalist crisis that we are experiencing today.

Howard J. Sherman, in Chapter 3, affirms Spector's analysis of capitalist crises as endemic to the capitalist system and shows in great detail, through charts and data, the nature and depth of this latest crisis of global capitalism. Sherman argues that the main cause of the Great Recession and financial crisis of 2007–2009 is to be found in the central flaw of the capitalist system itself, which is the profit motive for the private accumulation of capital. Capital accumulation at one pole and the exploitation of labor through the extraction of surplus value for the capitalists at the other, have left little in the hands of the workers in the form of wages, and led to a widening gap between capital and labor in the distribution of wealth and income, hence widening inequalities along class lines. Sherman shows that the resultant class polarization effected by enormous profits through frenzied financial speculation and accumulation of great fortunes at one pole, and low wages, high unemployment, foreclosures, low purchasing power, and mushrooming consumer debt at the other, is a sure formula for economic disaster that forces the economy into a recession, a great recession, or even a depression. He goes on to argue that the financial frenzy on Wall Street, the sub-prime mortgage crisis, the collapse of the housing market, and the unraveling of the U.S. economy during the Great Recession of 2007 to 2009 has, in turn, reverberated across the world and turned it into a global capitalist crisis of great proportions.

Expanding on Spector's and Sherman's accounts of the global capitalist crisis in earlier chapters of this book, James Petras provides in Chapter 4 a cogent analysis of the global political economy and argues that U.S. and global capitalism has entered a period that is evolving from a deep recession to a severe depression— one that has been fueled by military expansion, war, and naked imperialism. The capitalist state, he points out, is so deeply controlled and ruled by entrenched capitalist economic interests that it is virtually impossible to separate its actions from that of the capitalists who are destined to use the state as their instrument to advance their own class interests, even if it throws the U.S. domestic economy into a tailspin and force the United States into a Great Depression. Given the intersecting interests of the most powerful capitalists and their corporations in the global economy, the crisis of global capitalism in one major country—the United States—quickly affects other countries around the world, and that it consequently becomes a crisis of global capitalism, affecting all those involved in the system. Looking at this impact on Latin America, Asia, and the Middle East, Petras lays out the contradictions of this process across the third world. U.S. capital, and its political arm the capitalist state, Petras argues, holds a hegemonic position in the global political economy, and thus is able to impose its will on all others through its mighty military machine, at least for the time being. But, given its imperial overreach and the cost of policing the world, it runs the risk of collapse—similar to the fate of past empires that could not sustain their global domination through force—and a costly one at that.

The impact of the U.S. and global capitalist crisis on Europe is next taken up by Mike-Frank G. Epitropoulos in Chapter 5 to trace the origins of this most recent crisis and its ramifications for various economies in Europe. Focusing on Europe's distressed economies, in particular Greece, which is part of the troubled group of countries referred to as the PIIGS (Portugal, Ireland, Italy, Greece, and Spain), Epitropoulos provides a nuanced analysis of the Greek crisis that has pushed the country to the brink, necessitating an EU and IMF bailout of Greece—an action that is unprecedented in recent European history. Epitropoulos argues that Greece has been in the spotlight of the European sovereign debt crisis, and for good reason: it has become the ideological and political battleground of the opposing class forces in the world today. To uncover the origins and nature of the capitalist economic crisis in Greece, Epitropoulos contextualizes the Greek crisis by first considering problems at the global and the European Union (EU) level, as well as the PIIGS, and finally, the particular case of Greece.

After establishing the European backdrop and the structural problems of the PIIGS and Greece, in particular, he discusses the role of U.S. banks in the sovereign debt crises around the world. The roots of this economic crisis are found in the reckless behavior of capitalist behemoths like Goldman Sachs and J.P. Morgan, who generated and disseminated toxic assets to governments and investors across the world. The Greek government actually contracted with Goldman Sachs to hide debt, while incurring debt. Such actions, Epitropoulos argues, have been justly characterized as "economic terrorism" as the sovereignty and stability of nations are threatened for years to come. He points out that there has clearly been a battle over what narrative will prevail with regards to the capitalist economic crisis in Greece: the mainstream, neoliberal narrative holds that the situation is the product of a wasteful social welfare state and hedonistic Greeks living beyond their means; a more sober narrative focuses on the political-economic roots of global capitalism. As such, he posits that the case of Greece is also critical as a "demonstration effect" to the rest of the world that also endures the crisis in that a capitalist win against popular movements will translate into losses for grassroots democracy and the social state.

Epitropoulos points out that the capitalist offensive in Greece is being waged by the banks, the IMF, and the leaders of the EU, and that the rhetoric is that of "there is no alternative." But he also points out that there is a strong resistance movement in Greece, led by Leftists, labor unions, and a large swath of ordinary Greeks, and their message has been consistent: "We're not paying for the crimes of the rich thieves!" Given the high level of working-class consciousness in Greece, Epitropoulos contends that the class war is on, and that insurrection and revolution are real possibilities. But he is also aware that this volatility can also create openings for far-Right nationalists, neo-Nazis, and religious fundamentalists that can only stoke the flames of the political and economic fires burning in Greece, and prompt a military coup.

Finally, Epitropoulos argues that when one looks at the situation more closely, it becomes clear that there is no real "crisis" for capital in Greece: profits are up, bonuses are flowing, and the capitalist control of the state is naked and strong, and that there is no incentive for them to restore or enhance the welfare state, social programs, or democratic processes. In fact, he argues, they are employing the ultimate "shock doctrine" on a global level. But, he adds, it is also clearly a moment in time when the capitalist system can—and must—be challenged. Epitropoulos is certainly correct in pointing out that a lot is at stake in this class struggle: the hard-fought victories for higher wages, better working conditions, decent health care, social rights, and protection of the social safety net. This moment, he alerts us, offers Greece and the world the opportunity to not only fight to preserve those hard won rights, but also to push harder for more radical changes that favor people over profit.

Shifting the discussion to the periphery of the global capitalist system, Henry Veltmeyer in Chapter 6 focuses on the impact of the global capitalist crisis on Latin America. He argues that the current global capitalist crisis is but the latest and most virulent manifestation of an endemic propensity of the system to develop into a crisis, and that this particular crisis, which has quickly transformed from a financial into a production crisis of global scope with multiple dimensions, has uneven regional dynamics. Veltmeyer points out that in Latin America diverse popular and non- or anti-capitalist responses are paving the way for a possible way out of the crisis that challenge and go *beyond* the neoliberal capitalist model adopted to guide national policy.

Veltmeyer's argument is constructed in four parts. First, he establishes the premise that capitalism has an inherent propensity towards crisis. Then he reviews the recent literature on the crisis to identify two basic strands, monetary and structural, and argues that the latter gets closer to the real world—*the roots of the crisis*. He then turns to the dynamics of the crisis as it is unfolding in Latin America. The focus here is on the impact of the crisis on the economy and the diverse responses to it. In this context, he examines some of the popular alternative responses to the crisis that are emerging in the region, drawing conclusions that are summarized at the end of the chapter.

One conclusion Veltmeyer reaches is that neither definancialization, the reregulation of global capital in its speculative form, new checks on the excesses of neoliberal globalization, nor a counter-cyclical approach to the crisis with the restoration of credit or a production stimulus plan, will suffice to stave off the crisis. Another, and more crucial, conclusion that he reaches is that this might be the moment for moving *beyond capitalism* to socialism in some form. And a final, decisive (political) conclusion he reaches is that the *agency* for this development—

the way out of the crisis—is the active mobilization of the forces of change in the popular sector of society.

Veltmeyer points out that, although developments in the popular sector of diverse societies in Latin America are pointing the way forward, the problem is that the forces of change released by the legitimation crisis of capitalism in the current context (reflected in the widespread rejection of neoliberalism as an economic model), and the production crisis in its diverse manifestations, can be mobilized in different directions—to the right as well as the left. The current situation thus provides a major challenge for the left to take advantage of the opportunities brought by the existing conditions that prevail under the global capitalist crisis. Given the failure of center-left regimes in power now for more than a decade to effect changes that are transformational, Veltmeyer contends that to be effective, such changes will have to come from the mass movements that are based on labor and popular sectors of society and must be revolutionary in nature.

While the global capitalist crisis, which originated in the United States, had a negative impact on the U.S., Europe, and the less-developed economies of the periphery, it did not adversely affect China, as the Chinese economy has been effectively insulated from external shocks. In Chapter 7, Alvin Y. So shows that unlike the advanced capitalist countries which have experienced negative growth and high unemployment rates during the global economic crisis, China still managed to grow at an impressive rate of around 10 percent. So points out that at the onset of the crisis in the fall of 2008, the Chinese state quickly put up a massive stimulus program of US$586 billion to invest in infrastructure, agriculture, technology, environment, education, healthcare, and affordable public housing. As a result, the stimulus program, So explains, led to an enormous expansion of the state sector that led to industrial upgrading of labor-intensive industries and the rapid development of green industries. He goes on to observe that although conflict was intensified between the Chinese state and the transnational corporations, there was little social protest from workers and peasants because the state adopted a pro-worker and pro-peasant position.

However, in spite of having a robust economy during the global economic crisis of 2007–2009, China, So alerts us, does face a number of internal and external challenges in the near future: internally there are concerns whether China will experience economic decline when it exits from the massive stimulus program; whether China will have an overheated economy, with a high rate of inflation and the formation of a residential property bubble; and whether China could boost its domestic consumption and reduce its reliance on exports and foreign investment. Externally there are growing tensions between China and other rival states on currency, security, and territorial issues. However, so points out that since the Chinese state has a track record of managing crisis and resolving social and political problems, and since the state has not been weakened during the global economic crisis, it should be able to handle these internal and external challenges without much difficulty.

Finally, in assessing the rise of China through the economic, political, and cultural dimensions, So argues that the developmental state in China not only was able to seize the opportunity of the global economic crisis to strengthen its economy, but also its political power in the inter-state system and began to articulate a new set of values and model of development to challenge the United States.

Examining the impact of the global capitalist crisis on neoliberal globalization, Martin Orr in Chapter 8 places the "Great Recession" of 2007–2009 (and beyond) in the context of the decline of the United States as a world power in the last quarter of the twentieth century and into the twenty-first. He argues that conditions in the United States began deteriorating by the mid-1970s, and that the period since has been characterized by rising inequality and a widening gap between labor and capital, exploding public and private debt, and neglect of social services. The end of the Cold War enabled the U.S. to reassert itself, first under the banner of a multilateral neoliberalism, pushing governments to open their markets to Western capital. Stalled by opposition and enabled by the attacks of September 11, Orr argues that unilateral neoconservativism sought to force aside governments that refused to follow U.S. dictates, but this, too, failed in the face of resistance. Against the backdrop of growing inequality born of neoliberal capital flight and exacerbated by the diversion of taxes from social services to the military, Orr argues, the collapse of the housing market, unsustainable levels of household debt, and energy inflation combined to destroy demand, freeze credit, and bring down the economy. Capital has exploited the crisis by transferring public money to the banks, and by attempting to further increase inequalities by undercutting social spending.

Looking at the immediate future, Orr projects that as U.S. government policy seems intent on restoring the conditions that led to the crisis, a second and possibly deeper crisis seems likely. Finally, looking at the situation in the longer term, with U.S. wealth and influence squandered by neoliberalism and neoconservatism as other nations are growing in power, Orr concludes that the global capitalist crisis will usher in a fundamental restructuring of the global political economy, resulting from changes in the global balance of power, and this in turn will lead to major social transformations of epochal proportions during the course of the twenty-first century.

Clearly, the current global economic crisis is a crisis of the capitalist *system* on a world scale, and as such it affects all major components and institutions of global capitalism. This *systemic crisis* exacerbates and exposes the ever starker contradictions of capitalist society—of great abundance on a global scale of all the things people require, but of great want, deprivation, exploitation and oppression.

Finally, in the closing substantive chapter of this book, in Chapter 9, Walda Katz-Fishman and Jerome Scott make a compelling argument for the necessity of organized political action to effect change—one that is gradually becoming a reality as more and more people around the world join movements to change the course of history. They show in great detail that today, in 2011, four years into the deepest structural crisis of capitalism the world has ever experienced since the Great Depression of the 1930s, and responding to this economic crisis, massive social and ecological destruction, ongoing war, and growing repression on the part of the capitalist state, social movements and revolutionaries are in motion by taking the initiative to intervene in history to bring about change that goes beyond the current declining and decaying global capitalist system.

These realities, Katz-Fishman and Scott argue, present new possibilities for movement organizing, analyzing, visioning, and strategizing: twenty-first century global capitalism requires a coordinated global movement from the bottom-up with *working class leadership*, and as the mass movement develops and many forces come into play in this struggle, the path forward leads toward socialism as an objective necessity for the survival of humanity. This raises the questions that activists, revolutionaries, and social movements around the world are grappling with, and Katz-Fishman and Scott insist are key before a social transformation can take place: What is the vision of another world and another economy? What is the alternative to capitalism? Who are the forces that can make it happen? It is a core task of revolutionaries from deep within the mass movement, they argue, to use history and experience to raise class consciousness among the millions in motion and keep the movement on the strategic path toward the formation of an independent working class political force to transform global capitalism. In this context, Katz-Fishman and Scott see the World Social Forum as a new historic moment of social struggle and movement convergence—an alter-globalization from below—in opposition to the World Economic Forum, which represents the interests of capital and the capitalist state. In the new millennium, they point out, the social forum process coalesced: the U.S. Social Forum in 2007 and again in 2010 was a marker for U.S. social struggles and advancing an anti-capitalist mass movement connecting to global movements. They argue that the social forum process in the United States is a critical strategic tool for educating and coordinating a twenty-first century transformative movement from below, and that for this to occur revolutionaries must seize the opportunity to deepen consciousness and vision, convergence and capacity, and strategy. Thus, the social forum and the many fronts of struggle that converged, they point out, express and are interconnected with the movement in society that is in opposition to the capitalist crisis and is part of the developing anti-systemic movement toward socialism in the United States and the world. And this is evident in the most recent Occupy Wall Street movement, which has spread from New York City to some 20 states in the United States and to 80 countries around the world.

Katz-Fishman and Scott argue that all the various currents of struggle point in the same direction—the need for independent working class organization and politics, and the necessity to struggle against global capitalism and for socialism. The socialist alternative and vision of a cooperative, egalitarian, and collectively organized society is possible given the realities of today's economy, and is grounded in the social struggles of U.S. and global movements converging and strategizing in many spaces. A future without global capitalism is a historical necessity. The struggle between the forces promoting capitalist globalization from above and the forces of alter-globalization fighting against global capitalism from below—the popular movements of the world's working classes in all their diversity—has been joined in the twenty-first century. And the recent struggles against neoliberalism in Latin America, the uprisings, rebellions, and revolutions in the Middle East, and the riots, protests, and demonstrations in Greece, Ireland, France, and other European countries, and in the United States, point to the potential militancy of the working class and growing discontent and anger among working people that can translate into prolonged and protracted struggles against the capitalist state on a global basis, as the Occupy Wall Street movement demonstrates across the globe.

The book concludes with final observations on the current state and future direction of the world economy and the prospects for transformation of global capitalism in the twenty-first century. Outlining the process that will inevitably unfold in the coming years, the analysis provided in this concluding chapter lays bare the contradictions and crisis of the process in motion that will radically change the nature and structure of the global political economy and open up new and yet uncharted paths that stand before us in the years ahead.

Together, the nine cutting-edge essays that make up this book provide a rich compendium of informed analyses on the inner dynamics of advanced capitalism and the global capitalist crisis. Going beyond the boundaries of the current capitalist system, and looking toward future possibilities, the book ends on a positive note claiming that a new egalitarian economy and society is possible, and indeed necessary, and that this is certainly in keeping with a noble goal that can be attained if it is guided by the principles and precepts of a just ideology (socialism) that is put into practice under the leadership of the working class and its allies taking state power and shaping programs and policies that put people before profits. Thus, I argue that it is only through a new logic and a new social, economic, and political system—one based on the interests of the working class and the broad segments of the population—that we would be able to avert the kind of economic crises that we have been subjected to under global capitalism, and chart a course that is consistent with the promise of a just society in the not too distant future.

References

Amaladoss, Michael (ed.). 1999. *Globalization and Its Victims As Seen by Its Victims*. Delhi, India: Vidyajyoti Education and Welfare Society.

Berberoglu, Berch. 1992. *The Legacy of Empire: Economic Decline and Class Polarization in the United States*. New York: Praeger.

———. (ed.). 2002. *Labor and Capital in the Age of Globalization.* Lanham, MD: Rowman and Littlefield.

———. 2003. *Globalization of Capital and the Nation-State*. Lanham, MD: Rowman and Littlefield.

——. 2005. *Globalization and Change: The Transformation of Global Capitalism*. Lanham, MD: Lexington Books.

——. 2009. *Class and Class Conflict in the Age of Globalization*. Lanham, MD: Lexington Books.

——. (ed.). 2010. *Globalization in the 21st Century*. New York: Palgrave Macmillan.

Bluestone, Barry and Bennett Harrison. 1982. *The Deindustrialization of America*. New York: Basic.

Falk, Richard. 1999. *Predatory Globalization: A Critique*. Malden, MA: Blackwell.

Guthrie, Doug. 2006. *China and Globalization: The Social, Economic and Political Transformation of Chinese Society*. New York: Routledge.

Halliday, Fred. 2001. *The World at 2000*. New York: St. Martin's Press.

Hart, Jeffrey A. 1992. *Rival Capitalists: International Competitiveness in the United States, Japan, and Western Europe*. Ithaca, NY: Cornell University Press.

Harvey, David. 2003. *The New Imperialism*. New York: Oxford University Press.

Houtart, Francois and Francois Polet (eds). 2001. *The Other Davos Summit: The Globalization of Resistance to the World Economic System*. London: Zed Books.

Panitch, Leo and Colin Leys (eds). 2003. *The New Imperial Challenge*. New York: Monthly Review Press.

Petras, James. 2009. *Global Depression and Regional Wars*. Atlanta: Clarity Press.

Phillips, Brian. 1998. *Global Production and Domestic Decay: Plant Closings in the U.S.* New York: Garland.

Sassen, Saskia. 2009. "Too Big To Save: The End of Financial Capitalism." *Open Democracy News Analysis*, April 2.

Sklair, Leslie. 2002. *Globalization: Capitalism and Its Alternatives*. New York: Oxford University Press.

Stephens, Philip. 2009. "A Summit Success That Reflects a Different Global Landscape." *Financial Times*, April 3, 9.

Wagner, Helmut (ed.). 2000. *Globalization and Unemployment*. New York: Springer.

Chapter 2

The Origins and Development of the Global Capitalist Economy and Capitalist Crises

Alan J. Spector

To understand global capitalist crises, especially in the twentieth century, it is necessary to examine the evolution of capitalist processes within the industrialized countries in order to delineate how these processes have impacted, mutually saturated, and shaped the parameters of global capitalism in the twentieth and early twenty-first centuries.

While defining cataclysmic events are used to delineate the boundaries of different historical periods, reality is much more complex. Forces build up over time and interact with each other and transform each other. Some residues of past social processes and institutions are reformed in the newer period. So it has been with capitalism. One could say that the roots of capitalism go back to the 1400s or one could say they go back further, but there clearly have been watershed points in that history where qualitative changes took root. The processes of mercantile capitalism had already set in motion the dynamics where the contradiction between production for use (meeting the needs of the populace) and production for profit became sharper and more pronounced. In England, for example, between the mid-1700s and the mid-1800s, there were a number of "Enclosure Acts" which took what had been public land, used by poorer, rural people for grazing and farming, and eventually privatized it for the benefit of the wealthy. One consequence was more migration of the population to cities, where they became wage laborers. Another consequence was the further restructuring of the economy towards producing "for the market", particularly wool, rather than producing for the local economy. Whether it was the transformation of agricultural land in the Caribbean from forest to sugar cane, the "Enclosure" of land in England, or the development of beet sugar and Egyptian cotton for the market, major parts of the productive forces of society were oriented towards the market. The market, however, introduces considerable instability into these processes which in turn loop back and affect the production of goods.

In a simple sense, one can see that production is the "cause" and having something to sell in the market is the "effect". The feedback loop, the dialectic at work, however, is that if the products cannot be sold, then the firm cannot make a profit, and more dangerously, the firm itself is at risk of collapsing if it cannot pay its debts. All of these are among the inherent contradictions of capitalism.

The 1800s were a period of consolidation of the capitalist class in various European countries as well as the maturing of capitalist contradictions. Combined with modern transportation, communication, and weaponry, the great powers of Europe and the United States moved into nearly every part of the world—money in one hand, guns in the other—seeking to carve out empires. Other European powers and the United States were chipping away at the British Empire, which was gradually sinking into decline. Germany, in particular, was becoming a mighty industrial power. Politically and economically, the world became much smaller during this period. As capitalist processes continued to demand expansion, inevitable collisions between international companies and nations become more intense. At any moment, alliances might appear stable, but all sorts of events —economic crisis at home, discovery of mineral deposits in some other land, rebellion in some faraway part of the world, shifting of balance of power within a nation, rapidly developing technology, including naval capacity, airplanes, and weaponry—can all upset a seemingly stable world.

By the middle of the 1800's, mercantile capitalism was giving way to industrial capitalism, although aspects of mercantile capitalism have certainly persisted to this day. Industrial capitalism allowed for even more rapid, and therefore more unstable, accumulation (and loss) of wealth. The second half of the 1800s were marked by a number of "boom and bust" cycles and economic depressions (Duboff 1989). At its core, capitalism has a structural problem, a contradiction, where greater production can lead to greater actual profits in the short term (thereby encouraging even greater production), but the ratio of capital invested in production relative to the amount of profit made, and the flooding of the market with goods lead to a falling rate of profit. Attempts might be made at coordination, but the reality is that profit-seeking necessitates putting the interests of a firm above the interests of the capitalist system as a whole; hence attempts at planning rational production are undermined when firms must put short term actual profits ahead of longer term rates of profit. Markets get flooded and firms compete with each other and with their own previously purchased durable products. Short-term profits are important to service debts; one major short-term slump can permanently destroy a business and set in motion a domino effect where other businesses also collapse and major sections of the whole economy can collapse. Marxists refer to this "boom-bust cycle" as the "crisis of overproduction" when it reaches these crisis proportions.

As problematic as this was under agricultural/mineral extraction mercantile capitalism, the whole process became accelerated and even more unstable as rapidly developing technology to produce more products and deliver them to market became the norm under industrial capitalism. It was during this period that the cyclical boom and bust nature of capitalism, described by Marx, Engels, and others, came to shake whole societies. In the United States, the "Long Depression" which started in 1873 was a convergence of unstable speculative investments after the Civil War, the loss of investments from the failure to complete the Union Pacific Railway, and the collapse of the Austrian stock exchange, which resulted in an inability to keep investment capital flowing. After a relatively prosperous 1880s, the panic of 1893 in the United States caused another crisis, where lending and investment slowed to a crawl, the economy wound down, and unemployment soared (Glasner 1997). In 1897 there was a moderate recovery followed by another panic on Wall Street and banking crisis in 1907. The recessions/depressions under capitalism are not caused by a lack of wealth, resources, material, labor, or capital, but rather by an inability of capital to flow into investments, much as a person who experiences a sudden loss of blood could have enough remaining blood to sustain life, but not enough blood pressure to move that blood around. This is just a summary of core capitalist processes. One can easily find more comprehensive and deeper explanations available from many other sources.

The Twentieth Century: Finance Capitalism and Imperialism

The core dynamic of capitalism is the seeking of profits. The *rate of profit* is especially important as that greatly influences the ability of a business to attract investors and secure loans. When the rate of profit drops, even as absolute profits might remain positive, a business must take measures to reverse that drop or risk collapse or takeover. As capitalism gradually transformed from mercantile capitalism to industrial capitalism, so too did the ability to acquire great wealth quickly. One aspect of this was the concentration of more wealth in fewer and few corporations. In Europe and the United States, industrial capitalism was maturing into *monopoly capitalism*. There is an inherent contradiction in the whole process of capitalist competition. If competition develops freely, wealth and power can accumulate in certain corporations and banks that allow them to use their wealth to magnify and multiply their advantages, thereby further accumulating more wealth and power. This of course stifles competition as smaller companies cannot compete. Not only do the huge corporations enjoy direct economic advantages over their smaller opponents, economies of scale, etc.—they also have more leverage with suppliers, with retailers and with lobbying the government for policies and programs that would benefit them more. Of course, some smaller companies are more nimble, more flexible, and rise to seriously challenge the larger companies, but they are the exceptions. Often when they do emerge, they are bought up by the larger companies and absorbed into them. Competition among large cartels can be very intense. On the one hand, they might unite against common opponents, as when automobile companies unite to oppose the expansion of railway service, or when oil companies unite to open up new oil fields in other countries. On the other hand, the fewer and larger the remaining cartels are, the more intense is the competition among them, as their opponents also have enormous power. This all intensifies the needs for the larger corporations to maximize profits. It might seem counter-intuitive to those who think in individual, rather than systemic terms; an individual who is wealthy has no personal "need" to acquire more wealth. But a corporation locked in intense competition with other corporations has a constant need to maximize profits—not only to satisfy stockholders, but to service creditors and to outlast the competition. The larger the corporation, the greater the stakes. Along with this came the growing power of the banks.

This dynamic gradually evolved capitalism in Europe and North America towards a system where even greater fortunes could be rapidly gained (and lost) through banking in its various forms. Banks have access to huge amounts of capital, far more than any individual companies. Without needing to have huge sums of capital tied up in large buildings, land, machinery, and labor costs, banks could make their profit from borrowing money from savers at one rate of interest and investing it in other places at a higher rate of interest. This flexibility can help banks avoid stagnant investments; it can also lead to making risky, unstable investments. Because large corporations often might need a rapid infusion of large amounts of capital, banks were also able to negotiate for further economic power within those corporations by demanding seats on the boards of directors or the option to buy future stock at current prices, or various other rewards.

A corollary of the combined impact of the falling rates of profit endemic to overall capitalist dynamics and the growing power of transformation towards finance capital was the need to expand overseas economic activity. Ruling classes have organized wars to conquer other lands for all of recorded history, but each economic era has different purposes for those conquests. In pre-capitalist times, reasons included the taking of minerals, the taking of food, the taking of slaves. Related to these, of course, were the expansion of various religions and the expansion of political control through military power. As capitalist processes developed more through the 1500s–1700s, the modes of accumulating wealth changed. Huge trading companies—the Hudson's Bay Company, (British) East India Company, Dutch East Indian Company, and others—amassed big fortunes. Certainly through the 1800's, colonialism and the conquest of major parts of Asia and Africa (as well as the economic subordination of most of Latin America) by Europe and the United States was common. However, as capitalism in the centers of Europe and the United States evolved more into finance capitalism during the late 1800s, the specific needs of the banks and the industries were on profits as they related to investments. It is not that Britain needed to *consume* all the sugar from the Caribbean nor that France needed all the rice from Indochina in order to feed the French people; rather it was the profits that could be made, buying and selling on the global market. This of course further accelerated the ability to make, and lose, huge sums of money, and in turn took the instability to a higher level.

Capitalist Cycles in the Age of Imperialism

As described earlier using the United States as an example, the economic cycles (crises) within nations were temporarily alleviated by expanding to other countries. This was not simply a matter of greed nor a matter of choice. It was not simply taking the wealth from other lands for purposes of direct enrichment, although that remained an important aspect. Rather, the capitalist systems in Europe and North America had no choice. Going abroad meant the possibility of new markets (to sell the overproduced commodities) and cheap labor and abundant raw materials—and these would mean more profits to alleviate the falling rates of profit domestically. Those corporations which could successfully invest in other countries would grow; those that could not were vulnerable to collapse, takeover, or at best, stagnation. Simply put, capitalism had to expand or die, but in that expansion, it reached a new stage—modern imperialism. It was not and is not a matter of choice, any more than a child can choose to not age. The only alternative to ageing is early death. In the framework developed by Lenin, and practiced by large banks and corporations, imperialism is not something capitalism *does*, imperialist-capitalism, or modern *imperialism*, is what capitalism has *become* (Lenin 1997). This maturing of capitalism could be called the stage of *monopoly capitalism, finance capitalism, or imperialism,* as all three aspects developed, converged, reinforced and saturated each other until it became one integrated system.

The economic contradictions of capitalism which would have led it to collapse on the national level were thus transferred to the global level (Petras and Veltmeyer 2001; Berberoglu 2003). The result of this was the temporary alleviation of the sharpness of the contradictions and crises within the imperialist countries. In the longer run, however, these contradictions would emerge again, much larger, much more intensely, on a global level, where competition under crisis could explode not just into economic war between corporations, but world war among nations.

The U.S.-based National Bureau of Economic Research counts 21 distinct recessions from 1902 until 2001. A summary of these cycles, extended from 1854 to 2009 that demonstrates the persistence of "boom-bust" cycles is shown in Table 2.1.

Table 2.1 Capitalist Business Cycles in the United States, 1854–2009, by Duration

Duration in Months			
Contraction Expansion Cycle			
Average, all cycles	Peak to Trough	Previous trough to this peak	Trough from previous trough	Peak from previous peak
1854–2009 (33 cycles)	16	42	56	55*
1854–1919 (16 cycles)	22	27	48	49**
1919–1945 (6 cycles)	18	35	53	53
1945–2009 (11 cycles)	11	59	73	66

Note: *32 cycles, **15 cycles
Source: National Bureau of Economic Research, www.nber.org/cycles/cyclesmain.html.

Irrespective of how precisely one would define a recession or full scale economic depression, it is clear that the fundamental instability of the capitalist system has not been "solved" by the globalization of capital and the spread of capitalist relations across the world. What is important here to understand is that it is not merely the expansion of capital abroad that "solves" (or rather "eases") the inherent instability of capitalism, but rather whether those investments abroad are beneficial to the domestic economy. Furthermore, the raw materials may be important, especially if there is the possibility of war in the future, and in times of peace, controlling the flow of raw materials can offer a corporation and a national economy not only great wealth, but important control over the shaping of the economy (and military power) of other countries. Emphasizing only the relative amount of foreign investments commits an error of looking at a seemingly valid abstract model and mechanically applying it without taking into consideration the ways that seemingly small quantitative changes can have powerful qualitative effects. Similarly, the analysis that emphasizes the hegemony of powerful interests and their ability to unify also looks at a process in a mechanical way, failing to take uneven development and contradictions into account. Competition among firms is inherent in capitalism, and as united the powerful might appear to be, the uneven maturing of economic processes can accentuate and intensify latent contradictions within them, especially when they are subjected to outside stresses. Corporations and banks may have foreign owners and global interests, but they still must rely on national governments to help regulate the economy domestically and secure their interests globally, and those national governments in turn mediate among various capitalist groupings within each nation. Corporations, then, still generally have one primary national homeland to provide the political (and military) resources to protect their respective interests.

By 1900, capitalism in Europe and North America had evolved into finance capitalism/monopoly capitalism/imperialism with all its instabilities, and by then nearly all of the world was "claimed" by the United States or one or another of the powerful nations of Europe. Each nation's capitalism still had the need to expand and smaller collisions were occurring that would explode into World War I.

World War I was not simply an accident caused by an assassination. Nor was it merely a shifting around of balance of power or a clash of nationalisms. While the spark of the war is often posed in either "accidental" or "political rivalry" terms, it is clearer now that the rise of German capitalism and its need to expand was bumping directly into British imperialist interests. With the Ottoman Empire allied with Germany and the Serbs allied with Britain, the Balkans would be the arena where this proxy war, which would turn into a world war, began. The prize, however, was not simply the Balkans. German corporations had discovered oil in Mesopotamia, the region now encompassed by Iraq. Deutsche Bank sought funding to help build a Baghdad to Berlin railway, which would have helped strengthen the Ottoman Empire as well as supply the growing industrial engines of German factories. Britain's strength, that it had become a banking powerhouse, was also its weakness, as its industrial output lagged while Germany's soared.

Britain also needed oil; while Britain had a huge supply of coal, it was converting its navy, a major source of British power, from coal to oil. It had secured some oil contracts with Kuwait and Persia (now Iran). Politically, the British were actively trying to destabilize parts of the Ottoman Empire even as the Germans were attempting to strengthen the Ottoman Empire (Engdahl 2004). By the time this war was over, the "War to End All Wars", the Ottoman Empire was destroyed, Germany was in ruins, and while Britain did pick up some pieces from the defeat of Germany, the British Empire was irreparably weakened and the United States was better positioned to be the next preeminent world power. Yet the persistence of the underlying crises of capitalism would burst through again in the next decade with massive, world-shaking consequences.

After the Great War, Britain, France, and the United States feasted on the remains of Germany and its allies, especially the Ottoman Empire. Middle Eastern oil flowed their way. Germany was forced to pay heavy reparations. Economies of the United States and parts of Western Europe seemed to rebound as there were new "markets" in the form of reconstruction, and Germany seemed no longer to be an economic threat. This was a fertile ground for U.S. and British imperialist expansion until it ran its course up to the Great Depression.

The Great Depression and World War II

The Great Depression of the 1930s was arguably the most intensive and extensive economic collapse in modern times. For simplicity's sake, it is generally stated that it began with the stock market crash in New York in 1929. As stocks lost value, panic selling caused stocks to collapse. Businesses (and individuals) quite suddenly had access to less capital and were afraid to spend what little capital they had. As capital circulation slowed down, a self-reinforcing cycle intensified the slowdown and many businesses dropped below the survival point and went bankrupt. Unemployment was 30 percent or more in many places, and as business slowed down in the major industrial and financial centers, tariffs and other forms of nationalistic trade protection further limited imports, and the economic collapse became global. The Soviet Union, with a planned economy that was less susceptible to the instabilities of corporate capitalism, avoided the acute effects of this capitalist instability, although in the Soviet Union there were other serious economic and social problems. Japan also somewhat ameliorated the most intense effects of the depression through massive government spending, especially on military goods. Extending credit, especially through massive government spending can be a way to temporarily soften the acute impact of an economic downturn. If capital is not circulating and a chain reaction of businesses shutting down threatens to collapse major parts of the economy, some permanently, then any policy that can get capital circulating again might alleviate the immediate crisis. Economists call this "priming the pump". This economic policy, associated with the economist John Maynard Keynes, certainly can ameliorate an acute crisis of capital circulation, loans, investments, etc. (Keynes 1965). But the core problems associated with a poorly planned economy where each company is primarily concerned with short term profits and the consequential flooding of the market and falling rates of profit are not solved. If anything, they are forestalled and will emerge later with even greater magnitude and intensity, unless the system finds genuine new markets and genuine sources of cheap labor and raw materials to sustain the rates of profit.

As Table 2.2 shows, significant improvement in the money supply and in the Index of Industrial Production only began to move steadily forward as the United States began to gear up war production.

**Table 2.2 Leading Indicators of Economic Activity during the Great
        Depression, 1929–1940 (1935–39 =100)**

Great Depression Economic Data*	1929	1931	1933	1937	1938	1940
Real Gross National Product (GNP)**	101.4	84.3	68.3	103.9	103.7	113.0
Consumer Price Index	122.5	108.7	92.4	102.7	99.4	100.2
Index of Industrial Production	109.0	75.0	69.0	112.0	89.0	126.0
Money Supply M2 ($ billions)	46.6	42.7	32.2	45.7	49.3	55.2
Exports ($ billions)	5.24	2.42	1.67	3.35	3.18	4.02
Unemployment (% of civilian work force)	3.1	16.1	25.2	13.8	16.5	13.9

Note: * http://en.wikipedia.org/wiki/Economic_history_of_the_United_States-cite_note-32. ** in 1929 dollars.
Source: U.S. Department of Commerce, National Income and Product Accounts. Broadus Mitchell, *Depression Decade: From New Era Through New Deal, 1929–1941* (New York: Harper and Row, 1969), pp. 446, 449, 451.

While some claim that the depression was merely a problem of underconsumption and a clogged/stalled economy that was solved by massive government spending, which in turn created liquidity and increased the circulation of capital, bringing the economy back, the reality is that there was some slight improvement as a result of government programs—many people had very low paying jobs, rather than no jobs. The other reality is that it was only massive deficit spending on war materiel that began to bring the economy back in a significant way, and the significant economic improvement did not develop until after the war, with its massive destruction of property and productive forces, leading to a new growth-cycle based on postwar economic reconstruction.

The analysis that examines this depression within the context of capitalist crisis as outlined by Marx and others is especially useful. The unplanned economy, chaotic production, wild economic speculation and the drive for quick profits created a "bubble" of artificial wealth during the 1920s. In fact, for many in the United States and Europe, the 1920s were not particularly prosperous. The economic boom was uneven, with instability and economic hardship for many working class people in the United States, even as popular histories describe that era as "The Roaring Twenties". The door was slammed on immigration in 1924 because the real economy was not actually expanding, and the massive need for labor that expanding U.S. capitalism had for the previous 40 years had greatly diminished. In Europe, the 1920s were also unstable. Britain was able to take advantage of the massive reparations that Germany was forced to pay while in Germany the instabilities of the economy led to intense hyperinflation and eventually a collapse that helped bring the Nazis to power.

If the fundamental causes of the Great Depression follow the patterns as described in the analysis of capitalist crisis, so, too, do the realities of how the problems of the Great Depression were "solved," fit that analysis. As discussed above, the Keynesian economic policies only provided temporary relief from total collapse, but the instabilities remained. The instabilities manifest themselves as a "crisis of overproduction" and as falling rates of profit. Finding new markets can ease both the problem of "overproduction" and help raise the rate of profit. New sources of cheap labor and eliminating "non-purchasing" excess population also ease both the economic and political crisis that comes with economic instability. If Keynesian policies provide temporary relief, it is modern imperialism, the economic drive for cheap labor, raw materials and new markets mediated through political and military actions that could provide longer term relief for capitalism's problems. Germany and Japan may have restored a kind of "order" in their societies in the late 1930s, but the imperialist drive towards war was essential to their survival. For the Japanese ruling class, it was the massive assault on China and other parts of East Asia. For the Nazis, it was the March to the East to seize fertile land and eventually, to control Middle Eastern oil. World War II killed perhaps seventy to one hundred million people. Even in the United States, the number of military deaths exceeded 400,000, with many more permanently disabled. While exacting a terrible toll on families, it also had the effect of alleviating unemployment. Especially important, however, was the massive destruction of property, especially industrial property. Britain, France, Germany, Italy—most of Europe—as well as Japan experienced widespread devastation. Only the United States, and to an extent, the Soviet Union, (which suffered massive destruction but actually protected much of its industrial base), emerged from the war with their industry ready to produce. The massive destruction of the industrial productive forces during the war meant that the overproduction and flooding of the market could be forestalled for a while until capitalist production matured. The massive destruction created a "market" for new production. There was a tremendous need for consumer goods, and there was a tremendous need to rebuild the factories and transportation systems. It was this huge new market for goods that eased the classic crisis of capitalism, but only for a time.

The United States emerged as the big winner from the war, both economically and politically, although the Soviet Union, while suffering tens of millions dead and destruction of major population centers, also emerged in a position to actually become stronger. The Axis powers were, of course, no threat to the economic and political power of the United States, which sought to ally with especially Germany and Japan after the war as bulwarks against the Soviet Union. The other major Allied powers, especially England and France, may have been on the "winning side", but they emerged from the war much weakened. The United States was able to build up its industrial base and ease its economic problems by selling goods to the weakened countries of Europe. Furthermore, the independence of the former colonies of various European powers provided more openings for U.S. business to supplant the old colonial interests, although the old colonial powers often did maintain substantial economic investments in many of their former colonies. The same capitalist patterns of global competition would emerge, but it would take decades to mature as a result of the tremendous power of the United States and the weakened condition of the European powers.

Post-World War II to the Twenty-First Century

The period from the end of World War II to the early 1970s was the high point of U.S. capitalism and the high point of its global economic strength. The basis for this was laid, in part, at the Bretton Woods conference in July, 1944. While the war was still raging, the strong capitalist powers of Europe, led by the United States, convened this three week conference to develop common policies and structures of cooperation to avoid the kind of intense competitive nationalistic capitalist policies that intensified and prolonged the Great Depression. The Bretton Woods conference created a set of agreements to bring "order" to international trade and financial markets. Among other things, it discouraged countries from instituting various kinds of tariffs and from engaging in currency manipulation to give their products a competitive advantage on the world market. During that time, there was also an emphasis on encouraging governments to intervene in economic policies, even if this appeared to contradict the philosophy of pure "free enterprise". It was assumed that the devastating World War II was in large part the result of chaos in the economic processes within countries, and nationalist trade policies among countries, both of which caused plans to break apart and international conflict to ensue. While planning can certainly ameliorate some of the "spinning out of control" that can result from capitalist economic policies, it somewhat begs the question. Planning among participants can only be sustained if there is relative stability, either by having relative equality among the participants, or by having one or a few of the participants so powerful that the stability is maintained. But if one or some of the participants decide that they need to expand their own interests, or if they are forced to expand their own interests by economic crisis, and if those participants have grown in economic and political power to the point where they no longer believe that they must maintain the old order, then the economic competition becomes more intense again, even as all parties call for cooperation and unity. The processes of capitalism always lead to this unevenness, and stability is always temporary, but the postwar system did seem to ensure stability for a couple of decades (Gavin 2003; Hooks 1991). Key to this was keeping the price of gold somewhere around $35 an ounce. If it went much higher, investors would start buying more and more gold, the dollar would drop in value, and inflation would ensue. Furthermore, the stabilized price of gold meant that speculation both in gold and in currency would be discouraged, thus maintaining stability in the global economic order.

As is always the case in agreements of this sort, there are relative winners and losers, with the winners insisting on an "order" that primarily benefits the winner. In this case, the winner was the United States, which had been trying for decades to "open up" more trade with especially British, and to an extent, other European trade partners. A key way of preventing currency manipulation was taking world off the gold standard and instead, making the U.S. dollar the common core against which other countries would be valued; they, either by intention or by the instabilities of the market, would not be able to suddenly revalue their currencies in ways that would destabilize the whole global economic system. It was about this time that the International Monetary Fund (IMF) was also established to be the instrument that would oversee the implementation of these agreements. The plan for the IMF was to prevent individual countries from restricting the transfer of goods, to keep some countries from manipulating currency and allying with some countries against other countries through currency exchanges (Mason 1973). The IMF would also make short term loans to debtor nations so as to keep them from sliding over the edge into an economic collapse that could then threaten the whole system. However the IMF loans would have to be paid back, and they often came with "anti-inflationary" conditions that required the debtor countries to spend less on meeting the needs of the local population in order to keep inflation down and to keep their debt from spiraling out of control.

With U.S. industry intact, and most of Europe and Japan devastated, the 1940s was presumed to be the start of a supposed U.S. economic hegemony that might last a century or more. U.S. industry could produce and sell overseas, and its potential competitors not only could not compete, but in fact had to open the markets of their colonies and trading partners, and indeed their own internal markets to U.S. products. But the instabilities of capitalist processes continued to create unevenness that disrupted the smooth economic hegemony hoped for by the U.S. capitalist class.

There continued to be recessions, relatively mild, for the next twenty years. In the United States, there was a bipartisan consensus between Republicans and Democrats to continue to employ Keynesian government spending programs to keep capital circulating and keep the economy growing. Corporations enjoyed high rates of profit during the economic boom that accompanied the rebuilding of Europe and Japan after the war and that allowed U.S. corporations more free reign to invest in other parts of the world where labor was cheaper and markets to sell were developing (Levitt 1983). Wages of workers increased, in part because of labor union strength, but also because the corporations had the money to spend on increased labor costs. The prosperity also encouraged the capitalist class and the politicians to spend vast sums of money on government programs, including to lessen poverty, provide more health care, improve education, and increase educational resources, especially at the college level. The U.S. national debt increased significantly, but capital was circulating and the economic boom caused many in the corporate and political arenas to dismiss fears of major problems. When the U.S. government decided to escalate the war in Vietnam, the concerns about major expenses were met with calming rhetoric that the United States was so prosperous that it could afford both "guns and butter". Some in government were concerned about skyrocketing military expenses, others with skyrocketing domestic expenses, but both were maintained through the 1960s.

By the late 1960s, there were signs of a slowdown. The Vietnam War was dragging on and the money pumped into that war was stimulating the economy but not really producing much wealth at home. Inflation began to creep up. One major strategy of capitalist economic policy is to balance inflation with slowing the economy down, and balance slowdowns with pumping up the economy through more government spending if necessary (Weinberg 2003). Cutting spending was difficult during the war. Then, in the early 1970s, the Bretton Woods agreement collapsed (Gowan 1999).

The countries of Western Europe and Japan were experiencing strong economic growth. The U.S. was continuing to "print dollars" (go further into debt) to pay for the Vietnam War and for social programs. It was untenable for the other growing economic power to continue to accept the value of a dollar as defined by a \$35 per ounce of gold. Inflationary pressures to lower the value of the dollar grew as it became obvious that the United States had decreasing amounts of gold to back up the dollar. In 1970, the amount of gold that the U.S. had to back up the dollar dropped from 55 percent to 22 percent.

As a result of this growing instability, the value of the dollar dropped. Other currencies were also devalued somewhat in relation to the rising price of gold, but the dominance of the U.S. banks was clearly weakened. The IMF had become more the main banker for the world during the late 1960s, and now the European Economic Community (EEC) and Japan were increasing the value of their currency in relation to the U.S. dollar. Normally, this would weaken some transactions globally, as the dollar would be worth less and profits would be down, but strengthen other transactions as U.S. products would be more competitive on the world market. The negative effects of inflation would be offset somewhat by increased exports. In fact, this did not happen. Inexpensive Japanese autos and foreign steel continued to supplant U.S. sales around the world and even in the United States. More important to the balance of trade was the decision by OPEC (Organization of Petroleum Exporting Countries) to raise the price of oil by withholding supplies. OPEC felt strong enough to assert their independence from the U.S. and Europe, a change from what had gone on for decades before. This had a particularly negative impact on the U.S. economy, which needed oil for the

Vietnam War as well as for domestic consumption. Furthermore, major U.S. banks had been making important profits from reselling oil from members of OPEC and their ability to continue making those profits necessitated their raising prices in the United States.

Economic processes and needs produce political and military actions, but those political and military actions in turn exert an effect on the economic well-being of the parties involved. It was not only the growing economic strength of the EEC and Japan that weakened U.S. banking dominance. It was also the sense that the United States was not politically or militarily strong enough to prevent OPEC from raising its prices. Printing up money temporarily hid the damaging impact of the prolonged war in Vietnam, but it also showed a weakness in U.S. military strength. The increased price of petroleum forced the price up, which intensified inflation, while also making it expensive for businesses to sustain production and employment. The result was increasing unemployment combined with increased inflation. As troops began to return from Vietnam, the supply of labor further exacerbated the unemployment problem, but inflation, fueled by insecurity about the future, continued to compound on itself. Increased spending caused unemployment to drop temporarily in the late 1970s as inflation soared, and then the boom-bust cycle caused a drop in inflation and a further spike in unemployment in the 1980s that was only ameliorated by tax breaks and even more record spending which resulted in the federal debt tripling in just eight years, from $930 billion to $ 2.6 trillion. (As a point of comparison, twenty two years later, the federal debt now approaches $14 trillion and the price of gold is over $1,300 an ounce.)

To boost the U.S. economy during those years, there was considerable deregulation of major industries, including banking. The removal of some of these safeguards allowed for more risky investments and then led to the Savings and Loan crisis of the 1980s.

The 1990s saw the former USSR and China turn more towards capitalism. Superficially, this seemed to indicate a triumph for U.S. capitalism, but in reality, the new capitalist policies of those countries made them formidable competitors to the U.S. as Russia worked to expand its influence in the Middle East, and China began a massive investment program in Asia, Africa, and Latin America as well as buying up bonds, which keeps the U.S. economy afloat but keeps the dollar high, allowing Chinese goods to penetrate the world market, and make the U.S. economy very vulnerable to rapid devaluation if the Chinese decide to sell these bonds. The 1990s did see a small economic bubble (and a larger one in the stock market) in the U.S. that reflected more speculation and the creation of more "imaginary money" that kept capital circulating but at the expense of laying the basis for even more instability in the future. More and more investments flowed into financial markets as the rate of profit in domestic industries dropped and deindustrialization continued in the U.S. and Britain. Globally, the money-lending policies of the IMF created massive debt in the less-developed countries that could not be paid back even with strict austerity measures that depressed the living conditions of many in those countries (Stiglitz 2002; Goldman 2005). This policy, dubbed "neoliberalism", resulted in a severe intensification of poverty in many of these countries (Bello, Cunningham, and Rau 1994; Berberoglu 2005; Harvey 2005). Mexico, too, had a crisis, and in the mid-1990s, four Asian countries which had been seen as models of rapid economic development also experienced severe economic instabilities resulting from massive debt.

In the United States, the relative stagnation and decline of U.S. corporate profits in comparison to profits in the rest of the world, and the relative decline of profitability of U.S. domestic industries between 1960 and 2008 is shown in Table 2.3.

Table 2.3 Corporate Profits by Industry and Region, 1960–2008, Selected Years (in billions of dollars: quarterly data at seasonally adjusted annual rates)

	Corporate profits with inventory valuation adjustment without capital consumption adjustment		
	U.S. total	**U.S. manufacturing**	**Rest of the world**
Year	**(billions of $)** **(% increase)**	**(billions of $)** **(% increase)**	**(billions of $)** **(% increase)**
1960	51.5	23.8	3.1
	} 53.4	} 15.5	} 120.4
1970	74.4	27.5	7.1
	} 184.1	} 184.7	} 207.0
1980	211.4	78.3	35.5
	} 88.6	} 46.1	} 249.1
1990	398.8	114.4	76.1
	} 89.3	} 45.5	} 91.3
2000	755.7	166.5	145.6
	} 88.5	} 22.0	} 142.0
2008	1,424.5	175.5	377.2

Note: The percentage increase in profits for each decade was calculated by the author from data provided in the following source.
Source: Council of Economic Advisers, Economic Report of the President, 2010, Table B-91, page 436. Also available on-line at: http://www.whitehouse.gov/sites/default/files/microsites/economic-report-president-appendix-b.pdf.

Whereas profits from U.S. industries stagnated over the past three decades (increasing around 89 percent decade to decade), profits from investments in the rest of the world increased at a much higher rate, while profits from U.S. domestic manufacturing declined, especially during the 2000s, right up to the

Great Recession of 2007–2009 (Sherman 2010, Harvey 2010). The U.S. continued to be an economic powerhouse, but its relative strength was declining and its profits were based less on producing real "things" (manufactured goods) and more and more on unstable financial markets -- markets that are intertwined with the economies of other countries through a complex network of credit and debt, such that when a debtor has a crisis, so does the creditor.

The soaring stock market and the booming real estate market (together with an expanding enormous debt), based on speculative and questionable financial dealings, a bubbled-up economy that was soon to take a rapid downturn as first the "dot.com" stock market in high tech began to drop sharply, wiping out hundreds of billions of dollars of paper wealth that had been used to capitalize other investments (James 2009), and laid the basis for the global capitalist crisis that began to unfold in 2008—the topic that Howard Sherman will take up for a detailed analysis in the next chapter.

Conclusion

The zigs and zags of the global capitalist system during the twentieth century reveal the core economic contradictions of capitalism on a global scale. The combination of unplanned production for profit and increasingly productive technology has led to repeated crises of overproduction (actually wildly imbalanced production) and erratic falling rates of profit. These contradictions were globalized, thus elevating the internal contradictions of capital from the national to the global level. Various capitalist institutions and governments attempted to implement policies to minimize these problems with varying degrees of temporary success. Sometimes liquidity is encouraged, which leads to inflation, devalued currency, and a difficulty for the debtors to repay the debts, leading then to its opposite, an economic slowdown. Sometimes the economy is intentionally contracted to minimize inflation, but that leads to recession and sometimes the inability of debtors to repay debts. However, the economic developments are not simply a zig zag between two limits, nor simply cyclical. They are rather more like a spiral, repeating the same patterns, but spiraling up (or down) towards crisis.

The individual capitalist enterprises all want solutions that will help stabilize the entire system, but not at the expense of their individual enterprises. Hence the policies they propose and implement tend to benefit one or another segment of capital, sometimes at the expense of system-wide stability. Speculation is one aspect of this. This combination of individual interest policy-making, combined with the fundamental contradiction within capitalism of production for profit, increasingly efficient technology, overproduction, and falling rates of profit lay the basis for intensifying economic instability. These in turn intertwine with political problems brought on by working class rebellion, reaction from capitalists in the less-developed countries, and intense competition from other advanced capitalist countries. The world saw two devastating world wars during the twentieth century and quite a number of other, smaller wars that were actually proxy wars among bigger capitalist powers. The end of the twentieth century and the beginning of the twenty-first saw increasing economic instability in the United States, Europe, and much of what had been called the "developing world." But these economic problems, papered over by increased debt, were only a dress rehearsal for the massive crisis that would engulf the global capitalist economy less than a decade later.

References

Bello, Walden, Shea Cunningham, and Bill Rau. 1994. *Dark Victory: The United States, Structural Adjustment, and Global Poverty*. Oakland: California, Institute for Food and Development Policy.

Berberoglu, Berch. 2003. *Globalization of Capital and the Nation-State*. Boulder, CO: Rowman and Littlefield.

———. 2005. *Globalization and Change: The Transformation of Global Capitalism*. Lanham, MD: Lexington Books.

Brenner, Robert. 2003. *The Boom and the Bubble: The U.S. in the World Economy.* London: Verso.

Duboff, Richard B. 1989. *Accumulation and Power: An Economic History of the United States*. Armonk: M.E. Sharpe.

Engdahl, F. William. 2004. *A Century of War: Anglo-American Oil Politics and the New World Order* London: Pluto Press.

Gavin, Francis J. , 2003. *Gold, Dollars, and Power – The Politics of International Monetary Relations, 1958–1971.* Charlotte: The University of North Carolina Press.

Glasner, David. 1997. "Crisis of 1873". In Glasner, David; Cooley, Thomas F., eds. *Business Cycles and Depressions: An Encyclopedia*. New York: Garland Publishing.

Goldman, Michael. 2005. *Imperial Nature: The World Bank and Struggles for Social Justice in the Age of Globalization.* New Haven, CT: Yale University Press.

Gowan, Peter. 1999. *The Global Gamble: Washington's Faustian Bid for World Dominance.* New York: Verso.

———. 2010. *A Calculus of Power: Grand Strategy in the Twenty-First Century*. London: Verso.

Harvey, David. 2005. *A Brief History of Neoliberalism*. New York: Oxford University Press.

———. 2010. *The Enigma of Capital and the Crises of Capitalism*. New York: Oxford University Press.

Hooks, Gregory. 1991. *Forging the Military-Industrial Complex. World War II's Battle of the Potomac.* Urbana-Champaign, IL: University of Illinois Press.

James, Harold. 2009. *The Creation and Destruction of Value: The Globalization Cycle* Cambridge, MA: Harvard University Press, 2009.

Keynes, John Maynard. 1965. *The General Theory of Employment, Interest, and Money* New York: Harcourt, Brace, and World.

Lenin, V.I. 1969. *Imperialism: The Highest Stage of Capitalism*. New York: International Publishers.

Levitt, Theodore. 1983. "Globalization of Markets." *Harvard Business Review*.

Mason, Edward S. and Asher, Robert E. 1973. *The World Bank Since Bretton Woods*. Washington, DC: The Brookings Institution.

National Bureau of Economic Research, available at http://www.nber.org/cycles/cyclesmain.html

Petras, James and Henry Veltmeyer. 2001. *Globalization Unmasked: Imperialism in the 21st Century*. London: Zed Books.

Stiglitz, Joseph E. 2002. *Globalization and Its Discontents*. New York: W.W. Norton.

Weinberg, Meyer. 2003. *A Short History of American Capitalism*. Chicago: New History Press.

Chapter 3

The Great Recession and the Financial Crisis in the United States, the Epicenter of the Global Capitalist Crisis[1]

Howard J. Sherman

Every expansion in U.S. history has been followed by an economic contraction. If the contraction is relatively mild by historical standards, it is called a recession. If it is more severe, it is called a depression. When the contraction lasted ten years and official unemployment went up to 25 percent in the 1930s, it was called the Great Depression.

"Absolutely sound" was President Calvin Coolidge's assessment of the economy and the stock market merely a few months before Hoover swore in as President in January 1929. In the fall of 1929, Hoover's secretary of the Treasury, Andrew Mellon, reassured one and all that "there is no cause to worry. The high tide of prosperity will continue." Finally, in mid-October 1929, no less than Irving Fishing, the preeminent U.S. economist of his day, proclaimed that "stock prices have reached what looks like a permanently high plateau" (see Galbraith 1988: 15, 26, 41, and 70).

A few days later the stock market crashed, and the U.S economy sank into a depression that was to last a decade. By 1933, at least 25 percent of the labor force was unemployed and another 25 percent were on involuntary part-time work or were so discouraged that they gave up looking for jobs. The homeless, the hungry, and the desperate were never fully counted. The most famous pictures of the era showed long lines of people waiting for free bread or a bowl of soup. These breadlines, as they were called, would sometimes extend for blocks from the entrance of a soup kitchen.

The term "depression" was commonly used before World War II to refer to any economic contraction. From 1948 to 2001, there were 10 minor contractions.

---

1   This chapter is an edited and condensed version of the author's original book, *The Roller Coaster Economy: Financial Crisis, the Great Recession, and the Public Option* (Armonk, NY: M.E. Sharpe, 2010). Copyright © 2010 by M.E. Sharpe, Inc. Reprinted with permission of M.E. Sharpe, Inc. www.mesharpe.com All Rights Reserved. Not for Reproduction. The editor, Berch Berberoglu, edited various sections of the book in extracting text to compile the present chapter which is published here with the approval of the author.

Conservatives did not like the term "depression" because it reminded everyone of the horrors of the Great Depression which they would rather forget, while denying that the economy had any basic problem. So the conservatives invented the term "recession" to convey the idea that the problem was mild and temporary. Eventually the term "recession" was widely used.

In 2009, the United States was in the most violent contraction since 1929. It was even larger than the recession of 1982, which had been the biggest one since the 1930s. Conservatives want to call it a recession. But that word is not strong enough for most people. Paul Volcker, a past chair of the Federal Reserve System, has called it a "Great Recession" (Volcker 2009: 1).

In the first half of 2009, unemployment in the United States rose by half a million every month. The auto industry was especially hard-hit. Of the big three, General Motors (GM) sold the lowest number of vehicles in 49 years in 2008. Both GM and Chrysler, the third largest auto company, went bankrupt in 2009.

The reality reported every few days in all U.S. newspapers in 2008 and 2009 was that many firms, not just automobile makers, were firing thousands of people at a time. Citigroup, the giant banking conglomerate, decided to terminate 53,000 employees. Alcoa, the aluminum maker, decided to cut 15,000 workers, 13 percent of its worldwide workforce. DHL, the express shipper, decided to get rid of 9,500 workers, 73 percent of its U.S workforce. Dell computers announced it would lay off 8,900 workers, one-tenth of its workforce. Circuit City, the failing electronics retailer, announced it would let go of 8,000 workers, one-fifth of its work force (this is before it went out of business). And many, many more companies could be added to this list.

A "Great Recession" reflects actuality a lot better than just the term "recession." The Great Recession of 2007 to 2009 reflected new economic structures that have arisen in the last thirty years and have born a bitter fruit. More people have lost their jobs than in any other contraction since the Great Depression. Although it is not in the same class with the Great Depression, this Great Recession is bigger than any of the previous recessions in many ways. Americans have witnessed a deep contraction with an entirely different quality. An elephant is not just a bigger horse; it is qualitatively different.

Moreover, this contraction represented dramatic changes in the economic structure. The structure of the economy means the building blocks of which it is built and how they fit together. No contraction since the Great Depression has caused such a strong financial crisis. No other recession has seen millions of foreclosures that meant the end of the American dream of owning a house. No other recession has had so many large corporations teetering close to bankruptcy.

But there was also a financial crisis in the middle of the Great Recession. This crisis has been building for decades as the whole economic structure slowly changed. So the most accurate description of the 2007 to 2009 situation would be a Great Recession with a Financial Crisis. As a shortcut, we will use the term "Great Recession" in referring to the period 2007 to 2009.

History of the Roller Coaster Economy

In the United States, the transformation to a market economy took place in the nineteenth century. The United States in 1800 was mostly a land of self-sufficient farms. By 1900, the country had become a land of factories that had to sell their goods on the market in order to continue production. If millions of consumers did not buy enough automobiles, automobile workers lost their jobs. Thus, the transition to a market economy was one condition for a business cycle that would threaten most economic units.

In these capitalist economies beginning to take hold in Europe and the United States, where privately produced goods and services were sold in the market, the market became the chief means of generating income. Shop owners, factory owners, factory workers, those workers in their home all depended on the sale of the product of their labor to obtain an income. Whether products were sold depended on the purchasing decisions of millions of people. The buyers of products included fellow workers, factory owners, the land-owning aristocracy, shopkeepers, and professionals. The mass of these purchasing decisions made up the total, or aggregate, demand or spending-decision on the market economy.

In previous economic systems, the self-sufficient economic unit, the farmer or crafts person, produced a trickle of handmade items for known customers. When an economic unit consumed almost all that it produced, supply necessarily matched demand. Under capitalism, however, all the goods and services must be sold in the market if production is to continue. Production for the market, thus, is the first precondition for a business cycle.

With the coming of capitalism in Western Europe and the United States, another drastic change in economic institutions was the regular use of money in market transactions. Money was a necessary ingredient in the stew that led to the emergence of a business cycle of boom and bust.

The monetary system took the place of the barter system used in medieval feudal Europe and in the early Western United States. In the barter system, one good is exchanged for another good. Thus, a farmer brings pigs to the market and exchanges them for a cow.

Money replaced the barter system because money is much more convenient to use. But the widespread reliance on money allows economies to suffer from a lack of spending. Not enough aggregate demand expressed in money may lead to a recession or depression.

The problem in a capitalist economy is not a lack of money in the economy as a whole. There are people who wish to buy, but may have no money. Yet there are also people who have money but may not wish to spend it at present.

If people do not spend money income for consumer goods or services, they may still invest that money in equipment and buildings. If they do not spend their money income for consumption or for investment, then they leave it idle. Idle money reduces spending in the economy. Non-spending can slow or stop the flow of money through the economy at any point. When the flow of money slows or stops, so too does the flow of products through the economy, since products are only produced to be sold for money.

As the economy turns down in a recession, many people lose jobs and no longer have money to purchase even necessities. Without money to spend, these potential consumers are unable to buy products, which pile up in warehouses. This excess supply gets larger and larger as the economy slows. Many potential consumers in need go without because they do not have the money to buy these products.

The use of credit intensifies money problems. Relying on money and credit institutions makes an economy susceptible to the booms and busts of the business cycle. Financial crises can stop the whole economy when industry becomes dominant and relies on credit.

Production for the market and regular use of money must both be present if there is to be a roller-coaster economy with business cycles. But one more capitalist institution is necessary before a business recession or depression can occur. That necessary condition is production for private profit within a system of private ownership of production facilities.

Business cycles of boom and bust are found only in countries in which the economy is primarily run by private business motivated by profit. Businesses live and die for profit.

From 1800 to the U.S. Civil War in 1860, the British business cycle led the U.S. business cycle by a nose. Great Britain supplied most of the manufactured goods to the United States, while the United States shipped much food and raw materials to Britain. So a rise or decline in British business affected the smaller U.S. economy.

From the Civil War to World War I in 1914, the U.S. economy expanded rapidly, but did suffer several depressions. The worst was the depression of the 1890s, when the unemployment rate rose to 18 percent and stayed at double-digit levels for six years.

In the 1920s, the U.S. economy grew rapidly, but also endured three short recessions. Then the Great Depression struck, lasting a full decade from 1929 to 1939. Economies across the globe collapsed during the 1930s. From 1929 to 1932, gross domestic product, the broadest measure of national output, dropped 28 percent in the United States, 16 percent in Germany, 8 percent in Japan, and 6 percent in Britain (Aldcroft 1993: 64).

The official unemployment rate in the United States reached 25 percent, but the actual unemployment rate was yet higher. Businesses went bankrupt, banks foreclosed on mortgages, pushing homeowners out of their houses, wages fell, and prices dropped. The decrease in output in every sector of the economy was enormous. The output of the economy remained depressed for most of the ten years. Because people had little or no money to spend, there was little demand for what was produced. Even as people went hungry, farmers, at the behest of government officials, burned mounds of potatoes and tomatoes because no one could pay for them.

In 1941, World War II saved the United States from the Great Depression. The U.S. government bought 40 percent of the gross domestic product for war purposes at the height of the war effort. This massive government spending provided plenty of demand and jobs. The war pushed the official unemployment rate to 1 percent. By 1943, there was a shortage of labor because unlimited numbers of people were needed for the army and for production of war supplies.

Since the war, the U.S. economy has grown rapidly for long periods, punctuated by relatively mild and short recessions. These recessions meant misery to millions of people, but never threatened the economy with a long depression. All in all, from 1800 to the present, there have been thirty-six recessions or depressions, causing economic stagnation and human harm.

The Rise and Fall of U.S. Capitalism

During the golden age of U.S. capitalism, the first two decades after World War II, the U.S. economy grew rapidly. The growth lifted workers' incomes and alleviated poverty. U.S. banks and corporations loaned money to foreign banks and corporations. The United States was the largest creditor country in the world. The United States exported far more than it imported, so money flowed into the economy. This excess of exports over imports is called a favorable balance of trade or a trade surplus. The U.S. economy produced more than the rest of the world put together for a while, while also trading more than the rest of the world put together.

With its dominant position in the world economy, the U.S. economy grew an average of 4.4 percent a year from 1950 to 1969. The United States had strong trade unions and expanding government programs to protect employees. There were also programs to fight poverty, which spread the benefits of economic growth to most Americans.

The U.S. economy grew rapidly in the 1950s and 1960s, but in the following three decades, 1970 to 2000, it grew more slowly. Not only did GDP grow more slowly, but many other developments also weakened the U.S. economy. Production in other countries rose faster than U.S. production. Therefore, the U.S. share of world production dropped. The U.S. economy went from being the largest creditor to being the largest debtor. The United States changed from having the largest trade surplus to having the largest trade deficit. The percentage of workers in trade unions steadily declined.

Inequality between poor and rich Americans had declined in the period from 1950 to 1970. In the period from 1970 to the present, inequality between rich and poor rose continuously in every decade.

Over this long period, GDP growth slowed considerably from the 4.4 percent a year in the 1950–1969 period. It was only 3.4 percent a year in the 1970–2000 period. This decline may be seen very clearly in Figure 3.1.

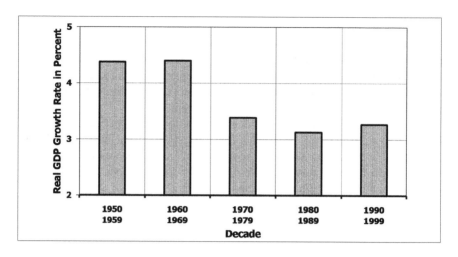

Figure 3.1 Gross Domestic Product, by Decade, 1950–1999
Source: Bureau of Economic Analysis, Department of Commerce (www.bea.gov).
Note: Gross domestic product. Percent change, quarter to quarter, 1950 to 1999 in billions of chained 2000 dollars. (Chained 2000 dollars means that all of the series is corrected for inflation with a base of the year 2000.) Seasonally adjusted quarterly data aggregated to decade data, at annual rates.

During this period of slower growth, unions and workers lost ground in the struggle over who gets what out of national income. This shift in income distribution happened partly because social spending programs and government protections were gutted.

From 1949 to 2001, there were nine recessions in the United States, with similar declines in most of the capitalist world. In these contractions, GDP suffered relatively mild declines. There was also a mild decline in the use of productive capacity, with more equipment and buildings idle. The unemployment rate rose in each of these recessions. But the decline in jobs ranged from 5 to 10 percent unemployment rates. This was far below the 25 percent unemployment of the Great Depression, so it was considered very mild, except by the millions of people who lost their jobs for a year or more.

The U.S. economy grew more slowly in the expansion of 2001 to 2007 than in any of the earlier recessions since World War II. GDP grew at an anemic rate of 2.49 percent a year in that expansion. It is important to understand that what made most Americans unhappy with the expansion under President Bush was that most of the income generated by an increased GDP went to the wealthy and much less went to the middle class and the poor.

The basic cyclical rise and fall of employment has been repeated in the latest expansion and contraction. But some trends of the last couple of recessions became far more pronounced in the Bush expansion and the Great Recession.

In both the expansion of the 1980s and that of the 1990s, employment was slow to recover from the previous recession, but this trend was emphasized dramatically in the expansion from 2001 to 2007. The number of jobs actually continued to decline in the first two years of the expansion, an unprecedented event. Moreover, the number of jobs did not recover to the prerecession peak until 2005, about four years into the recovery. The time it took to recover to the former job level was about twice as long as in the average of the previous five cycles.

The previous five expansions had added over 2.5 percent new jobs a year to the labor force. The 2001 expansion, however, added less than 1 percent of new jobs a year. Why was this expansion so jobless by comparison to earlier ones? Fewer jobs were needed because of the lower economic growth. Furthermore, global competition led firms to do everything possible to use new technology that would replace workers with machines. Moreover, with increased global competition, U.S. firms exported jobs to other countries with lower wages; for example, many U.S. corporations hired computer savvy employees in India.

While the Bush expansion of 2001 left millions of disappointed workers with poor-paying jobs or no jobs at all, the Great Recession, beginning in late 2007, was much worse. It was a major factor in the defeat of the Republican Party in the 2008 presidential elections.

The Great Recession of 2007 to 2009

How did GDP behave in the Great Recession and during the financial crisis of 2008? This question is answered pictorially in Figure 3.2.

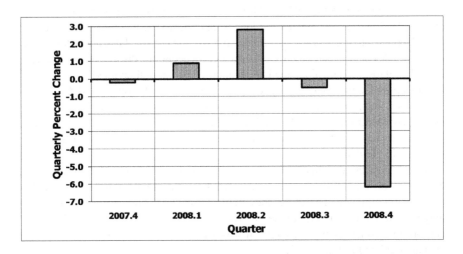

Figure 3.2 Gross Domestic Product in the Crisis, 2007.4–2008.4

Source: Bureau of Economic Analysis, U.S. Department of Commerce (www.bea.gov).
Note: Real gross domestic product. Percent change, quarter-to-quarter, 2007.4 to 2008.4, in billions of chained 2000 dollars. Seasonally adjusted quarterly data, at annual rates.

The Great Recession began in the last quarter of 2007, but became much worse in 2008. There was a slight decline of GDP at the peak in the fourth quarter of 2007. But there was still a little growth in the first half of 2008. Then there was a tiny decline of in the third quarter of 2008. In the last quarter of 2008, GDP declined at an annual rate of 6.3 percent. This decline was a striking loss to society. It meant that the economy was engulfed in the worst downturn since the Great Depression.

By the time the recession began in the fourth quarter of 2007, housing prices had been declining for more than a year. Corporate profit was becoming stagnant. The risky mortgages were held by financial companies, so when the mortgages were foreclosed, it caused a financial panic. Other factors played more important roles than housing in causing the recession, but housing certainly was one of the chief actors starting it.

All cyclical downturns have most features in common, but also some unique features. In 2007, before the beginning of the Great Recession in December, one could see the usual signals of economic distress. Most forms of aggregate revenue, such as all consumer spending, had slowed their rate of growth. Most parts of aggregate cost, such as oil prices and interest rates, were rising rapidly. Profit comes from revenue minus cost. So aggregate profit slowed down and then fell. In addition, however, in this particular expansion, housing prices had been falling since 2006, while banks were issuing an amazing flood of dangerous-looking loans—usually signs of a recession turning into a depression.

The contraction from 2007 to 2009 is called the Great Recession for obvious reasons. By 2009, it was already the longest and most severe contraction since the Great Depression of the 1930s. The financial crisis, the housing bust, and a downturn in the global economy combined to create a level of economic distress unprecedented since the 1930s. In 2008 alone the U.S. economy lost 2.6 million jobs. Not since the Great Depression has the economy lost jobs every month of a year as it did in 2008.

During 2008, the number of jobs in the whole economy declined every single month. By December, more than half a million jobs were being lost each month. Newspapers reported thousands of job losses every day. A total of 2.6 million jobs were lost in 2008 alone.

Every day large firms announced that they were laying-off thousands of workers. The unemployed then had much less income than when they were previously employed. Therefore, they bought less goods and services than when they were at paid work. Of course, the reduction in total national demand caused corporations to let go more workers. It was a vicious downward spiral. The exact data are depicted in Figure 3.3.

According to Figure 3.3, unemployment rose during every one of the first five quarters of the Great Recession. The biggest increases were in the third and fourth quarters of 2008, when the intense financial crisis was spreading disaster all around. The number of job losses, however, continued to climb throughout the first quarter of 2009.

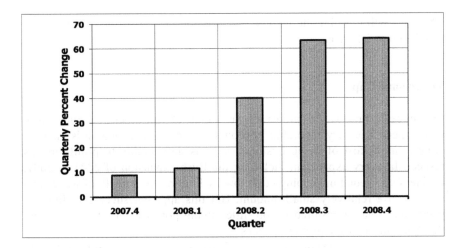

Figure 3.3 Unemployment Rate in the Crisis, 2007.4–2008.4

Source: Bureau of Labor Statistics, U.S. Department of Labor (www.bls.gov).

Note: Unemployment rate is the ratio of all unemployed workers to all members of the civilian labor force. Percent change, quarter to quarter, 2007.4 to 2008.4, seasonally adjusted quarterly data, at annual rates.

The decline in GDP in the Great Recession of 2007 to 2009 has been greater than in any of the last nine recessions. Unemployment appears to be growing to a higher level than in any of these earlier recessions.

    The signs of economic distress were not confined to the labor market. In the fall of 2008, consumer spending registered a large decline, unlike the tiny decline in the 2001 recession. As household incomes declined, workers lost jobs, and consumers cut back on spending. Worried consumers reduced their household debt for the first time since the Great Depression. As consumers scrimped, retail sales plummeted. Major retailers, even eBay, let go of workers while others, such as Circuit City, went out of business. Prices fell significantly in 2008, the first annual drop since 1949. All the major capitalist economies went into recession in 2008 and got worse in 2009.

    The crisis of 2008 and the following recession illustrate dramatically the main point of this chapter. Capitalist economies are vulnerable to a cycle of expansion and recession or even severe recession. One important clue to the mystery of recessions and depressions is the fact that in every expansion, as in the 2001 expansion, the GDP rises fairly rapidly in the first half of expansion, then more and more slowly in the last half. The exact same trend is found in many other major economic variables, such as consumer spending. This clue shows that the causes of recession and depression are to be found in the underlying trends in the preceding expansion. Far more dramatic clues to the causes of the Great Recession, and all such contractions, will be given in the following sections, where we will examine the income gap, the housing crisis, the credit balloon and the financial crisis.

The Income Gap

Employee income is the largest single source of consumer spending, so in this respect it is very favorable to profits. But employee income is also the largest single cost of doing business, so it is unfavorable to profits in this respect. In every expansion, including the Bush expansion of 2001 to 2007, business succeeded in keeping costs low by limiting the growth of wages and salaries to a relatively small amount. But this apparent success in limiting wages and salaries resulted in too little buying power to buy the increasing flood of consumer goods and services.

In the Bush expansion of 2001 to 2007, there was a rapidly increasing income gap between wages and salaries on the one hand and corporate profits on the other hand. The fact that this gap rose dramatically in the Bush expansion is crucial. It reduced the buying power of most Americans. This meant less ability to buy consumer goods and services, which caused that sector to slow its growth to a crawl. The income gap also meant less buying power to purchase new homes. It eventually limited construction and forced people to get very risky mortgages to finance their new homes. This was a major force underlying the financial crisis to come.

In the 1950s and 1960s, the income of the average worker rose every year. Thus, middle-income workers had the money to afford a modest home and education for their children.

From 1970 to the present, however, wages and salaries (adjusted for inflation) have stagnated. The average middle-income worker no longer puts away some savings. Most people of average income now go into debt. This is a very drastic change in the economy and society.

In terms of income, there are two Americas: the enormous class of workers and the tiny class of capitalists. It will be shown that most of the wealth goes to rich individuals, who own the giant corporations, while the average worker has a far smaller income based on the labor that is done by the worker.

As long as workers work for a firm, some of their product becomes profit. This institutionalized giveaway helps to explain the increasing trend toward inequality. "The increase in inequality," according to Larry Summers, the top economic adviser to President Obama, "meant that each family in the bottom 80 percent of the income distribution was effectively sending a $10,000 check, every year, to the top 1 percent of earners" (see Leonhardt 2009).

In 2005 the poorest 20 percent had less than 4 percent of all income. In the same year, however, the richest 20 percent had over 50 percent of all income. And the richest 1 percent, the superrich, had 21 percent of all income to themselves. Those are enormous differences in income. Wealth, on the other hand, is all that has been saved out of income during a person's lifetime. Since most people are unable to save because they must use their whole income for necessities, only the rich can save large amounts and pile up wealth.

Wealth is, therefore, much more unequally owned than is income. In 2004, the top 1 percent of Americans owned 34 percent of all the wealth. When averaged out, the bottom 60 percent, including most of the middle-income group as well as the poor, had no wealth at all. That average of the wealth of the lowest 60 percent of Americans comes to zero because it includes not only the savings of those who are fairly well off, but also the debts and liabilities that everyone has.

Not only is there inequality in America, but this richest of all countries also has a large amount of outright poverty. According to the U.S. Census Bureau, the average poverty threshold for unrelated individuals in 2007 was an income of $10,787, and for a family of three with one child, the poverty-level income was $16,689. In 2007, 12.5 percent of the U.S. population lived in poverty, according to official government data. Nearly 11 percent of families lived below the poverty level.

For female-headed households, the numbers are even worse. In 2007, a little over 28 percent of female-headed households lived below the poverty threshold. Even more surprising is the number of working people who live below the poverty threshold. Just over 11 percent of people living below the poverty level worked year-round, full-time jobs.

The average hourly wage (for nonsupervisory workers) in 1972 was $19.32. In 2007, 35 years later, the average hourly wage had dropped to $17.88. (These figures are in real dollars, that is, adjusted for inflation. Adjusting for inflation will always mean here using the appropriate price deflator supplied by the government.) As real wages declined, aggregate U.S. production actually rose by 180.7 percent over the same period.

Although ordinary production-line workers suffered in this period from stagnant real-wage rates, corporate chief executive officers (CEOs) did very well. The salaries of CEOs rose from 41 times the average wage in 1960 to 326 times the average wage in 1997 and to 411 times the average wage in 2005. The one thing that ordinary workers were able to increase was their debt. The debt of the average household rose from 29.5 percent of personal income in 1949 to 65 percent of personal income in the mid-1980s and then to 113 percent of personal income in 2007.

It is worth stressing that the members of the richest 1 percent—from millionaires to billionaires—make most of their income from property ownership, mainly from ownership of corporations. The only apparent exception is the salary of CEOs, but these enormous salaries are actually corporate profit for the most part. Corporations also often give CEOs the option to buy stock at very favorable prices.

On the other hand, the income of the bottom 90 percent comes primarily from wages and salaries. The bottom 90 percent, however, receives only negligible amounts of property income.

The division of income was examined above in terms of individuals at different levels of income. But there are also data on the aggregate amount of income by class. An economic class is any group of people with common interests. There are a number of significant classes in the United States, including workers, farmers, small business people, and capitalist owners of corporations. This section focuses on the working class and the capitalist class, which are vital for understanding the business cycle.

Workers labor all the normal working day for a corporation or some other business. But under the economic system of capitalism, everything produced by workers goes to the capitalist. When the goods or services are sold, the capitalist then pays the worker a certain wage or salary. After paying for wages and salaries, as well as raw materials and equipment, the capitalist keeps the rest of the revenue. That revenue is called "profit".

Wage and salaried employees are over 90 percent of the population, but they get much less than that share of the national income. Capitalists who own significant capital are only about 1 percent of the population, but they have a very large percentage of the national income.

Over the five cycles from 1970 until 2001, the gap between workers' income and the whole national income has grown rapidly. In other words, property income has increased much faster than workers' income.

Much of the gap is due to the rapid rise of corporate profit. The increasing gap between all national income and employee income reflects the simple fact that wages and salaries have grown slowly, while corporate profit has grown rapidly.

During the 2001 to 2007 expansion, corporate profit increased its pace of growth to an astonishing degree. In mid-expansion, corporate profit rose 20 percent in 2004 (see Figure 3.4). Employee income grew less than corporate profits every year except 2001 during the recession, when profit actually fell. Thus, as in every postwar expansion, profits grew faster than wages, salaries, and benefits. The difference from previous expansions was that the gap between the slow rise of wages and salaries and the extraordinary rise of profit was enormous in the Bush expansion.

The increasing gap between profit and employee income is a very powerful clue to explain the behavior of consumer spending. Thus, this gap is a major key to the unraveling of the mystery of why an expansion ever ends and a recession or depression begins.

The Great Recession began in the fourth quarter of 2007 and continued its economic contraction into 2009. The financial crisis, which was part of the Great Recession, became a panic in the fourth quarter of 2008. For this reason employee income and corporate profit both fell in 2007 and 2008, but the biggest decline was in the fourth quarter of 2008.

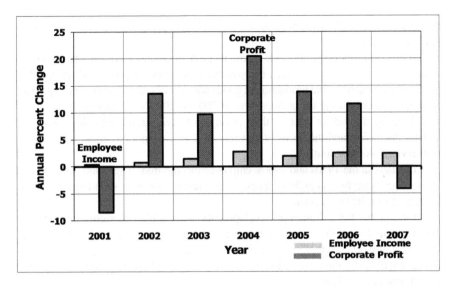

Figure 3.4 Employee Income and Corporate Profit, by Year, 2001–2007
Source: Bureau of Economic Analysis, Department of Commerce (www.bea.gov).
Note: Employee income is all wages, salaries, and benefits. Profit is corporate profit before taxes. Percent change, year-to-year, 2001 to 2007, in billions of actual dollars.

When employee income falls, it sets up a vicious circle in the economy. The vicious circle of the Great Recession went this way. Less employment leads to less aggregate employee income. Less income leads to less spending. Less spending means fewer sales and profits across the economy. The story begins again when less sales lead to less employment. Every unemployed person means a further reduction of consumer spending.

Why did the vicious circle accelerate downward? When millions of workers, from low paid to high paid, lost their jobs in 2007, this had to lead to less consumer spending. In late 2008 and early 2009, every day of the week thousands of workers lost their jobs. Every day of the week, one could see that less and less people brought home paychecks. Lost income meant less spending. Lower consumer spending leads to less profit, less production, and more workers losing their jobs.

The Consumption Gap

The largest single element of expenditures in the U.S. economy comes from the American consumer. Consumer spending was the Energizer Bunny that kept the economy growing through the 1990s and for the first seven years of this century. After that expansion, however, the Great Recession of 2007 to 2009 witnessed the disastrous economic consequences of what happens when consumers cut back on spending.

When consumption is cut back below its peak, it creates a consumption gap. In other words, it is the gap between the possible production of goods and services for people to use and the actual production of goods and services under the present capitalist economic system. In the Great Recession of 2007 to 2009, the actual production was held down by the lack of demand from paying customers. In the capitalist economic system, the desires and the needs of consumers, if they cannot pay money for goods and services, do not count.

Long ago, in the 1950s and 1960s, employee income from wages and salaries rose almost every year by a significant amount. As a result, consumer spending rose most years by a significant amount.

In the early 1970s, however, developments in the global economy changed all that. For one thing, other countries began to catch up with the United States, so the U.S. share of world production and trade began to fall. Due to that competition and the weakening of labor unions by various means, real wages and salaries showed very little growth from then till now.

Since employee income is the largest source of consumer spending, there was a big decline over the decades in the growth rate of consumer spending. The weakened growth of consumer spending was one of the major causes of the Great Recession of 2007 and the country's inability to recover from the downturn in 2008 and 2009.

During the 2001 to 2007 expansion, the gap between the growth rate of employee income and corporate profit was enormous. With less and less of the national income, workers had less to spend on consumption. They used an increasing amount of credit to fill the gap. Yet even with credit, the weak recovery—plus the very weak growth of jobs and employee income—resulted in a very slow growth of consumption compared with earlier cycles. These trends can be seen in Figure 3.5.

Figure 3.5 shows that consumption during the Bush expansion moved upward rapidly in the first half of the expansion. Its highest growth rate was reached in the middle of the expansion. After reaching a peak growth rate in 2004, consumer spending rose more and more slowly up to the peak of the expansion in 2007.

The slower growth of consumer spending, down to a much lower growth by the end, was one factor leading to the Great Recession, which began in the fourth quarter of 2007. Thus, the consumer gap not only means less consumption for individuals, but also poses an increasing danger to the economy. It was not the only danger, but it was an important one.

What happened to consumer spending from the beginning of the Great Recession in the last quarter of 2007 through the financial panic in the last quarter of 2008? The answer is shown in Figure 3.6.

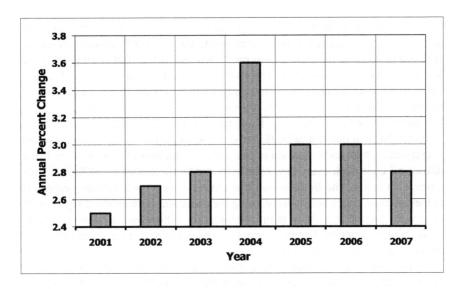

Figure 3.5 Consumer Spending by Year, 2001–2007
Source: Bureau of Economic Analysis, Department of Commerce (www.bea.gov).
Note: Consumer spending, percent change, year to year.

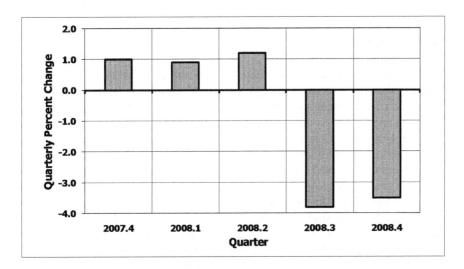

Figure 3.6 Consumer Spending in the Crisis, 2007.4–2008.4
Source: Bureau of Economic Analysis, Department of Commerce (www.bea.gov).
Note: Consumer spending, percent change, quarter to quarter.

As usual, consumers attempted to carry on in the Great Recession as they had been doing in the late expansion. For the first three quarters of the Great Recession, consumers managed to continue the slow growth pace. How did they do that when people were beginning to lose their jobs? Those with savings dug into their savings to pay the bills. Those who had no savings resorted to an increase in their credit. If they could get credit no other way, some people took out a larger mortgage. Somehow the average consumer kept up almost the same standard of living for some time in the crisis.

In the last two quarters of 2008, however, the Great Recession became apparent to everyone. Job losses became enormous, and large numbers of workers were being thrown off their work every day. Finally, by the fourth quarter of 2008, there was a freeze on credit. The freeze meant that almost no one could borrow, regardless of their income. Since people were losing their jobs and were unable to get credit, they were forced to reduce their consumption. There was a large decline in aggregate consumption. People reduced every kind of spending, from children's toys to medically prescribed drugs.

Such a slowing of consumption growth, followed by a large two-quarter decline, had been unknown since the Great Depression. When credit dried up and more and more people lost their jobs in the second half of 2008, the resulting collapse of consumption pushed the economy into the Great Recession. This event provides another clue toward a solution of the mystery of the onset of the Great Recession.

The Housing Crisis

As this chapter is being written, the U.S. economy is in the grip of a virulent housing crisis. In this crisis, housing construction is declining, housing prices are falling, and foreclosures are skyrocketing. The crisis is hurting people and it is hurting the rest of the economy. How did this happen?

In the 1950s and 1960s, average income rose year to year. More and more middle-income workers bought homes. From the 1970s to the present, however, the average worker's income stagnated, so workers did not earn enough money to buy a house. They used credit to fill the gap. After 2006, however, many people could not pay their mortgages and millions lost their homes.

During the expansion of 2001 to 2007 housing construction rose much of that period until 2006. The path of housing construction in the expansion is shown in Figure 3.7. The graph reveals that housing construction rose a tiny bit even in the recession year of 2001. Then it continued to rise faster and faster, reaching about 10 percent growth in 2004 in the mid-expansion. It was a bright spot in the recovery and helped to raise the general rate of growth during a weak recovery. In 2005 it still agreed with GDP and consumption in that it continued to grow, but more slowly.

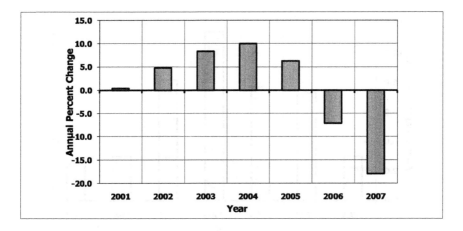

Figure 3.7 Housing Construction by Year, 2001–2007
Source: Bureau of Economic Analysis, Department of Commerce (www.bea.gov).
Note: Housing construction is defined as real residential private domestic investment, percent change, year to year, 2001 to 2007, in billions of chained 2000 dollars, seasonally adjusted.

In the last two years of the expansion, however, it deviated strongly from other sectors. The long rapid growth and the bubble in housing were over. Housing construction began its decline in 2006. It led the cycle by a considerable amount, falling while the expansion continued. In comparison with the last five cycles, it fell much sooner in the expansion and fell much stronger than in the earlier cycles. It was perhaps the major contributor to the business cycle contraction that began at the end of 2007.

In fact, as we shall see later, the decline of housing construction, the fall in housing prices, and the great increase in foreclosures set off the financial crisis. It was not the sole cause of that crisis by any means, but it pushed a steadily weakening and increasingly fragile financial structure over the brink.

Housing prices for the period 2001 to 2007 are depicted in Figure 3.8 showing that they went slowly upward in 2001, even though it was a recession year. The bubble in housing prices then continued to grow rapidly until it reached almost 12 percent annual growth in 2004. At that point, housing prices began to weaken. There were three years of slower and slower growth of housing prices. Housing prices rose at a slow crawl up to the cycle peak, and then fell precipitously during the recession.

Housing construction led the way down in the period before the Great Recession began in the fourth quarter of 2007. What happened next is shown in Figure 3.9, which shows that in the first half year of the recession housing construction fell at a very rapid pace. The average decline was at a rate of about 25 percent a year. This strong decline began before GDP or most of the economy had fallen very far, so housing was still a downward leader.

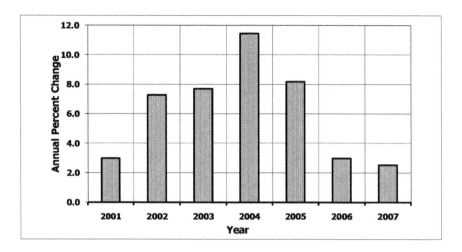

Figure 3.8 Housing Prices by Year, 2001–2007
Source: U.S. Census Bureau (www.census.gov).
Note: Sales price of houses sold, percent change, year to year, 2001 to 2007, in current dollars.

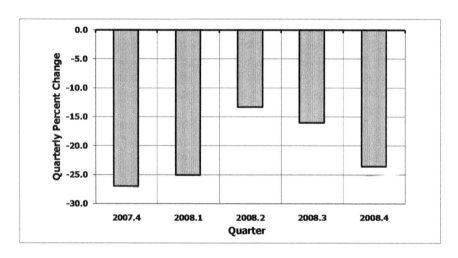

Figure 3.9 Housing Construction in the Crisis, 2007.4–2008.4
Source: Bureau of Economic Analysis, Department of Commerce (www.bea.gov).
Note: Residential construction is defined as real residential private domestic investment, percent change, quarter to quarter, 2007.4 to 2008.4, in billions of chained 2000 dollars, seasonally adjusted quarterly data, at annual rates.

The main reason for the housing decline was that the average middle-income worker, lacked the money to buy a home at the inflated, bubble prices. Now the situation had worsened because many workers had lost their jobs. Furthermore, banks were becoming afraid to lend much credit through mortgages because they finally realized that this was a very risky market.

One important indicator of the risk being taken was the rise in the number of subprime mortgages – loans on houses in which the borrower has less funds and lower income than the bank considers safe for making a loan.

In the expansion of 2001 to 2007, however, banks and other lenders assumed that people would get better and better jobs as time went on. So they gave mortgages with small down payments and assumed that the homeowners would get higher and higher wages or salaries so that they could make their payments of interest and principal of the loan. This bank behavior worked fairly well as long as the economy kept rising, so that people received more and more income. As soon as income started to stagnate in 2006 and to fall in the recession, the subprime loans could not be paid back. People lost their homes. Without these payments, banks and other home mortgage lenders got weaker and weaker, till many went bankrupt.

In the second quarter of 2008, the economy did a little better and the recession took a breather. So the rate of decline of housing construction slowed, but was still well over 10 percent a year. After that, as the economy got much worse, the decline of housing construction was at 24 percent a year in the fourth quarter of 2008.

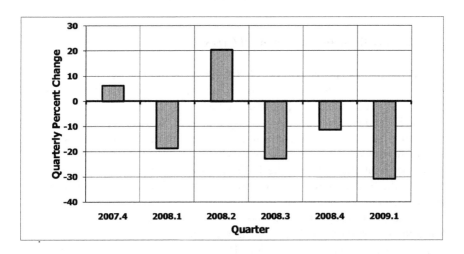

Figure 3.10 Housing Prices in the Crisis, 2007.4–2009.1
Source: U.S. Census Bureau (www.census.gov).
Note: Average sales price of houses sold, percent change, quarter to quarter, in annual rates, 2007.4 to 2009.1, in current dollars, at annual rates.

In brief, housing construction and the general business cycle interact. In this case, housing construction led the downward economic spiral. The bad mortgage loans hurt the financial system, which hurt the rest of the economy. When the economy did a little better in the first half of 2008, it caused housing to decline a little slower. When the rest of the economy declined faster in the last half of 2008, so did housing construction.

The extreme rise in housing prices from 1970 to 2001 was an important part of the extraordinary boom in housing. Their subsequent rapid decline in 2008 and 2009 was an important part of the extraordinary crash in the housing market.

Figure 3.10 reveals how housing prices acted in the first five quarters of the Great Recession. Figure 3.10 tells a very clear story about housing prices. Housing prices continued to extend the bubble by a tiny bit even in the last quarter of 2007, when the Great Recession officially began. Then the bubble started to break in the beginning of 2008. When GDP recovered a little in the second quarter of 2008, housing prices breathed their last gasp upward. In the next three quarters of the severe recession, housing prices declined rapidly. By the fourth quarter of 2008, housing prices declined at an annual rate of 30 percent! So the great boom in housing was followed by the crash in housing.

For the entire period from the 1970s to 2007, the growth of real wages and salaries has been sluggish to nonexistent. This meant that it was harder and harder for the average American to buy a home because housing prices continued to rise faster than most other prices.

So what fueled the great housing boom? Obviously, the answer is increasing credit in the form of mortgages. This was a major part of the story of the credit balloon.

The Credit Balloon and the Financial Crisis

To understand the financial crisis of 2008 to 2009, one must understand the Federal Reserve System, which is supposed to regulate finance. There was a bad financial crisis in 1907, which led to the birth of the Federal Reserve.

The Federal Reserve System was begun in 1912. It was supposed to prevent financial crises by requiring banks to keep minimum necessary reserves and by lending to banks as a last resort to save them.

In the Great Depression of the 1930s, however, the Federal Reserve failed to preserve the banks. They were all closed, and then slowly reopened with many new regulations and safeguards.

By the 1960s, people began to forget the terrible financial crisis of the 1930s. Since the 1960s, there has been a broad movement of all kinds of conservatives to end as many regulations as possible. By 2007, most financial regulations were gone. It was explained that competition made the system self-regulating, so no regulations were needed. Even the few remaining regulations were evaded by the financial institutions to a remarkable degree. Each new president, from President Reagan through President George W. Bush, got rid of more regulations.

When consumers borrow money from a financial agency, they obtain a certain amount of credit. Consumer credit grew enormously from 1970 to 2001. Why did consumer credit rise so rapidly? Earlier we showed that the real income of the average worker grew very little in that period. Just to keep up with family needs, most Americans felt pressure to get more and more credit.

The really interesting question is whether the ratio of debt to an average person's income rose or fell. What actually happened in this long period? In the 1970–1975 cycle, the ratio of consumer debt to national income was 64 percent on the average. This means that the debt owed by the average person was almost two-thirds of income in an average year. That is a lot of debt burden. By 2001, people owed an amount equal to their yearly income. In fact, the average person had to pay 14 cents of every dollar earned for interest payments.

The amount of credit kept growing regardless of the cycle of expansion and recession. It just grew a little faster in expansions than in recessions. This was not a cyclical problem, just the long-run growth of a credit bubble of amazing proportions.

In fact, as long as people could get more credit it merely helped the expansion continue. It was only when, in 2008, people lost their jobs and banks no longer extended more credit that the situation became a disaster.

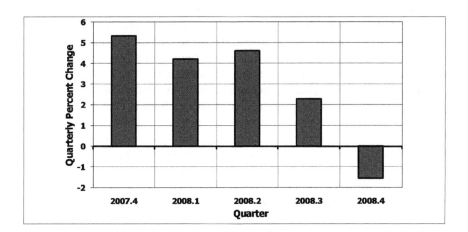

Figure 3.11 Consumer Credit in the Crisis, 2007.4–2008.4
Source: Federal Reserve Board off Governors, table G.19, series G19/CCOUT/DTCTL.M (www.federalreserve.gov).
Note: Consumer credit means consumer credit outstanding, the total consumer credit owned and securitized. Percent change, quarter-to-quarter, 2007.4 to 2008.4, in billions of current dollars, seasonally adjusted monthly data, aggregated to quarterly data, at annual rates.

Why was this process headed for disaster? The problem was that the vast increase of credit over such a long time made the economy exceedingly fragile. It became a bubble ready to burst with any sudden pinprick. When the Great Recession struck, people could not maintain the payments to their banks for loans and to corporations for things they had bought.

The Great Recession began in the fourth quarter of 2007. The progress of consumer credit in the Great Recession is shown quarter by quarter until the end of 2008 in Figure 3.11.

Consumer credit continued to rise at about the same rate in the first three quarters of the Great Recession. Then its rate of growth diminished. Finally, in the fourth quarter of 2008, the bottom of the credit market dropped out. A disaster occurred. For the first time in many years, consumer credit actually declined by a significant amount. But because of mounting job losses, household incomes were falling nearly as quickly.

The decline of consumer incomes and the decline of consumer debt came as a vast surprise to most people. When retailers have grown accustomed to expanding sales every quarter, they plan their inventories on that basis. They order what they expect to need from manufacturers. When sales fall off because of lack of credit, they suddenly find they have relatively large inventories of goods that cannot be sold at the current price. Their profit is reduced by fewer sales and by lower prices.

As the retailers cut back their orders, manufacturers cut back their production and laid off large numbers of workers. The manufacturing corporations cannot pay back their own loans from banks. At the same time, the consumers cannot pay back their loans to banks. Every actor in the economic drama is hurt. There is a vicious spiral downward of less buying power, fewer purchases, less production, more unemployment, and still fewer loans to individuals.

There was no cyclical pattern in corporate credit from 1970 to 2001. Corporations kept borrowing more and more throughout the period from 1970 to 2007. The rate of growth was about the same in expansions and recessions. The corporate credit bubble grew and grew in an extraordinary manner from 1970 to 2001. In the 2001 to 2007 expansion, personal saving hovered around zero percent of national income. Usually it was just above zero, but it was below zero in some quarters. Below zero meant that the average person's debts grew faster than the person's income.

If corporations did not get their investment money from personal saving, where did they get it? For a time, much of it came from the corporation's own profits. But by the 1970s, this source became far smaller than credit.

The largest corporations acquired high "leverage" and were proud of that. Leverage meant that they had borrowed billions of dollars from other people, and then used it to expand rapidly. By these means they made amazing amounts of profit. So to make maximum profit, corporations just kept borrowing more and more. The bubble kept growing.

As a result, the corporations became more vulnerable and fragile. They bet on rapid expansion of their sales. A small decline would mean that they could not repay their debt, could not pay the interest on the debt, and could not pay their employees or their suppliers. When the decline came in 2008, many corporations were quickly ruined.

In the recession of 2001, many companies desperately needed credit to keep them running in the mildly declining economy of the recession. They needed the new credit to pay back old loans, to pay employees, and to pay for supplies. From 2002 to 2007, credit grew every year. Not only did credit grow, but also its rate of growth continued to rise. From less than 1 percent in 2002, when the expansion was extremely weak, the annual growth rate of corporate credit grew and grew to the boom rate of almost 14 percent in the peak year of 2007. Corporations continued to get higher profits from more leverage through more credit. This was a fragile bubble that was ready to burst.

In the first four quarters of the recession in 2008, corporate credit moved at a slower growth rate in every quarter. Corporations wanted to borrow more because their income had dropped. They did not have enough income to pay the interest and principal of their debts and also to pay employees and suppliers. Banks, however, were less and less willing to advance more credit as corporate profits looked worse and worse.

In the fourth quarter of 2008, outstanding corporate credit rose only about 1 percent. Since corporate income was declining, but corporate credit was tiny, companies could no longer pay their workers, their suppliers, or interest payments to the banks. Most corporations let go large numbers of workers. Many companies went bankrupt. The ceasing of payment to the banks was one of the causes of the financial crisis.

Changes in economic structure set the stage for the financial crisis, while cyclical problems set it off. There were four main changes in the structure of the economy that led to the crisis. First, the long-run stagnation of real wages and salaries meant that the corporations could no longer take for granted continued growth in the demand for goods and services. Thus they could no longer count on growing income and consumer spending to solve all problems. Second, the dangerous and extraordinary growth of the credit bubble occurred.

Third, most financial regulations and safeguards had disappeared after several decades of work by their opponents. This meant that banks could and did make extremely risky loans to increase their short-run profits. Fourth, there was an extraordinary boom in housing that lasted almost four decades (with a few minor declines). This could be seen in the large increase of home prices over the period.

Then there were immediate cyclical problems. The first problem was that lack of consumer income had been solved by an enormous increase in consumer credit for 40 years. The rapid growth of consumer credit postponed the recession, but its price was increased economic fragility. When employment and income fell in 2007 and 2008, consumers could no longer pay their debts to industrial corporations, such as General Motors, or to financial institutions, such as Bank of America. This severely weakened the financial system.

The second problem came from the huge bubble of corporate debt. As shown above, when corporate income declined in the severe recession, companies could not pay their bills or debts. Many went bankrupt. The effect on the financial system was powerful. The weakened or even bankrupt corporations could no longer supply a flow of money payments to the banks and other financial institutions (such as the immense insurance company, AIG).

As if the declining ability of consumers and corporations to pay the banks was not enough, the third problem came when the housing increase slowed and then turned down. The biggest single asset of the banks and other financial institutions was the mortgages they owned. The housing industry had expanded without stop for more than 35 years. Housing prices had risen all that time. The supply of credit to buy homes through mortgages had risen all that time.

Millions of people had mortgages. In many cases, it was clear that they would have trouble paying them on their existing income. The lenders assumed that workers' income would slowly rise, so they could pay, though perhaps with difficulty. Moreover, the price of the house would continue to rise. Therefore, even if the home-owner could not pay the mortgage, the house could be foreclosed. Foreclosure was considered safe by the lenders because the price of houses would continue to rise.

Thus, there were millions of risky mortgages. On top of this risk, the financial institutions evolved a scheme in which one sold mortgages to another, with each firm making a profit along the way. So one mortgage supported a pyramid of financial transactions all over the world. When the housing market went bad, big banks in Germany suffered as much as big banks in the United States.

And housing did go bad. As we have shown earlier, housing construction began to decline in 2006 and has continued to decline until now in 2009. Housing prices rose monstrously for almost forty years, but have declined more than one-third since 2007. This decline in housing, with hundreds of thousands of foreclosures amid falling price knocked out the supports from the flimsy palace of finance.

Finally, it must be emphasized that the financial crisis and panic greatly worsened the recession. Constriction of credit by the financial institutions meant that ordinary people could no longer get additional credit to support their normal way of life, especially when they lost their jobs. This meant less spending on goods and services, further harming the industrial corporations. The industrial corporations were caught between two fires. On the one hand, consumer support for goods and services sales was falling. On the other hand, banks and other lenders were refusing to make loans to get the corporations through the hard times. The financial crisis provided considerable justification for calling the severe downturn a Great Recession.

The mortgages and other bad loans of the financial system came to be called toxic assets. The spread of these toxic assets, along with the problems in consumer and corporate finance, led to a crisis in the whole financial sphere around the world.

How the Great Recession Spread in the Global Economy

Recessions and depressions spread through the global economy by three different mechanisms: trade, investment, and finance.

The first mechanism is trade. When a recession in the United States reduces U.S. imports, it hurts the trade of other countries and reduces their profits and their employee income. The other country in turn will reduce its imports and this hurts the rest of the world, including the United States.

This mechanism operated at top speed in the Great Recession and financial crisis of 2008. U.S. production led the way downward, so U.S. imports started falling soon after the beginning of the recession. For a little while, it looked like other countries might be able to skip the U.S. recession. U.S. imports, however, provide a big money inflow to many other countries. So these countries soon found their exports dropping and money from trade with the United States disappearing. As they went into the Great Recession for this and other reasons, their own imports declined, which meant that the United States could export that much less to them.

A second mechanism to spread recessions is the investment process. When U.S. business no longer sees profit ahead, it reduces its investment in the expansion of U.S. industry. On the other hand, the Great Recession in the United States not only reduces the profit of U.S. investors, but also reduces the profit of those foreign investors who had previously invested from abroad in the United States. With less profit, they have less to invest in their own country.

Investment not only relies on objective estimates of future conditions, but also is always over pessimistic or overoptimistic. A poor profit outlook in the United States may cause a major convulsion in the U.S. stock market. In the modern world, the pessimism spreads immediately to the rest of the world. So all stock exchanges follow the first one to make a big move up or down.

A full-scale discussion of foreign investment in each country of the global economy would require a discussion of the imperialism and colonialism of the nineteenth and twentieth centuries, the very rapid increase in foreign investment since the 1970s by all the major developed countries, and the spread of a small number of giant corporations that operate within and dominate over most countries (Sherman 1991).

Because of the entanglement of all countries in the global economy, the Great Recession of 2007 to 2009 spread from the United States to other countries in various ways. As the U.S. stock market continued to fall, foreign investors left it in droves and did not soon return. They did their best to get all their money out of U.S. corporations. The collapse of confidence in U.S. profits sent shudders throughout all stock markets and all forms of investment around the world. The investment panic spread, not only because of the actual decline of profits, but also because of the fear and uncertainty about the future.

In addition to the developed capitalist countries, each of which had its own growing problems even before the U.S. recession, the underdeveloped countries often base their entire economy around trade in one or two main exports. When the United States suddenly stopped buying many raw materials, and when other developed countries also stopped buying these materials, the economies of many underdeveloped countries collapsed much further than the economies of the developed capitalist countries. People in the underdeveloped countries suffered far more terribly on the average than those in developed countries, even though people suffered plenty in the developed countries.

The third mechanism for the spread of recessions in the global economy is international finance. The international financial market operates in many ways. To give one example, the crisis in the U.S. mortgage sector caused by too risky mortgages was spread to a number of European banks because they had bought large numbers of these mortgages when they looked like an eternal source of wealth. When the people who had taken loans against the mortgages could no longer pay back interest or principal, the banks were left holding hundreds of billions of dollars of worthless assets.

There are international transactions of trillions of dollars a day. These involve all financial institutions everywhere in the world in a close web of activity. When one goes down, the ripple spreads rapidly. As more banks fail, those others with deposits or investments in them might also fail. Again there is a vicious circle downward.

The trade deficit itself was a drag on the U.S. economy because it meant that many billions of dollars flowed out of the country. That outflow of dollars was counteracted by the equally immense flow of billions of dollars back into U.S. financial markets.

Those dollars flowing back into the United States propped up the economy and the expansion of 2001 to 2007. They left the U.S. economy dependent on foreign capital from China, Japan, and Europe to keep it going. Should those countries stop investing the dollars they accumulate from selling their exports in the United States and invest elsewhere, the U.S. economy would be left in shambles.

The unprecedented size of the U.S. trade deficit made these financial flows especially dangerous. By 2007, the U.S. trade deficit relative to the size of the U.S. economy had reached 6 percent of GDP. The last time prior to this decade that the U.S. trade deficit had been above 4 percent of GDP was in 1816, when British imports flooded into the United States after the end of the War of 1812.

Here is the present danger. The U.S. economy racks up a record trade deficit. Buying foreign exports increases the supply of dollars in foreign hands. At the same time, the United States must attract enough dollars from abroad to pay for the deficit in its current trade account. The deficit was more than $700 billion in 2007. In other words, the U.S. trade deficit creates the supply of dollars abroad, but that generates the U.S. need for dollars from abroad to pay for its deficit.

Dollars are lured back into the U.S. economy from overseas in two ways. Foreign investors can buy stock in U.S. corporations or they can buy government bonds from the U.S. Treasury. Because profits in the U.S. stock market were risky and uncertain throughout the Bush expansion even before collapsing in 2008, almost all the money from overseas investors came from buying U.S. corporate and Treasury bonds.

The monies to be invested in the U.S. economy can be envisioned as a giant swimming pool of savings. An increasingly large share of the water in the U.S. savings pool now comes from abroad. When foreign capital is a substantial part of the water in the U.S. savings pool, the sheer volume of capital that can flow out of the country is much larger. This made the U.S. stock market and other asset markets more volatile.

Through much of the expansion of 2001 to 2007, foreigners were happy to purchase the gobs of debt issued by the U.S. Treasury and corporate America to cover the trade deficit. That kept U.S. interest rates low. Much of that flood of savings from abroad went into residential real estate. International buyers bought up mortgage-backed securities. This swelled the housing bubble, whose collapse contributed so mightily to the financial crisis.

Global investors' stock and bond investments became overloaded with U.S. assets. By 2007, foreign investors held more than half of U.S. Treasury bonds.

China alone held nearly $1.8 trillion in U.S. assets. The growing dependence of the United States economy on foreign capital was a sure warning sign of the financial crisis that soon came.

In the summer of 2007, capital flight struck. Foreign investors slashed their holdings of U.S. securities by a record amount. The dollar's value fell, declining relative to other currencies for most of a year. As it became clear that the unpaid mortgage interest would cause widespread losses for investors, large numbers of foreign investors sold their U.S. assets, intensifying the crisis. The withdrawal of foreign investors helped cause the stock market collapse as well. With the departure of foreign savings from the U.S. economy, the supply of credit for buying automobiles, for student loans, and even for corporate loans dried up, making matters worse.

Decline in each country reverberated to all the others. This process was one major factor that resulted in the ever-deeper vicious circle downward.

Then a curious thing happened. Foreign investors returned to the United States as their economies collapsed. They did not invest in the U.S. housing market or buy U.S. stocks or corporate bonds. Rather, like domestic investors, foreign investors flocked to the safest haven in the financial world, U.S. Treasury bonds.

That turnaround had two dramatic effects: (1) with the return of foreign savings to the United States, the value of the dollar appreciated and that made U.S. exports more expensive and imports a bargain; as a result, the trade deficit worsened, further slowing the U.S. economy; (2) the stampede into Treasury bonds allowed the federal government to borrow at extremely low interest rates, close to zero percent. How the government spends that money will determine the nature of the recovery that eventually emerges from the crisis.

To sum up how the Great Recession in the United States spread to the global economy, it is important to note the following five mechanisms, which together played a key role in impacting economies in the rest of the world.

First, imports rose faster than exports in the expansion of 2001 to 2007 and in most previous expansions. The rise in imports led to increasing trade deficits in each expansion. The outflow of money through the trade deficit tends to lower U.S. domestic demand profits.

Second, in contractions, imports go down faster than exports, so the trade deficit decreases. The decrease in the trade deficit in contractions, however, has been less than the increase in expansions in the last six U.S. business cycles. Thus, in the period since 1970, the trade deficit has tended to get larger and larger over time.

Third, raw material prices usually rise more than consumer prices in an expansion. This hurts the profits of corporations in the developed capitalist countries. It is another factor leading from prosperity to recession or depression. In recessions, prices of raw materials go way down. This decrease cushions the profits of corporations in the developed capitalist world, but it creates great suffering for the people of the underdeveloped countries.

Fourth, international investment is now closely intertwined in the global economy. So a recession or depression beginning in one country soon reduces investment in all countries.

Fifth, the international financial sector is also closely tied together. So failures of banks in one country tend to spread very rapidly around the global economy. If the U.S. economy looks too fragile at any time, a great deal of money could flow out in a short time.

It is worth emphasizing that all these mechanisms operated to spread instability around the world in the Great Recession of 2007 to 2009. So there was a worldwide Great Recession. It should also be said that these mechanisms spread the crisis only after it started in the United States. It would not have affected other countries to such an extent, however, if they were not already in a weak and fragile condition.

Concluding Comments

In searching for the causes of the Great Recession, we have seen that accompanying the housing bubble, the credit balloon, and the consequent financial crisis, excessive consumer credit during the expansion has clearly played a major role in triggering the Great Recession. The increase of consumer credit has made each expansion more and more fragile. This has been also the case with corporate credit. The increase of corporate credit, likewise, has made each expansion more and more fragile. Finally, the stock market has risen rapidly and become a tenuous balloon at the peak of each expansion, especially at the last two cycle peaks. When the stock market begins to fall, the wealth effect drags down consumer spending. The wealth effect includes the rising consumer optimism from a rising stock market, but also the reluctance of consumers to spend when their stock values decline. In the Great Recession of 2007 to 2009 stocks fell more than 50 percent. In addition to removing money from consumption and from investment, a fall in the stock market also destroys the confidence of corporate investors, so it makes recovery far more difficult.

Figure 3.12 tells a dismal story about the stock market in the Great Recession. Of the five quarters in the graph, two show a very slight expansion of stock prices as profit expanded slightly. Then, however, the economy grew worse. In the fourth quarter of 2008, in which GDP and profit took a nosedive, the stock market crashed and lost value at an annual rate of 70 percent. In other words, as the economy declined, so did the stock market, but more rapidly.

The coming together of all these factors in the U.S. economy during the first decade of the twenty-first century brought about the catastrophic crash of the financial system that resulted in the Great Recession of 2007 to 2009, which in turn set the stage for the spread of the economic crisis throughout the world.

This chapter has shown in detail why the expansion of 2001 to 2007 turned into the Great Recession and financial crisis. It was shown that in the expansion the income gap increased, the consumer gap increased, the credit bubble grew stupendously and then broke.

Every one of the behavior patterns discussed above has been shown to be the product of the economic institutions of capitalism (see Sherman 2003).

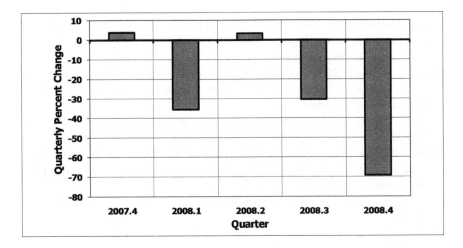

Figure 3.12 Stocks in the Crisis, 2007.4–2008.4

Source: Yahoo Finance (www.yahoo.com).

Note: Stocks means Standard and Poor's 500 corporation stock index, percent change, quarter to quarter, 2007.4 to 2008.4, monthly data aggregated to quarterly data, at annual rates.

Finally, the financial crisis was the result of long-run structural changes in capitalism. These changes included the changes in the money and banking system that allowed financial institutions to leverage their capital into a huge pyramid built on a small amount of initial capital. The structural trends also included changes in industry that resulted in the weakening of labor unions and the bargaining power of all employees

These changes were accompanied by an amazing housing bubble and housing crash. The housing crisis, as well as the changes in the banking system toward more risky loans, led to an equally amazing credit bubble and credit crash. Since the same trends occurred in most countries around the world, the Great Recession and financial crisis became worldwide. The problems of each country reverberated to harm the others.

References and Select Bibliography

Aldcroft, Derek H. 1993. *The European Economy, 1914–1990*, 3rd ed. London: Routledge.

Bureau of Economic Analysis (BEA). U.S. Department of Commerce. www.bea. gov.

Galbraith, John Kenneth. 1988. *The Great Crash, 1929*. New York: Houghton-Mifflin.

Jenkins, Holman W., Jr. 2008. "How to Shake Off the Mortgage Mess." *Wall Street Journal*. July 30. http://online.wsj.com/article/SB121737434767195077.html?mod=todays_columnists.

Leonhardt, David. 2009. "A Bold Plan Sweeps Away Reagan Ideas." *New York Times,* February 26. www.nytimes.com/2009/02/27/business/economy/27policy.html.

Mitchell, Wesley C. 1951. *What Happens During Business Cycles: A Progress Report*. New York: National Bureau of Economic Research.

National Bureau of Economic Research (NBER). 2008. "Determination of the 2007 Peak in Economic Activity." Business Cycle Dating Committee. December 11. www.nber.org/cycles/dec2008.html.

———. 2009. "Business Cycle Expansions and Contractions." www.nber.org/cycles/.

Pollin, Robert. 2007. "Global Outsourcing and the U.S. Working Class." *New Labor Forum* 16 (1):122–125.

———. 2008a. "The Housing Bubble and Financial Deregulation: Isn't Enough Enough?" *New Labor Forum* 17 (2): 118–121.

———. 2008b. "How to End the Recession." *The Nation*. November 24, 13–16.

Sherman, Howard J. 1991. *The Business Cycle: Growth and Crisis Under Capitalism*. Princeton, NJ: Princeton University Press.

———. 2003. "Institutions and the Business Cycle." *Journal of Economic Issues* (3): 621–642.

Volcker, Paul. 2009. www.huffingtonpost.com/2009/04/23/volcker-us-world-in-a-gre_n_1900761.html.

Chapter 4

The Global Capitalist Crisis and World Depression[1]

James Petras

Introduction

All the idols of capitalism over the past three decades have crashed. The assumptions and presumptions, the paradigms, and the prognosis of indefinite progress under liberal free market capitalism have all been tested and have failed. We are living the end of an entire epoch: Experts everywhere witness the collapse of the U.S. and world financial systems, the absence of credit for trade and the lack of financing for investment. A world depression, in which upward of a quarter of the world's labor force will be unemployed, is looming. The biggest decline in trade in recent world history—down 40 percent year to year—defines the future. The imminent bankruptcies of the biggest manufacturing companies in the capitalist world haunt Western political leaders. The "market" as a mechanism for allocating resources and the government of the U.S. as the "leader" of the global economy have been discredited (*Financial Times* 2009b). All the assumptions about "self-stabilizing markets" are demonstrably false and outmoded. The rejection of public intervention in the market and the advocacy of supply-side economics have been discredited even in the eyes of their practitioners. Even official circles recognize that "inequality of income" contributed to the onset of the economic crash and should be corrected. Planning, public ownership and nationalization are on the agenda, while socialist alternatives have become almost respectable.

The Global Capitalist Crisis

With the onset of the global economic crisis, all the shibboleths of the past decade are discarded: As export-oriented growth strategies fail, we see the re-emergence (actual and potential) of import substitution policies and the panoply

---

1   This chapter is an edited and condensed version of the author's original book *Global Depression and Regional Wars* (Atlanta: Clarity Press, 2009). Copyright © 2009 by Clarity Press, Inc. Reprinted with permission of Clarity Press, Inc., www.claritypress. com (all rights reserved, not for reproduction). The editor, Berch Berberoglu, extracted and edited text from various sections of the book to compile the present chapter, which is published here with the approval of the author.

of developmentalist models which had been forced into academic and political obscurity by the IMF-enforced restructuring and Friedmanite economics that have assailed developing countries since the early 1980s. As the world economy "de-globalizes" and capital is "repatriated" to save near-bankrupt head offices, "national ownership" is proposed. As trillions of dollars/euros/yen in assets are destroyed and devalued, massive layoffs extend unemployment everywhere. Fear, anxiety and uncertainty stalk the offices of state, financial directorships, management suites of the factories, and the streets ...

We enter a time of upheaval, when the foundations of the global capitalist system are deeply fractured, to the point that no one can imagine any restoration of the political-economic order of the recent past. The future promises economic chaos, political upheavals and mass impoverishment. Once again, the specter of socialism hovers over the ruins of the former giants of finance. As free market capital collapses, its ideological advocates jump ship, abandon their line and verse of the virtues of the market and sing a new chorus: the State as Savior of the System—a dubious proposition, whose outcome will not be socialism, but only a prolongation of the pillage of the public treasury and postponement of the death agony of capitalism as we have known it.

The crash of the U.S. financial system is symptomatic of a deeper and more profound collapse of the capitalist system that has its roots in the dynamic development of capitalism over the previous three decades.

Contrary to the theorists who argue that the nub of the problem is that "finance" and "post-industrial" capitalism have "destroyed" or de-industrialized the U.S. economy and put in its place a kind of "casino" or speculative capital, we have actually witnessed the most spectacular long-term growth of industrial capital, globally employing more industrial and salaried workers than ever in history. Driven by rising rates of profit, large-scale and long-term investments have been the motor force for the penetration by industrial and related capital of the most remote underdeveloped regions of the world. New and old capitalist countries have spawned enormous economic empires, breaking down the political barriers of states and the cultural barriers of peoples to incorporate and exploit billions of new and old workers in a relentless process. As competition from the newly-industrialized countries intensified, and as the rising mass of profits exceeded the capacity to reinvest them most profitably in the older capitalist centers, masses of capital migrated to Asia, Latin America, Eastern Europe and, to a lesser degree, into the Middle East and Southern Africa, to reap the greatest gain or (as explained to abandoned first-world workers) to remain competitive.

Huge surplus profits spilled over into services, including finance, real estate, insurance, large-scale real estate and urban lands, driving up prices and creating bubbles everywhere.

The dynamic growth of capitalism's technological innovations found expression in its greater social and political power—dwarfing the organization of labor, limiting its bargaining power and multiplying its profits. With the growth of world markets, domestic workers were seen merely as "costs of production" rather than final consumers upon whose purchasing power sales depended. Wages stagnated; social benefits were limited, curtailed or shifted onto workers. Under conditions of dynamic capitalist growth, the state and state policy became their absolute instrument: restrictions, controls, regulation were weakened. With the heads of multinationals at the helm of government, the process dubbed "neoliberalism" opened new areas for investment of surplus profits: public enterprises, land, resources and banks were privatized.

As competition intensified, as new industrial powers emerged in Asia, U.S. capital increasingly invested in financial activity. The financial circuits elaborated a whole series of financial instruments, which enticed investment from the growing wealth and profits generated by the productive sectors by offering even higher returns.

U.S. capital did not "de-industrialize"—it *relocated* to China, Korea and other centers of growth, not because of "falling profits" but because of surplus profits and greater profits overseas. U.S. and European manufacturers invested in Asia to export back to their home markets—shifting the structure of internal capital toward commerce and finance, and domestic purchasing power toward credit card debt. Diminished wages paid to the workers led to a vast expansion in the ability of banks to sell debt, billed as "credit". Financial activity grew in proportion to the entrance of commodities from the dynamic, newly industrialized countries. Industrial profits were re-invested in financial services or in Treasuries, facilitating the government's ongoing pursuit of war. Profits and liquidity grew in proportion to the relative decline in real value generated by the shift from industrial to financial/commercial capital.

Super profits from world production, trade, finances and the recycling of overseas earnings back to the U.S. through both state and private financial circuits created enormous liquidity. It was far beyond the historical capacity of the U.S. and European economies to absorb such profits in productive sectors.

The dynamic and voracious exploitation of the huge surplus labor forces in China, India, and elsewhere and the absolute pillage and transfer of hundreds of billions from ex-communist Russia and "neoliberalized" Latin America filled the coffers of new and old financial institutions.

Over-exploitation of labor in Asia, and the over-accumulation of financial liquidity in the U.S. led to the magnification of the paper economy and what liberal economists later called "global disequilibrium" between savers/industrial investors/exporters (in Asia) and consumers (debtors)/financiers/importers (in the U.S.). Huge trade surpluses in the East were papered over by their purchase of U.S. T-notes. The U.S. economy was precariously backed by an increasingly inflated paper economy.

The expansion of the financial sector resulted from the high rates of return of the "liberalized" global economy imposed by the power of diversified investment capital in previous decades through its instruments, the International Monetary Fund (IMF) and World Trade Organization (WTO). The internationalization of capital, its dynamic growth and the enormous growth of trade outran the stagnant wages and declining social payments from exploitation of the now huge surplus labor force. Seeking to maintain the high rates of return to which investors had become accustomed, finance capital sought to bolster its profits via inflated real estate based on expanded credit, highly leveraged debt and outright massive fraudulent "financial instruments" (collateralized debt obligations bundling securitized mortgages whose actual value could not be ascertained by investors). The collapse of the paper economy exposed the overdeveloped financial system and forced its demise. In quick order, many of the major investment banks of the western world, and notably in the United States, Merrill Lynch, Lehman Brothers, Bank of America, Bear Sterns and others, deflated, restructured, collapsed or were absorbed.

The loss of finance, credit and markets reverberated through all the export-oriented industrial manufacturing powers. The lack of social consumption that resulted from application of the neoliberal prescription and the resultant weakness of internal markets globally denied the industrial countries any compensatory markets to stabilize or limit their fall into recession and depression. The dynamic growth of the productive forces based on the over-exploitation of labor led to the overdevelopment of the financial circuits, which set in motion the process of "feeding off" industry and subordinating and redirecting the accumulation process toward highly speculative capital.

Cheap labor—the primary source of profits, investment, trade and export growth on a world scale—could no longer sustain both the pillage by finance capital and provide a market for the dynamic industrial sector. What was erroneously dubbed a financial crisis or even more narrowly at first a "mortgage", "sub-prime lending" or housing crisis, was merely the "trigger" for the collapse of the overdeveloped financial sector, awash in derivatives and credit default swaps, and a host of mechanisms which had become directed toward speculation rather than the management and insurance of real production. As a result, the financial sector, which grew out of the dynamic expansion of "productive" capitalism, later "rebounded" against it. But it was the historic links and global ties between industry and financial capital that led inevitably to a systemic capitalist crisis; the crisis was embedded in the contradiction between impoverished labor and concentrated capital. The current global economic crisis is a product of the "over-accumulation" process of the capitalist system in which the crash of the financial system was the "detonator" but not the structural determinant: the exploitation of labor. This is demonstrated by the fact that industrial Japan and Germany experienced a bigger fall in exports, investments and growth than "financial" U.S. and Britain.

According to free market theorists, the capitalist system in crisis destroys capital in order to "purge itself" of the least efficient, least competitive and most indebted enterprises and sectors, in order to re-concentrate capital and reconstruct the powers of accumulation. However, free market ideology aside, in the real world, political conditions permitting, this re-composition of capital grows out of the pillage of state resources—so-called bailouts and other massive transfers from the public treasury (read "taxpayers"), *which results from* the savage reduction of social transfers (read "public services") and the cheapening of labor through firings, massive unemployment, wage, pension and health reductions, and the general reduction of living standards in order to increase the rate of profit.

The World Depression: A Class Analysis

The aggregate economic indicators of the rise and fall of the world capitalist system are of limited value in understanding the causes, trajectory and impact of the world depression. At best, they describe the economic carnage; at worst, they obfuscate the role of the leading (ruling) social classes, with their complex networks and transformations, which put into place the global trade and financial architecture, directed the neoliberal expansion and then managed the resultant economic collapse and the role of the wage and salaried (working) classes, which produced the wealth to fuel the expansive phase and now pay the cost of the economic collapse.

It is a well-known truism that those who caused the crisis are also those who have been the greatest beneficiaries of government largesse. The crude and simple everyday observation that the ruling class "made" the crisis and the working class "pays" the cost is, at a minimum, an implicit recognition of the utility of class analyses in deciphering the social reality behind the aggregate economic data.

From Over-Accumulation to the Dominance of Finance Capital

Following the recession of the early 1970s, the Western industrial capitalist class secured financing to launch a period of extensive and deep growth covering the entire globe. German, Japanese and Southeast Asian capitalists flourished, competed and collaborated with their U.S. counterparts. Throughout this period the social power, organization and political influence of the working class witnessed a relative and absolute decline in its share of material income. Technological innovations, including the re-organization of work, compensated for wage increases by reducing the "mass of workers" and, in particular, their capacity to pressure the prerogatives of management. The capitalist strategic position in the management of production was strengthened: they were able to exercise near absolute control over the location and movements of capital.

The established capitalist powers—especially in Britain and the U.S.—with large accumulations of capital and facing increasing competition from the fully recovered German and Japanese capitalists, sought to expand their rates of return by moving capital investments into finance and services. At first, this move was linked with and directed toward promoting the sale of their manufactured products by providing credit and financing toward the domestic purchases of automobiles or "white goods". Less dynamic industrial capitalists relocated their assembly plants to low-wage regions and countries.

The result was that industrial capitalists took on more of the appearance of "financiers" in the U.S. even as they retained their industrial character in the operation of their overseas manufacturing subsidiaries and satellite suppliers. Both overseas manufacturing and local financial returns swelled the aggregate profits of the capitalist class. While capital accumulation expanded in the "home country", domestic wages and social costs were under pressure as capitalists imposed the costs of competition on the backs of wage earners via the collaboration of the trade unions in the U.S. and social democratic political parties in Europe. Wage constraints, tying wages to productivity in an asymmetrical way, and labor-capital pacts increased profits. U.S. workers were "compensated" by the cheap consumer imports produced by the low-wage labor force in the newly industrializing countries and by access to easy credit at home.

The Western pillage of the former USSR, with the collaboration of gangster-oligarchs, led to the massive flow of looted capital into Western banks throughout the 1990s. The Chinese transition to capitalism in the 1980s, which accelerated in the 1990s, expanded the accumulation of industrial profits via the intensive exploitation of tens of millions of wageworkers employed at subsistence levels. While the trillion-dollar pillage of Russia and the entire former Soviet Union bloated the West European and U.S. financial sectors, the massive growth of billions of dollars in illegal transfers and money laundering toward U.S. and UK banks added to the overdevelopment of the financial sector.

The rise in oil prices and "rents" among "rentier" capitalists added a vast new source of financial profits and liquidity. Pillage, rents, and contraband capital provided a vast accumulation of financial wealth disconnected from industrial production. On the other hand, the rapid industrialization of China and other Asian countries provided a vast market for German and Japanese high-end manufacturers: they supplied the high quality machines and technology to the Chinese and Vietnamese factories.

U.S. capitalists did not "de-industrialize"—they de-industrialized *the United States*. By relocating production overseas, importing finished products and focusing on credit and financing in order to achieve domestic sales, the U.S. capitalist class and its members became diversified and multi-sectoral. They multiplied their profits and intensified the accumulation of capital, even as they fled U.S. taxation.

On the other hand, workers were subject to multiple forms of exploitation: wages stagnated, creditors squeezed interest, and the conversion from high wage/high skill manufacturing jobs to lower-paid service jobs steadily reduced living standards.

The basic process leading up to the breakdown was clearly present: the dynamic growth of western capitalist wealth was based, in part, on the brutal pillage of the USSR and Latin America, which profoundly lowered living standards throughout the 1990s. The intensified and savage exploitation of hundreds of millions of low-paid Chinese, Mexican, Indonesian and Indochinese workers, and the forced exodus of former peasants as migrant laborers to manufacturing centers led to high rates of accumulation. The relative decline of wages in the U.S. and Western

Europe also added to the accumulation of capital. The German, Chinese, Japanese, Latin American and Eastern European emphasis on export-driven growth added to the mounting "imbalance" or contradiction between concentrated capitalist wealth and ownership and the growing mass of low-paid workers.

Inequalities on a world scale grew geometrically. The dynamic accumulation process exceeded the capacity of the highly polarized capitalist system to absorb capital in productive activity at existing high rates of profit. This led to the large scale and multiform growth of speculator capital in order to maintain the same rate of return to which investors had become addicted, leading to massive investment and price inflation in real estate and commodities, and a range of financial restructuring related to hedge funds, securities, debt-financing, mergers and acquisitions—all divorced from real value-producing activity.

Speculator financial activity with massive liquidity offered a "short-term solution": profits based on debt financing. Competition among lenders fueled the availability of cheap credit. Real estate speculation was extended into the working class, as wage and salaried workers, without personal savings or assets, took advantage of their access to easy loans to join the speculator-induced frenzy based on an ideology of irreversible rising home values.

The inevitable collapse, detonated by failures to make debt payments first occurring at the bottom of the speculative chain, reverberated throughout the system. From the latest entrants to the real estate sub-prime mortgage holders, the crisis moved up the ladder affecting the biggest banks and corporations, all of whom had been deeply engaged in leveraged buyouts and acquisitions. All "sectors", which had "diversified" from manufacturing to finance, trade and commodities speculation, were downgraded. The entire panoply of capitalists—both industrial and financial—faced bankruptcy, as German, Japanese and Chinese industrial exporters who exploited labor witnessed the collapse of their export markets.

Indicators of the Onset of Depression

Indicators of the deepening depression in 2008–2009 were to be found everywhere:

- Consumer bankruptcy filings rose 33 percent from a year earlier, while business filings rose 64 percent (Reuters 2009b).
- The IMF reported in April 2009 that banks around the globe will need to write down about $4.1 trillion in loans and securities (Reuters 2009a).
- The losses arising from banks having to mark their investments down to market prices totaled over $3 trillion in 2009—equivalent to a year's worth of British economic production (*Financial Times* 2009c: 9).
- Financial *assets* worldwide *fell* by more than $50 trillion in 2009—a figure of the same order as *annual global output* (*Financial Times* 2009c: 9).
- The face value of all derivatives contracts across the world outstanding at the end of 2008—a measure that counts the value of a derivative's

underlying assets—totaled more than $680 trillion, according to the Bank for International Settlements in Switzerland. The biggest banks and brokerage firms, including JPMorgan Chase, Citigroup and Goldman Sachs, as well as major insurers, are all major players in derivatives (Labaton and Calmes 2009).

- For 2009, the U.S. was projected as running a budget deficit of 12.3 percent of gross domestic product—a giant fiscal deficit that will ultimately ruin public finances.

From late 2007 to early 2009, the world markets were in a vertical fall:

- The TOPIX fell from 1,800 in mid-2007 to 700 in early 2009.
- Standard and Poor's fell from 1,380 in early 2008 to below 700 in 2009.
- The FTSE 100 fell from 6,600 to 3,600 in early 2009.
- The Hang Seng fell from 32,000 in early 2008 to 13,000 at the start of 2009 (*Financial Times* 2009a: 27).
- In the fourth quarter of 2008, GDP shrank at an annualized rate of 20.8 percent in South Korea, 12.7 percent in Japan, 8.2 percent in Germany, 2.9 percent in the UK and 3.8 percent in the U.S. (*Financial Times* 2009: 27).
- The Dow Jones Industrial Average declined from 14,164 in October 2007 to 6,500 in March 2009.
- Year on year declines in industrial output were 21 percent in Japan, 19 percent in South Korea, 12 percent in Germany, 10 percent in the U.S. and 9 percent in the UK (*Financial Times* 2009a: 27).
- Net private capital flows to less-developed capitalist countries from the imperial countries were predicted to shrink by 82 percent, and credit flows by $30 billion (*Financial Times* 2009a: 27).
- The U.S. economy declined by 6.2 percent in the last three months of 2008 and fell further in the first quarter of 2009 as a result of a sharp decline in exports (23.6 percent) and consumer spending (4.3 percent) in the final quarter of 2008 (British Broadcasting Corporation 2009).

With over 600,000 workers losing their jobs monthly in the first three months of 2009, and many more on short hours and threatened with job loss subsequently, real and disguised unemployment reached 20 percent by late 2010. All of the signs point to a deep and prolonged depression:

- Automobile sales of General Motors, Chrysler and Ford were down nearly 50 percent year to year (2007–2008). The first quarter of 2009 saw a further decline of 50 percent.
- Foreign markets are drying up as the depression spreads overseas.
- In the U.S. domestic market, durable goods sales declined by 22 percent (British Broadcasting Corporation 2009).
- Residential investments fell by 23.6 percent and business investment was

down 19.1 percent, led by a 27.8 percent drop in equipment and software.
• Between December 2007, when the recession began, and May 2009, 5.7 million jobs have been lost. Job losses were large and widespread across nearly all major private-sector industries.

The rising tide of depression is driven by private business-led disinvestment. Rising business inventories, declining investment, bankruptcies, foreclosures, insolvent banks, massive accumulative losses, restricted access to credit, falling asset values and a 20 percent reduction in household wealth (over $3 trillion) are causes and consequences of the depression. As a result of collapse of the industrial, mining, real estate and trade sectors, there are at least $2.2 trillion of "toxic" (defaulting) bank debt worldwide, far beyond the bailout funds allocated by the White House in October 2008 and February and March 2009. But if one takes into account the credit default swaps which may be tied purely to speculation (where the owners of CDS don't even own the assets whose standing they purport to be "insuring"), there is a much bigger hole if these contracts are to be upheld. According to Bloomberg, the Fed has already lent or committed $12.8 trillion, an unsupervised/unauthorized by Congress expansion of the money supply, making the government programs insignificant in comparison (except that they incur debt rather than induce inflation).

U.S. Recession/Depression: The Domestic Consequences

The U.S. economy is rapidly descending from a recession into a depression. Hundreds of thousands of workers are losing their jobs each month. One out of five workers are out of work or working part time. One out of every ten homeowners cannot meet their mortgage payments and faces eviction. Bankruptcy rates are at depression levels. Credit is drying up. Major banks survive only because of the trillion-dollar government bailouts. Unemployment, bankruptcy, credit freeze, corporate losses and debt—a general depression—has devastated the U.S. domestic economy, severely damaged the "real economy" and the stock market as well. Massive state spending and subsidies to banks have failed either to stimulate the financial system or to encourage lending to the productive sectors and to finance household consumption. In fact, some have argued this is because the derivatives-based debt is in the trillions of dollars, and that financial recuperation would not be feasible even with government assistance, without the cancellation of these contracts. Others have argued not only that the recipient banks are using the funds to take over other banks, but to make non-banking-related purchases elsewhere in the real economy. U.S. Treasury bonds are now paying negative interest rates, far below the rate of inflation. The multi-billion-dollar Wall Street swindles have destroyed confidence between banks and investors, lenders and borrowers, government and industrial firms. The capitalist system has broken down. As an economic system it no longer performs its most basic functions at a minimum level of efficiency—to produce, lend, employ, consume, trade and house.

The traditional "monetary stimulus" of central banks—interest rate reduction—has clearly failed. Even though U.S. interest rates are reduced to 0.25 percent (almost zero), the Federal Reserve admits these measures have not even slowed the descent into a deeper recession. The U.S. capitalist state has resorted to unprecedented printing of money to finance its gaping 3 trillion dollar deficit for fiscal year 2010 and to avoid the collapse of basic federal, state and local government services. However, the bulk of this unprecedented printing is going to loans and other commitments made by the Fed to banks, whose names and the quantities involved the Fed has refused to divulge. Major firings of public employees and the closure of social services have multiplied as social services have been slashed.

What is striking about the U.S. political-economy in this deepening recession are: the divergence in performance between the stock market and the real economy; the vast reduction in public spending in the civilian economy even as there is an increase in military spending; the reduction of civilian employees and the escalation of troops sent to war. In other words, the capitalist state is allocating its scarce resources to rebuild the empire and engage in multiple wars even as it starves the civilian administration of resources at a time when it verges on bankruptcy and the productive domestic economy collapses in a deepening recession.

A similar divergence in state policy is evident with relation to the vast sums allocated to support the financial sector and the total neglect of the productive economy. As a number of big banks appear to have been pulled back from the brink of collapse, they still face outstanding derivatives which are scheduled to come due in the near future, while thousands of major manufacturing, mining, construction, and transport enterprises have gone bankrupt or are on the verge of failure with virtually no state support.

This peculiar and specific character of the U.S. capitalist crisis leads to several tentative observations:

1. Military-driven empire building is the primary priority driving state policy over and above the domestic (and even export) productive economy. While the military budget and personnel grow, private investment funds and employment in productive sectors shrink.

2. The military-imperial complex is relatively, and perhaps temporarily, independent or 'autonomous' from the domestic productive economy. Its growth and overseas expansion take place despite the contraction of the economy. In fact, there seems to be an inverse relation: As the domestic economic crisis deepens, the military-imperial complex expands. Those who believed that the economic recession would undermine military-driven empire building and wars, forcing the government to concede defeat, withdraw or "negotiate" with adversaries and submit to multilateral coordinated decisions, have been proved wrong. One might concede that a prolonged recession/depression may ultimately force the government to retrench military empire

building in the face of mass unemployment and even mass hunger. However, even that is uncertain given the lack of any mass protests and the reduction of the bureaucratized private trade union sector to below 5 percent of the labor force. There is no protest even with the massive layoffs of unionized automobile, steel and other industrial workers.

There is no pre-determined point at which sufficient political pressure might arise to reverse the predominance of military imperial priorities over the civilian domestic economy. How many imperial wars, of what duration, will be counterposed to what percentage of unemployed and underemployed workers to set in motion a political shift toward confronting the domestic recession/depression? Will it be two or three wars versus 20–30 percent unemployment and underemployment? The Imperial Wars will go on; the domestic economy will continue to decline. In current circumstances no planners can believe the lesson of the Great Depression—that only World War II brought an end to it. There are no economic benefits to be derived from the current wars similar to those that resulted from World War II (where America faced no significant costs, but rather reaped huge benefits from exports and reconstruction, etc.) These new wars are fought for military objectives. There are no economic benefits in fighting wars in Afghanistan and Pakistan. U.S. efforts to encircle China have failed in the face of the lucrative trade and investment agreements signed with its neighbors and the tremendous debt dependency of the U.S. on China.

The State's highest priority is placed on the military-imperial and financial sectors despite the breakdown of the domestic economy and the drain from the prolonged and failing imperial wars in the Middle East. This suggests that we are dealing with *deep political-economic structural relations within the U.S.*, which cannot be changed or reversed by any particular elected political official. Deep structures cannot be uprooted in the current context; new "economic stimuli" can only activate short-term projects, whose scope and depth are limited by the voracious demands of the imperial wars and the dysfunctional financial system.

Regional Impact of the Global Capitalist Crisis

It has been argued that "economic development outside the process of globalization is no longer possible" (Steill 2007). However, a short review of the impact of the global crisis on other regions of the world reveals the disastrous consequences inflicted upon the regions due to their linkage to first-world capital and the accelerated processes of de-globalization which are actually in progress, and leads rather to the conviction that "globalization" as an imperial project is presently moribund.

The worldwide depression has both *common* and *different* causes, affected by the interconnections between economies and specific socio-economic structures. At the most general global level the rising rate of profits and the over-accumulation of capital leading to the financial/real estate/speculative frenzy and crash affected most countries either directly or indirectly. At the same time, while all regional economies suffered the consequences of the onset of the depression, regions were situated differently in the world economy and subsequently the effects on them varied substantially.

Latin America

The spread of imperial capital throughout the world led to the rapid spread of the financial crisis and breakdown among those countries most closely linked to the U.S. and European financial circuits. Globalization tied Latin American economies to world markets at the expense of domestic markets, and increased their vulnerability to the vertical fall in demand, prices, and credit witnessed today. Globalization, which earlier promoted the inflow of capital, now, with the onset of the depression, facilitates massive capital outflow.

The United States, which is absorbing 70 percent of the world's savings in its desperate effort to borrow and finance its monstrous trade and budget deficits, has squeezed out its Latin American trading partners from the global credit market. The depression demonstrates with crystal clarity the pitfalls of imperial-centered globalization and the stark absence of any remedies for its collaborators in Latin America. The disintegration of the imperial-centered global economy is evident amidst rising protectionism and the billions of dollars in state subsidies used to prop up the imperial states' own capitalists in the banking, insurance, real estate and manufacturing sectors. The world depression not only reveals the intrinsic fault lines of the globalized economy, but ensures its ultimate demise into a multiplicity of competing units: nations, each depending on their own treasuries and state sectors to pull them out of the deepening depression at the expense of their former partners. The world depression is spurring the return of the nation-state, as "de-globalization" accelerates.

Parallel with, and intimately related to, the demise of the world market is the rise of the *capitalist state* as the center-piece for salvaging the national treasury and exacting an exorbitant tribute from the pension, health and wage funds of billions of workers, pensioners and tax-payers. Growing *state capitalism* in times of capitalist collapse only emerges to *save the capitalist system from capitalist failures*, as its promoters argue. In order to do so it exploits the collective wealth of the entire people. *Nationalization* or *statification* of insolvent banks and industries is the culmination of predator capitalism, not the opening steps of a progression towards socialism. Instead of individual enterprises or even sectoral exploitation of wage and salaried workers, it is now the *capitalist state* that preys on the entire class of the producers of wealth.

Latin America's options revolve around recognizing and accepting that *globalization is dead*, that only under popular democratic control can nationalization function with a socialist orientation, with a view to generating wealth and creating employment, instead of serving to channel and redistribute resources upward and outward to the failed, bankrupt capitalist class in the developed countries.

Asia

The Great Depression of 2009 has adversely affected every economy in Asia that is dependent on the international financial and commodity markets. Even the most dynamic countries, like Japan, China, India, South Korea, Taiwan and Vietnam, have not escaped the consequences of drastic declines in trade, employment, investment and living standards. Two decades of dynamic expansion, high growth, and rising profit margins, based on export markets and intense exploitation of labor, led to the over-accumulation of capital. Many Asian and Western pundits argued for a "new world order", led and directed by the emerging Asian economic powers, especially China, where power would be increasingly based on their purported "regional autonomy". In reality, China's dynamic industrial growth was deeply embedded in a world commodity chain in which advanced capitalist economies, like Germany, Japan, Taiwan and South Korea, provided precision tools, machinery and parts to China for assembly and subsequent export to U.S., European and Asian markets. "Decoupling" was a myth.

Export-driven growth was fueled by savage exploitation of labor, the dismantling of vast areas of social services (namely free health care, pensions, subsidized food and lodging and education) and the extensive concentration of wealth in a tiny elite of newly rich billionaires (*Economic and Political Weekly* 2008). China and the rest of Asia's growth were based on the contradiction between the *dynamic expansion of the forces of production* and the increasing *polarization of the class relations of production*. The high rates of profit led to high rates of investment, the over-accumulation of capital leading to huge budget and trade surpluses which spilled over into the financial sectors, overseas expansion (or money-laundering) and real estate speculation.

Asia's economic edifice was precariously situated on the backs of hundreds of millions of laborers with virtually no consumer power and an increasing dependence on overseas export markets. The world crisis especially deflated the export markets, exposing the Asian economies' vulnerabilities and causing a massive fall in trade and production, and a huge growth in unemployment. The efforts of China and the other Asian countries to counteract the collapse of the export markets by massive injections of public capital to stimulate financial liquidity and infrastructure development have been insufficient to stem the growth of unemployment and the bankruptcy of millions of export-linked enterprises.

The Asian capitalist classes and their government elites are entirely incapable of "restructuring" the economy and social structure toward substituting domestic demand as the external market collapses. To do so would mean several profound transformations in the class structure. These include the shift from investments based on high profitability toward low-profit-margin productive and social services for the hundreds of millions of low-income workers and peasants. It would require the transfer of capital back from private real estate, stock markets and overseas bond purchases (like U.S. Treasury Notes), where it presently resides, to finance universal health care, education and pensions and the restoration of land to productive use rather than to dispossession and real estate speculation.

The entire dynamic growth of Asia, built around capital concentration, high profits and low wages, is trying to survive based on deepening the impoverishment of labor via massive firing of workers, huge reverse flows of migrant labor back to the devastated countryside and the growth of the surplus labor force. The expulsion of labor, the usual capitalist solution, merely re-locates and intensifies the contradiction, heightening the conflict between urban-based industrial/finance capital and hundreds of millions of impoverished, unemployed and underemployed workers and peasants. The states' injections of capital to stimulate the economies pass through the "filter" of regional state elites and the capitalist class, which absorbs and uses the bulk of this capital to buttress faltering enterprises—with negligible impact on the mass of unemployed workers.

The Middle East

The oil-producing countries accumulated vast "rents", which they re-cycled into large-scale finance, real estate and military purchases in and out of the region. Profits concentrated in the hands of billionaire absolutist rulers led to highly polarized class relationships: super-wealthy rentiers and low-paid immigrant laborers limited the size and scope of the domestic markets. To break out of the crisis of over-accumulation and falling profits, the ruling elites adopted two strategies that temporarily avoided the crisis: large-scale export of capital to rent, interest and dividend-yielding sites throughout the world—first to the U.S. and Europe and later to Asia and Africa—and the recycling of profits into real estate, tourist and banking centers of pharaonic scale and splendor in the Gulf States, leading to an enormous real estate bubble.

The collapse of the Middle East "rentier (or non-productive) oligarchies" began with the frenzied commodity oil boom between 2004–2008, which heightened a construction and real estate boom, as well as the accumulation of debt and labor importation. The result was the onset of a regional economic crisis, in which budget and trade surpluses were replaced by mounting deficits. At no point did the Middle East economies diversify from their foundation based on "rents" to create a diversified economy centered on production and the creation of a dynamic mass-based regional market. The rentier ruling classes face a growing mass of unemployed domestic and immigrant workers (who will likely be sent home), and the massive flight of thousands of expatriate European financiers, real estate professionals and other non-productive hangers-on.

No longer the beneficiaries of the petro-dollar boom—as prices, profits and rents collapsed—and no longer the powerful bankers and holders of debt, the Gulf Arab ruling class had too few external and internal resources and outlets to project a "recovery program" for the immediate future. This led to deepening crisis in the form of high unemployment, rising poverty, and mass deprivation that eventually triggered the mass protests, rebellions, and revolutions that toppled dictatorships across the Middle East—from Tunisia to Egypt to Yemen—as well as uprisings in Bahrain, Syria, and elsewhere in the region.

Lessons From the Collapse of Wall Street

The collapse of the stock market and the loss of hundreds of billions of dollars managed by Wall Street investment banks illustrate the pitfalls and dangers of free market capitalism which face the entire working population of the United States and, through the United States, the world.

1. *The near bankruptcy of Social Security.* The attempt by the White House and leading Republican and Democrat congressmen as recently as three years ago to "privatize" Social Security—essentially to turn over the management and investment of trillions of dollars in Social Security funds to Wall Street—with the argument that private investors would earn more for retirees, would have led to the bankruptcy of the entire Social Security fund. Privatization would have provided yet another income stream to the major private investment banks on top of that already forced into the market by the Federal Reserve's enforcement of low interest rates, enabling them to prolong their binge of highly-leveraged speculation and invention of even riskier financial instruments, leading to an even greater calamity than the disastrous results we witnessed in 2008–09. While private pension funds go belly-up, Social Security continues. It is the private pensions which have gone bankrupt, not the publicly managed Social Security fund, contrary to the statements of the experts and critics of Social Security. Clearly, the current private debacle argues for public control and management of pension programs.

2. *The insecurity of private pension funds.* All the major private pension funds for public and private employees, including TIAA-CREF, CALPERS and labor union pensions, have shown negative growth over the five-year period from 2004 to 2009. Clearly, linking pension funds to the stock market has severely reduced the living standards of retirees, forcing many to remain in the labor force into their seventies and beyond or to sink into poverty. Pensions linked to publicly funded productive activity would avoid the losses and risks embedded in investing in the stock market for old age security.

3. *The loss of a real economy manufacturing base.* The conversion of the U.S. into a "service" economy as opposed to an advanced and diversified manufacturing economy is the root cause of the collapse of the U.S. financial system and the continuing long-term recession. From the 1960s onward, the state adopted policies that promoted finance, real estate and insurance (the so-called FIRE sectors), which raised rents, redirected subsidies, provided tax concessions and subsidies, and destroyed and displaced industry. The

re-conversion of the FIRE economy back to a balanced manufacturing economy and welfare state, essential for reversing the collapse of the U.S. economy, will require a major political upheaval.

4. *Corporate flight.* The massive flight of capital from productive sectors to FIRE was accompanied by the huge surge of capital overseas, as competition forced corporations to seek out the multitude of advantages of production in less-developed countries (cheap labor, tax concessions, lax regulation), leaving the domestic economy overly dependent on "services" (sold to Americans as the knowledge economy), particularly volatile and risky "financial services" and debt-based rather than wage-based sales to domestic consumers. The conversion of the U.S. from a diversified economy to a FIRE monoculture increased the vulnerability to a general collapse if and when the financial/real estate market went under. Recovery and sustained growth can only occur with the return to a diversified economy, and the retention of capital from overseas flight. This is not happening and will not happen because of higher rates of profit abroad and the deep structure of the economy—namely the dominant position of finance capital. Only with a new political leadership which breaks with Wall Street can we envision the kind of large-scale, long-term public investment and incentives for the productive and social service sectors.

5. *The pursuit of military-driven empire building*, at the expense of joint ventures and reciprocal trade agreements with countries with expanding markets, strategic energy sources, and large populations and markets, created enormous budget and trade deficits and alienated potential sources of markets and strategic commodities. Trillion-dollar military expenditures in pursuit of prolonged, costly colonial wars diverted funds from the application of technological advances and high-end manufacturing which would have lowered costs and increased market competition. Equally important, by shifting from market-driven domestic expansion to overseas military-driven expansion, the entire axis of economic power shifted from industrial to financial capital. Finance capital, which was essential to funding government budget deficits incurred through military expenditure, grew in influence— Wall Street replaced the steel-belt as the axis of power in Washington.

The "power elite" is only as powerful as it is able to manipulate, intimidate and beguile the more than three hundred million U.S. citizens into thinking that they are indispensable to running the American economy—rather than complicit, in a class sense, in milking it for private gain:

> According to the man who may be the leading expert on banking fraud, there is also no innocent explanation for the events leading to the current economic crisis. Last week on his PBS show, Bill Moyers interviewed William K. Black, the senior regulator during the savings and loan scandal in the late 1980s. Mr. Black, who wrote a book based on his experiences and called it *The Best Way to Rob a Bank is to*

Own One, said the fraud and deceit that resulted in the world banking system's dire distress makes Bernie Madoff look like a piker. In fact, says Mr. Black, who is the former director of the Institute for Fraud Prevention, what we have experienced was caused by "calculated dishonesty" on the part of corporate CEOs, aided and abetted by politicians and regulators who tore down the barriers to financial shenanigans—perhaps the most important example being the repeal of the Great Depression-inspired Glass-Steagall Act that separated commercial banking from investment banking. This cleared the stage for the fraudulent investments that made a lot of people very, very rich in what we can now see was an immense Ponzi scheme, many times the size and scope of the scam pulled off by Mr. Madoff.

When asked by Mr. Moyers whether he was alleging that Timothy F. Geithner and others in the administration, and the banks, are engaged in a cover-up to keep us from knowing what went wrong, Mr. Black said, "Absolutely." The rulers are frightened to admit that many of the large banks are insolvent. They have ignored the proven methods for dealing with bank fraud and have instead adopted what they used to laugh at when the Japanese did it: covering up bank losses by lying about them and injecting money into failed institutions. Even though it's working exactly as one would expect—just as it did in setting Japan into a long, deep recession—they don't know what else to do. (Smith 2009)

While the overwhelming initial popular rejection of the Wall Street bailout suggests that the ruling oligarchy is not invincible, what must next become a popular conviction is that they are *not competent* to do other than maximize their own private interests.

The world's future is not safe in their hands.

References

British Broadcasting Corporation. 2009 (February 27).
Economic and Political Weekly. 2008 (Mumbai, December 27).
Financial Times. 2009a (February 25).
——. 2009b (March 9).
——. 2009c (March 10).
——. 2009d (March 11).
Labaton, Stephen and Calmes, Jackie. 2009. "Obama Pushes Broad Rules for Oversight of Derivatives," *New York Times* (May 13).
Reuters. 2009a. "No Quick Solution to the Financial Crisis: IMF" (April 21).
——. 2009b. "U.S. Bankruptcies Highest Since 2005" (June 10).
Smith, Ron. 2009. "A Fraud That Makes Madoff Look Small Time," *The Baltimore Sun* (April 12).
Steill, Benn. 2007. "The End of National Currency," *Foreign Affairs*.

Chapter 5

The Global Capitalist Crisis and the European Union, with Focus on Greece

Mike-Frank G. Epitropoulos

In the run up to the U.S. Presidential elections in the Fall of 2008, the "shocking" news broke that the country's "housing bubble" had burst, and that the economy had gone into a recession. In short order, the revelations of what had been playing out on Wall Street and the magnitude of their market manipulations led economists and politicians to sound the alarm bells of dire *economic crisis.* Clearly, this situation demanded immediate political attention, and it got it. Under President George W. Bush—in public consultation with presidential candidates Barack Obama and John McCain, and the leadership of both parties—the economic and political elite secured the Troubled Asset Relief Program (TARP). Led by the likes of Treasury Secretary Henry Paulson (formerly the CEO of Goldman Sachs) and Federal Reserve Chairman Ben Bernanke, those in command swiftly and successfully "socialized" the costs of Wall Street's reckless behavior, invoking the mantra of "too big to fail" and making sure that none of the perpetrators would be held accountable. This scenario not only opened the door of the White House to Barack Obama, but it set into motion—or at least accelerated—global capitalist crisis and class war that hadn't been seen at this level in the Western world for a very long time.

The so-called "toxic" loans that are at the root of this economic crisis are the product of financial deregulation begun under President Bill Clinton and continued and expanded under George W. Bush. The clear beneficiaries are the bankers, financiers, and speculators of the capitalist class. These "toxic" loans are essentially fraudulently-generated "bad paper" loans that the financial services industry packaged and repackaged for sale to investors and institutions alike. They were facilitated in this process by corrupt credit rating agencies and other middle-men. At every step of the way, these players took their fees and their commissions while they knowingly sold bad paper, representing nothing other than claims on future earnings (Korten 2009).

The bloated banks and financial services companies of Wall Street and the rest of the capitalist West certainly did not confine their business and their "products" to any one country. Capitalism is a global enterprise that seeks profit maximization and capital accumulation wherever it can find it. And being keenly *class conscious*, capitalists are willing to exercise their influence in the political arena, to serve their interests and exact punishment on potential rivals. Thus, the vast sums of paper money that had been accumulated by Wall Street and European banks were continuously being lent to both individual consumers and sovereign nations. Cheap money proved addictive for both.

In Europe, the introduction of the euro—and more fundamentally, the primacy of *economic* union over *political* union—allowed weaker member states to post rapid growth numbers and realize material gains out of sync with realities on the ground. Most of the so-called "PIIGS"—Portugal, Ireland, Italy, Greece, and Spain—were just such countries. For its part, Greece had been one of the fastest growing countries in the eurozone, and after successfully hosting the 2004 Olympiad as the smallest country to ever do so in the modern era, foreign capital flowed to the country (albeit less than economists expected, because of the Greek bureaucracy). The same expectations had been raised for Ireland, which had been held out as a shining example of economic growth (Garofalo 2010); and Spain with its own housing bubble (Krugman 2010b).

The net result was that the PIIGS as a group, benefiting from the disproportionate strength of the euro, combined with strong national accounting numbers, were prime candidates for money from global capital. Their ability to borrow large sums of money at low rates of interest allowed the PIIGS to accumulate and run large structural deficits. So, by early 2010, as the global capitalist crisis continued to foment, fears of sovereign debt crises developed in Europe, especially among the PIIGS (Forelle 2010; Matich 2010; Newmark 2010).

The irony here is that the *fears* are primarily those of the "pushers" of the loans—the global capitalist creditors. At the same time, European capital and its political establishment, the EU, feared and continues to fear, the integrity of the euro. All of this had also fueled predatory financial speculators to bet against these countries being able to overcome their debt, eroding those countries' credit ratings even further. Some, like financial analyst Max Keiser and commentator Alex Jones of PrisonPlanet.com and InfoWars.com, have appropriately labeled these people and their practices, as "economic terrorists". What is worse is that often the same financial entity "giveth" and "taketh," hedging their bets—throwing caution to the wind and throwing people and countries into tailspins.

All of this led to a crisis of confidence in the PIIGS that widened bond yield spreads and risk insurance on credit default swaps. In the European context, it is Germany and France to whose banks most of this sovereign debt accrues, but the global capitalist ties must not be overlooked (Wolff 2010a). This is because the class conscious capitalists are not pushing this narrative of what went down (Bello 2010). Their narratives aim to not only exploit the "shock" in the terms of Naomi Klein in *The Shock Doctrine*, but also aim to establish a *demonstration effect*, lest anyone challenge the system and/or the notion that there "*might*" be an *alternative!* (Klein 2009).

No, financial lobbyists around the world are taking this opportunity to use the economic crisis as a lesson to rail against all public spending and social programs (Matich 2010; Newmark 2010; *The Economist* 2010). This is a war that not only is against non-capitalist, alternative systems, but even—*or especially*—against

Keynesian economics and economists! Yes, even Keynesians have become *"persona non grata"* in our times! (Hahnel and Doherty 2010). So, instead of reining in speculative capital and re-regulating the banks and financial services sector, that are the cause of the economic problems, capitalists went with "open hands" to take their bailouts, exact their bonuses, and then blame everything on high taxes, burdensome regulation, labor unions and pensions. They have kept profit a private matter, while socializing the costs.

In this chapter, with this backdrop, I will focus on the impact of the global capitalist crisis on the Greek economy, and how this has impacted the social and political spheres there. The situation is truly unbelievable in many ways, and it is surely a trying time for not only Greeks, but working people everywhere. Beyond assessing the impact on Greece, I will develop the political response of the Greek working class and the Greek masses in general, along with their formal political parties and a wide range of social movements. This will surely include how different groups and groupings in Greece are reacting to the "Troika" of the IMF, the European Central Bank (ECB), and the EU, who have usurped control of the country's economic policies with the blessing of the Greek government.

This will take our discussion into the topic of *"what is to be done?"* There is clearly potential for an explosive, even "revolutionary" situation, as it is highly unlikely that austerity measures on the backs of the working class and those who can least afford it will save Greece from eventual default. This volatile situation could take any of many forms, from the potential for a socialist direction, to another military coup and dictatorship. The situation on the ground in Greece is what will determine the outcome.

Origins and Nature of the Crisis

Greece has long had a bloated public sector that has employed disproportionate numbers of the population. This schema has not operated on market or even traditional public sector principles, but rather on *rousféti* — or patronage — principles of political convenience. This means that there were typically more civil servants employed than were necessary, their working hours were shorter, and their service more lax than one would expect or like. All of these things have become targets for neoliberal reform around the world, as we are seeing the "shock doctrine" introduced and forced upon people in these countries that find themselves in a bind (Klein 2008).

Next, as the aforementioned *rousféti* would indicate, the Greek state has long been known as a bastion of corruption. In many economics and business textbooks, Greece is held out as a leader in black market economic activity. And, under the previous conservative New Democracy (ND) government, Finance Minister Giorgos Alogoskoufis "redefined" the always problematic measure of social and economic well-being, the Gross Domestic Product (GDP), by essentially adding an estimated amount of Greece's well-known "black market" activities (Matich

2010). In doing so, the government proudly announced that Greece and Greeks were 25 percent wealthier overnight in 2006! (Epitropoulos 2006). What was important was that the Greek government was on board with the global, neoliberal program that was catering to and pampering both domestic and foreign capital, and Washington.

Beyond this, Greece is at the top of the list in military spending as a percentage of GDP in the EU. All of this is occurring while Greek teachers are next to last in salaries in the EU. In fact, in the past few years, riot police have beaten and tear-gassed teachers and students more frequently than any other group. The point here is that both ND and their counterparts in Greece's two-party stranglehold, the Pan-Hellenic Socialist Movement (PASOK) have consistently been more in line with the neoliberal economic agenda and tougher in the social arena than their reputation in the West as the "black sheep of Europe" would suggest (Kushlis 2010).

So the powder keg of social discontent needed only a spark to set off its fury and frustration. In December of 2008, 15-year-old Alexis Grigoropoulos was shot and killed by a police officer in Athens. Since the shooting occurred in the Exarchia neighborhood of downtown Athens, many identified the incident with the anarchists whose center of activity is there. The police claims that the youth had attacked them did not jibe with eyewitness accounts of the event. Greek society was outraged by the incident, and protests ensued across the country for weeks. The murder of Alexi was the spark that triggered these demonstrations and riots, but the causes were many and had been simmering under the surface of Greek daily life for a long time. Among those were the neoliberal policies of the New Democracy (ND) government, police brutality, overt corruption and scandals, and poor job prospects and working conditions for youth, to name just a few.

While the youth and students from universities down through the elementary schools took the lead in organizing and conducting the demonstrations and riots — many of which caused significant property damage, which led to a backlash against the protesters in some circles —a broad spectrum of Athenian society, including Left political parties, unions, parents, and immigrant groups also joined in. It was this broad-based anti-government and anti-brutality outpouring that also acted as a check against abuse and misrepresentation of events by the mainstream media in Greece. When the media portrayals of events didn't correlate with what the people in the streets and their families directly experienced, the media's legitimacy suffered and they were forced to modify and retract earlier reports of events. The legitimacy of both the media and the government suffered as parents listened to their kids, and as people from across all walks of life and classes condemned the killing of Alexi, the government crackdown on dissent, and sensationalized and inaccurate media depictions of the protests (Epitropoulos 2010).

With the veneer of the post-Olympiad "boom years" stripped away, the harsh realities of Greece became obscenely blatant (Petras 2010a). Scandals had begun piling up: the Vodafone wire-tapping case; the Olympic security scandal involving questionable contracts to U.S.-based Science Applications International

Corporation (SAIC) with ties to Blackwater (now XE Services) and smaller Greek firms; the 2008 Siemens corruption and bribery scandal that implicates Greek politicians of the two main parties (ND and PASOK) and is connected with both the 2004 Olympic contracts and the subsequent sale of the national telephone company, Hellenic Telecommunications Organization (OTE); the Vatopedi monastery scandal, and the Culture Minister Zahopoulos' corruption and sex scandal, to name but a few (Lewis 2010). This subset of scandals cost billions of euros, sold out national sovereignty, threatened security, and took lives—but no one was sent to jail, no one paid a price, and the wrath of the state's security apparatus was directed towards teachers, workers, students, farmers and immigrants.

As mentioned earlier, the narrative of the mainstream press, politicians, and Wall Street is that years of unrestrained spending to build a welfare state led Greece to accumulate a sovereign debt it cannot afford (Wolff 2010b). The country's national debt is estimated to be approximately €300 billion, with a national budget deficit at 12.7 percent. As the economic crisis hit and unraveled, this meant that the flow of cheap and worthless loans were drying up, and—more importantly—that Greece's (and the other PIIGS') credit ratings had been downgraded (Bello 2010; Hudson 2010; *The Economist* 2010). In fact, at the time of this writing, Greece has the lowest credit rating of any country in the eurozone.

So, in this European Union that was designed to be "economics first" and "democracy second", the "black sheep," Greece, had to be made an example of for two main reasons: first, to keep the hands of government regulation off of international capital (both U.S. and EU) and shift the blame for the hard times about to be exacted upon the working classes onto the welfare state, social spending, and labor; second, the case of Greece becomes a prototype test case in the global capitalist battle against a historically resistant and militant culture (not labor movement). The table is set for an epic tragedy pitting profit against "democratic impulses" in the birthplace of democracy (Bello 2010). How the battles play out can potentially affect other workers' and popular struggles in the other PIIGS' countries and the rest of the world, so the stakes are correspondingly high. Let us consider what has been brewing elsewhere in Europe for a moment.

Europe as the Backdrop to the Greek Crisis

In the past few years, Europe has faced serious riots not just in Greece, but also in France, England, Italy, Spain, Ireland, and Iceland. The root causes of these various confrontations have been the brutally anti-people/pro-profit neoliberal agenda. There has been overt concern about these uprisings in both Europe and the United States as we have entered the greatest economic downturn since the Great Depression. In France, President Sarkozy backed down on education reforms, saying that, "We don't want a European May '68 in the middle of Christmas," and that, "...The slogan of the Greek students about 'the €600 generation' could easily catch on here," referring to the increasing number of Greek youth who are relegated to low-wage, part-time, no-benefit jobs.

For U.S. intelligence and security officials, Greece has long been a focus of attention, going back to the U.S. government's *de facto* support for Greece's military junta (1967–1974). Today the United States views Greece as a centerpiece of "counterinsurgency" doctrine, especially with regard to suppressing leftist forces. Among the more familiar tactics employed in such counterinsurgency efforts is infiltrating opposition groups with provocateurs. In the context of the December 2008 riots in Greece, Paul J. Watson of Prison Planet reported that "police masquerading as anarchists were committing acts of wanton violence to inflame tensions and provide a pretext for a brutal crackdown on legitimate demonstrators protesting against police brutality and the mishandling of the economic crisis (Watson 2008). These are the kinds of tactics that lie at the heart of many counterinsurgency strategies, and can be expected as government responses to anti-authoritarian dissent, especially during a period of economic crisis. Recently, Jose Trabanco, an independent writer based in Mexico, reported in an article on the website of the Centre for Research on Globalization on official concerns about potential civil unrest in the United States, as elites begin to grasp the magnitude of the economic crisis (Trabanco 2009). This may not square with recent positive economic news, but we should be just as wary of numbers and projections from the White House as we are from credit-rating agencies.

Greeks, like other Europeans, have a history of bold protest, direct action, and civil disobedience. They have shown willingness to fight for their own class interests, time and again. And this current crisis is no different. It is fine that Greek Prime Minister George Papandreou, German Chancellor Angela Merkel, and even President Barack Obama pay lip service to cracking down on financial speculators and the big banks. But none of them has moved seriously to regulate, restrict, or punish them. In the United States, we bailed out the banks with taxpayer money. In Greece, the government is introducing punitive austerity measures on the working and middle classes to pay for the "accounting magic" that Wall Street consultants, like Goldman Sachs and JP Morgan, provided to the previous government (Hudson 2010). And this is the crux of why Greece is in the spotlight now.

U.S. Banks as the Force Behind Greece's Troubles

In the U.S., we all witnessed how the banking sector of contemporary capitalism responded—*with class consciousness, of course!* After successfully changing rules and regulations in the banking and accounting spheres of operations, they exploited the system by knowingly engaging in the creation, multiplication, and dissemination of "toxic assets," while collecting fees, commissions, and bonuses every step of the way. These same banks also conveniently and consciously hid both *losses* and *potential losses* so as to show more profit and remain under the radar in this "phantom wealth" economy (Korten 2009). In fact, Goldman Sachs secretly bet on the looming U.S. housing crisis that it helped create (Gordon 2010).

In response, as mentioned earlier, the Bush Administration and former-Goldman-CEO-turned-Treasury-Secretary Henry Paulson played the role of "financial terrorist" as he warned (or threatened?) that unless the state came through with TARP for the "too big to fail" banks, we would face, "… collapse and martial law." That role could also be seen as "delivery boy" for big capital that best understands its class interests and the true importance of the role of the state. Initially, Paulson's hubris had him arrive with a mere three-page TARP proposal, amounting to a *carte blanche* with no potential legal review. A revised document subsequently passed TARP, however, securing the *socialization of the cost* of capital's mischief. Further, Fed Chairman, Ben Bernanke, was able to waive (future) losses for banks, ensuring their profit status as part of the bailouts. And unlike the Savings and Loan scandal, there has not been a single arrest, indictment, or conviction of any of the key players that orchestrated this scheme.

After wreaking such havoc and securing their bailouts and bonuses, the banks and Wall Street elected "their man" in Barack Obama. Goldman Sachs was Obama's number one private contributor in the 2008 presidential contest (Center for Responsive Politics 2010). And though his capitalist backers may not be happy with his rhetoric or his entire political platform, they are certainly happy with the frivolous reforms for the financial sector, and the "compromise" extension of the Bush-era tax cuts. Repeal of those tax cuts on the top five percent of U.S. income earners had been a centerpiece of Obama's 2008 campaign. So, instead of taking those dollars into the public coffers, we are *borrowing* from the rich *with interest* on the backs of the working class's future earnings.

The phantom wealth that the toxic assets of the deregulated housing market created was also sold through international funds. These banks *knowingly* sold countries like Greece these shady, toxic assets with the fraudulent stamps of approval of equally-corrupted credit rating agencies (Hudson 2010). It is these very same banks that want to be repaid, but are exacting their booty in terms of *real* pension funds, *real* assets, and the *real* wages of Greece's (the PIIGS', and America's) working classes. In essence, these private financial interests have come to *own* Greece, and now Greece's economic policy apparatus, through *fraud*. But what is worse in the Greek (and the PIIGS') case than that of the U.S. is the two-fold narrative emphasis: (1) the crisis is the fault of the welfare state, socialist policies, and living decadently, and (2) the working classes and popular, democratic resistance must be thwarted and demonstrably be made examples of to prevent or to halt the movement toward socialism (Bello 2010).

The Greek national budget deficit that has been a global concern for quite some time now stands at about 12.7 percent, about as large as that of the U.S., *and* about what it had been *years prior* in Greece. Other countries of the PIIGS have had greater deficits. Greece—and probably many of these other countries—fudged their numbers to hide their situation from the markets. There was ND finance minister George Alogoskoufi's famous, magical revision of the country's GDP by

25 percent for starters, but the government went calling on the best "cheaters" in the business: Goldman Sachs and J.P. Morgan (Epitropoulos 2006, 2010).

But when financial speculators started to raise the *ante*—betting against Greece and the euro—the pressure on the euro (as a currency) and the EU mounted. The EU, of course, placed the stability of the euro and eurozone at the top of its priority list. After all, Greece had, indeed, violated the monetary union guidelines and misreported the country's official economic statistics—again, with the paid assistance of Goldman Sachs and other banks, which helped create the mess. Such arrangements and shady dealings are not the traits solely of Greece, however, as other EU countries, and the entire global capitalist regime have exhibited such activity.

On April 27, 2010, Standard & Poor's downgraded Greece's credit rating to "junk" status, and downgraded its view on Portugal as well (Wachman and Fletcher 2010). This occurred as the EU power center in Germany grappled over, whether and how to arrive at a "Greek bailout" package. As the dominant economic power in the EU, Germany has a lot at stake in the viability of both the euro and consequently Greece, and the rest of the PIIGS. The political dimension of *how* to deal with the situation was and remains a difficult one. It is especially difficult in light of the aggressive nature of contemporary global financial speculators, especially those in the United States.

The Banks, the IMF, and the Politics of the Greek Bailout

The Greek parliament passed the Economic Protection Bill, estimated to save an initial €4.8 billion, on March 5, 2010. Then, on April 23, Prime Minister George Papandreou appealed to the EU and the IMF for the activation of the bailout package—the IMF was more than happy to expedite the appeal (*Irish Times* 2010a; Melander 2010). Here is where the historic conditionality's "devil-in-the-details" reared its ugly head. Not only had Greece ceded its national sovereignty and autonomy in economic policy to the so-called, "TROIKA"—consisting of the European Union, European Central Bank, and the IMF—but, they also began doing the dirty work by imposing punitive austerity measures on the Greek people—particularly the working class.

The neoliberals, big banks, and financial speculators that fueled the crisis now want to be paid in real wealth. They want the Greek people, and in particular the working class, to pay. Their narrative about what is wrong in the global economy *must* win, as much as their personal holdings *must* increase. So, the mainstream media went into action establishing and spreading the scenarios of how Europe's "socialist black sheep" and "lazy, hedonistic workers" had wrecked the country and now threatened the euro, the EU, and the entire global economy. All the while the laundry list of scandals, corruption, and thievery of Greek and global politicians, capitalists, and speculators kept their names clean, their practices unscathed, and themselves out of jail.

Of course, all of this political and economic turbulence had led to an electoral victory for PASOK and George Papandreou in October of 2009. Like his father and grandfather before him, Papandreou rode a wave of populist anxiety and anger as the Right and ND had been disgraced and discredited (Papandreou 2010a). His campaign emphasized a liberal social democracy with special concern for the nation's health care and educational systems. But like his ND counterparts and his forefathers before him, Papandreou claimed to have discovered a more dire economic situation than expected and almost immediately invoked, "T.I.N.A.— *there is no alternative.*" The modern Greek "*shock doctrine*" had to be swiftly implemented. As delineated by Naomi Klein, this exploitation took "text-book" form in the name of "austerity" measures and "economic reform" (Klein 2008). A punitive package of measures was readied just as the Greek government *signed over* its economic policy sovereignty to their new masters—the Troika (Hudson 2010; Jessen 2010; Mavroudeas 2010).

The financial markets made clear that they would stop lending to Greece, or make borrowing so cost-prohibitive that their financing options would dry up. The Greek government could have started with a serious crack-down on tax evasion, but that didn't occur. The Bank of Greece released data in 2010 that admits that the middle and working classes pay *more than* the Greek upper class in taxes (Epitropoulos 2010). It is apparent, then, that Papandreou—president of the Socialist International—is unwilling and/or afraid to tax Greece's richest enterprises and citizens. Instead, PASOK employed slogans like, "Hope!" and appeals to national pride—even invoking a "call to arms"—in the now-*national* effort to combat the "*krisi*" (crisis).

Who was the "enemy" in this struggle? The banks? The lenders? The speculators? Unscrupulous politicians and shady businesspeople? Tax-evaders? Maybe organized crime syndicates?

No. The narrative of capital had been cemented. At fault were the "*kalo-perasakides*" of Greece ("happy-go-lucky" Greeks). The roots of this problem: the Greek welfare state, the unions, and "too much" democracy (Bello 2010, Lewis 2010; Matich 2010; Newmark 2010; *The Economist* 2010).

The Greek government began implementing what the financial gods of the Troika had decreed: *living standards were to be slashed, wages and salaries reduced, retirement ages raised and pensions cut, taxes raised, social programs cut, public entities privatized, and a special penalty for the Greek hedonists—hiked taxes on tobacco, alcohol, and fuel!* All of this was put together in conjunction with the Troika of the dominant eurozone governments and the IMF. All of this falling on the backs of those *least* able to pay and *least* responsible for the crisis.

So, *who wins* and *who loses* is clear. *Who plays* and *who pays* is just as clear.

The bailout packages for Greece, Ireland and the subsequent PIIGS that fall victim to this crisis are essentially TARP-like arrangements for global financial capital—especially German and French banks and global currency speculators (Wolf 2010a, 2010b). The exploitation phase of this "shock" is in full swing. Workers and the public sector are under assault. The two-party duopoly is invoking

T.I.N.A. and manipulating the people. And Greeks, who had indeed been "living high" off of the euro and the 2004 Olympics, are in "shock"—do they resist or submit? Do they give up *"kalo-perasia"* ("living well") and get "down-and-dirty" to challenge the system and the *de facto* foreign governance, or do they succumb and fulfill the desired *demonstration effect* for the world to see?

The rhetoric of the government and the Troika would have us believe that the austerity measures and bailout will allow Greece to reduce its debt and become independently solvent by 2013. They also have no choice other than to exude nothing but optimism *vis-à-vis* these packages and their affects on the euro. But to actually reduce these inflated, "phantom" debts, there will have to be *real economic growth* and improvement. Are these reasonable expectations, given the range and magnitude of the austerity measures and the current global capitalist economy?

Keynesian economists, such as Paul Krugman and Joseph Stiglitz, have been warning that austerity measures, coupled with deregulation of markets and privatization of state services, are precisely what *are not* called for at this time (Krugman 2010a; 2010b; Stiglitz 2010; Hahnel and Doherty 2010). They have sounded the alarm bells about misguided trust in the unfettered, *laissez-faire* "free market" approaches to our current structural economic conditions. In fact, Krugman says of the U.S. and Obama's economic recovery plan that we are spending "too little, too late" (Krugman 2010a). But as Naomi Klein shows in *Shock Doctrine,* the views of the Keynesians have not only fallen on deaf ears, but these prominent, Nobel Prize-winning economists have fallen out of favor with the corporate-controlled mainstream media and have become *persona non grata* within the economics profession (Hahnel and Doherty 2010; Klein 2008). These economists aren't socialists, nor are they radicals, but because the class war is on, the gloves are off. The name-calling and red-baiting discredit even milquetoast liberals, and the reified deification of markets continues unabated.

IMF-Imposed Austerity and Class Struggle in Greece

Predictably, the Greeks have not taken this lying down. While it is clear that the Greek elites have shored up their positions and sided with the global class war against the working classes and the public sector, Greek unions and Leftists of various stripes have been engaging in a wide-range of strikes, direct actions, and campaigns that have closed down the city-center of Athens, airports, seaports, government offices, archaeological sites, courts, and schools. While frowned upon by mainstream politicians, media, and international capital, these actions, too, reflect *class consciousness and resistance.*

The workers and the people whose wages and living standards are being slashed understand the likely economic consequences of the austerity measures. They understand the consequences more clearly than anyone else as they sit in the dark without heat or air conditioning in attempts to save money to meet their basic needs (Egger 2011; Jessen 2010). As mainstream Keynesian and radical analysts alike predict, the Troika's austerity measures are likely to first have the Greek economy *contract*—with higher unemployment, slashed wages and benefits, and higher taxes all reducing demand and closing more small- to mid-size Greek-owned businesses. Next, and in progression, this contraction will likely lead to further reductions in wages reflecting the aforementioned contraction (Wolff 2010b). Then, the hope of attracting foreign direct investment will also likely *not* materialize unless the Greeks truly fall to Third World levels. Finally, if these are the likely economic outcomes of the austerity measures, government tax revenues will be further eroded, pressuring the state to seek more loans and increase budget deficits once again. Because Greece does not have its own currency so as to devalue its economy in the name of competitiveness, some are calling this, "*internal devaluation*," with the people—not the capitalist classes—paying the freight (Mavroudeas 2010).

If these are indeed the likely consequences of the austerity measures, why do the EU and IMF, along with the Greek government exude such confidence in the plan? Are critical social and economic analyses simply hyperbole perpetrated to exact marginal political gain and to enflame and stir up the public?

There is ample evidence on the table to arrive at the conclusion that global capital's plan is to extract as much real wealth (first) and future wealth (second) in the short run as they can—this means by their 2013 initial target date (Bello 2010; Hudson 2010). This might be extended, but that is largely dependent on the political backlash (or not) of the working classes. Wall Street and the Troika realize that the Greek (or other PIIGS') debts cannot be paid in the end—especially if they expect it to be paid under the conditions of austerity that have been laid out. In the long-run, they understand that economies need *capital* and *spending*—not austerity—to recover.

Do we not have eyes to see what U.S. capital and the banks did? They went with "hands open" for their TARP and bailouts, ensuring "hands off" for financial regulators, and bonuses to keep flowing into their coffers. Without state intervention—that many call "socialist"—the whole financial system might have taken them (and all of us) down. As Michael Hudson succinctly observes:

> Bank lobbyists know that the financial game is over. They are playing for the short run. The financial sector's aim is to take as much bailout money as it can and run, with large enough annual bonuses to lord it over the rest of society after the Clean Slate finally arrives. Less public spending on social programs will leave more bailout money to pay banks for their exponentially rising bad debts that cannot possibly be paid in the end. It is inevitable that loans and bonds will default in the usual convulsion of bankruptcy (Hudson 2010).

From this, we can see that while we write about the global capitalist "crisis," the political and economic elite on both sides of the Atlantic are laughing as they mesmerize and scare people, enjoy profits and personal bonuses, and assure that their phantom loans get paid back with real assets. They do this while demonizing anything public and deepening the true crises of the working class, the middle class and the state.

As James Petras observes:

> Paradoxically, the CEOs used the pretext and rhetoric of "crises" coming from progressive journalists to keep workers from demanding a larger share of the burgeoning profits, aided by the ever growing pool of unemployed and underemployed workers as possible "replacements" (scabs) in the event of industrial action (Petras 2010b).

The same holds true for Greece, the PIIGS, and the rest of the world. The "crisis" we are talking about is disproportionately being experienced within the ranks of the working classes—*not the warring capitalist classes*. They continue to accelerate exploitation whenever and however they can. And they have been very successful, so far facing little resistance. But without a *real, productive* economy with workers and consumers, this bonanza will be short-lived.

Class Struggle and the Prospects for Change

My argument of the value the Greek case has, as a *demonstration effect* to the capitalist classes, rests upon how the Greek people will respond to the ongoing crisis (Epitropoulos 2010). That message was delivered by the so-called "socialist" Papandreou, who ran on a populist message, emphasizing the prioritization and revamping of the health care and educational systems and promising to address poverty, only to reverse direction and provide cover for the banks on the one hand (at the EU and global levels) and for Greek capital and the wealthy (domestically) on the other (Petras 2010a). All the while, the diagnosis is the same, as is the prescription—*the Greek people must pay*.

However, the Greeks reacted with outward expressions of defiance. The parties of the Left—(Communist Party of Greece [KKE] and the "Coalition" [SYRIZA])—along with many disgruntled elements of PASOK openly criticized the government's actions *vis-à-vis* the Troika and the austerity measures. These parties have organized various actions and protests through their affiliated groupings, such as P.A.M.E. (The All-Workers Militant Front), in addition to many informational and lobbying events throughout Greece. They have also been openly suggesting a coordinated effort, with allies from other PIIGS' countries to affect change at the EU level, while they work on the ground in Greece.

But the general strikes, work stoppages, and sit-ins organized by trade unions, like GSEE (the General Confederation of Greek Workers), anarchists, and people from across the political spectrum have been more disruptive, and have garnered more attention from the media and authorities. Greeks have been striking and demonstrating against the severe austerity measures. Many of these actions have turned violent and people have been killed.

Greeks are mobilizing and are acting in ways that reflect *class consciousness* and are fighting for their interests. Protests, rallies, and direct actions that have drawn over half a million people at a time have gained international attention. Yet, election results in late 2010 yielded the same blue (ND) and green (PASOK) victors, leaving the red (KKE, SYRIZA) and black (anarchists) in much the same place electorally.

Thus, it appears that while Greeks may be "class conscious" and protest under radical banners of anarchism, socialism, or communism, the system pulls votes back to the main parties electorally. This makes the size, frequency, and volatility of the protests and actions even *more impressive because it is reasonable to believe that the fact that PASOK and Papandreou are in office has kept many more people and workers off the streets who would otherwise be there* (Kushlis 2010).

This is the backdrop against which most mainstream politicians and political analysts in Greece are able to make public appearances at home and abroad and argue that the protests and protestors are not representative of the Greek people, but rather are a disgruntled segment of the population. As one apologist, Giorgos Yfantis, president of the Hellenic Center for European Studies, said, "…a majority of Greeks realize it is a dire, grave situation, that we've been living beyond our means, and that it's time to fix our house" (Omadeon Worldpress 2010). Again, this all may be true, but it implies that those who set this economic fire must go free and that the Greek people must endure a prolonged period of immiseration. Others have characterized this type of response as, "Stockholm Syndrome," wherein prisoners come to identify with their captors . Implied here, again, is that *there is no alternative* to the existing system.

It is also true that to this point the sum of all of the street protests and direct actions have done nothing to stop the Troika or the *demonstration effect* being leveled on the Greek people. Elections "show" victories for the two parties that have ruled and exploited the situation throughout. The bailout money and any other savings that accrue from cuts to social programs, pension funds, and privatizations will flow to the German, French, and Wall Street bankers, as the exploitation of Greece is ratcheted up and democracy of any sort continues to be decimated. Much of this is why the Greek unions are weaker than they otherwise might be and why many Greeks identify with anarchists who don't trust the political elite. Of course, this vacuum also allows openings for other elements like far-Right nationalists, neo-Nazis, and religious extremists, who are also suffering along with the rest of society.

Conclusion

Greece, the PIIGS, and the entire world find themselves in a time when all contradictions are openly laid out on the table and competing narratives and ideologies are being tested. Ireland was the second of the PIIGS to succumb to a three-year bailout package, estimated at between €80-90 billion, accompanied by a drastic €15 billion four-year austerity plan (Doyle 2010, Fahy and Ross-Thomas 2010, Prasch 2010). Protesters immediately took to the streets in anger. In Portugal, in late March, 2011 the government was forced to resign, as their political parties rejected further austerity policies designed to avoid the third bailout in the E.U., after Greece and Ireland. In England and Italy, university students have also been protesting increased tuition and changes in higher education, occupying tourist sites and battling with police (Coughlin 2010, Znet, Many Authors 2010). On March 26, 2011 more than 250,000 people took to the streets in London to protest the toughest spending cuts since World War II. The mass demonstrations across London were organized by the British Trades Unions Congress (TUC) and included teachers, nurses, firefighters, public sector workers, students, and pensioners. In France, a unified trade union movement has mobilized millions of people to confront the neoliberal Sarkozy government (DiMaggio 2010, Wolff 2010c). In the United States, the labor union members have turned out in tens of thousands in Wisconsin, Indiana, Michigan, Ohio, and elsewhere to protest against anti-labor legislation intended to end collective bargaining and slash public employee benefits. Finally, across North Africa and the Middle East, millions of people have rebelled against neoliberal policies, poverty, and corruption by dictatorships that have been in power for decades in Tunisia, Egypt, Yemen, Bahrain, Syria, and elsewhere in the region. The world is clearly expressing a backlash against austerity measures, budget cuts, and the "shock doctrine" agenda of Wall Street, the IMF, and global capital as they affect countries across the globe (DiMaggio 2010).

But to those who question whether there are viable alternatives, consider the case of Iceland. In a March 2010, nation-wide referendum, Icelanders emphatically rejected a $5.3 billion payback to British and Dutch banks, with over 90 percent of the people on board (Quinn 2010a, 2010b). Though this essential default is risky and will likely make it extremely difficult for Iceland to find international financial capital, Icelanders rejected the deal as "unfair" and refused to pay for the illegal and reckless behavior of their bankers and politicians. They have opted for an *autonomous, independent* road that will also certainly be extremely difficult.

This is similar to the equally-risky example set by Argentina, who in 2003, defaulted on its debt by paying twenty-five cents on every dollar it owed. It took guts and jeopardized Argentinean "*kaloperasia*," but it worked, and turned their economy around. And as Walden Bello put it, "the Argentinean solution is certainly fraught with risk, but the consequences of surrender are *painfully clear* if we examine the records of countries that submitted to IMF adjustment" (Bello 2010; emphasis added).

The economic crisis in Greece (and elsewhere) does not appear to be going away any time soon. Marginal improvements have appeared and will appear again as short-term macroeconomic figures skew the national and international debate. Capital is winning, as costs and risk is socialized, and the working classes pay in the form of lowered standards of living and increasing exploitation and economic instability. The resistance has brought us to near-revolutionary situations, with the potential for socialist revolution. This volatility also exposes Greece (and other societies) to the possibility of new military *coups* or other brands of far-Right reaction.

As uncomfortable, tiring, or challenging as it may be, taking back the reins of government for the Greek people—through whatever means—will determine whether the country will be run by international bankers and Wall Street or by popular interests. The Troika—the EU, ECB, and IMF—are unelected agents of global capital that clearly aim to extract as much *real* wealth as they can, while concurrently *rolling back* as much social democracy as they can. This is a short-run street fight based on wealth and power, and does not appear to be a sustainable regime that will "heal" the economy. It is clear that elected leaders are plundering their countries on behalf of capital, shifting the burden onto the people and particularly the working class. It is equally clear that there is hot resistance and thirst for change, with sketchy organizational capacity, as institutions, political parties, and unions have all fallen under the sway of the "lesser of the evil" capitalist parties around the world.

The global capitalist system is broken—*and they're still making money!* In fact, they are using the "crisis" to impose yet another global "shock doctrine." Phantom wealth economics is still the game *de jour* and governments aren't addressing it— they're even mocking the Keynesians now. The ghosts of the nineteenth century aristocrats, "fat cats," and bankers have fought back. Debt slavery is the whip that conditions today's world.

What is required is a commitment to justice and bold, direct action. The debt schemes only look to be worsening until confronted by a counter-force. At stake are people's wages, food, and living standards. If political parties, unions, or capitalism itself are not capable of addressing these issues, then they must be replaced or we are in for a long stretch of depression and suffering. Protecting creditors and speculators at the expense of the people must be stopped.

Preceding the October 27, 2011, bailout agreement by the Troika, hundreds of thousands of Greeks flooded Syntagma Square in Athens to protest the proposals. On November 1, Prime Minister Papandreou called for a national referendum on Greece's sovereign debt bailout and for an immediate vote of confidence, and this sent shock-waves through financial markets around the world.

The Greeks will hopefully provide us with a contemporary expression of *democratic action* that *revolutionizes* their political economic system. There is a Greek folk song that goes:

> One hour of *freedom* is better than forty years
> of *slavery* and *prison*.

Does this spirit still ring true *anywhere*? Or have we grown so soft, as "*kaloperasakides*," that we fall into the aforementioned "Stockholm Syndrome"? If the adage that, "we are all Greeks," is to hold, we can only hope that they (and the PIIGS) will provide us with a *demonstration effect* that holds high *democracy* and social *justice* once again.

References

Bello, Walden. 2010. "Greece – Same Tragedy, Different Scripts." *Philippine Daily Enquirer.* Retrieved September 18, 2010 (http://opinion.inquirer.net/viewpoints/columns/view/20100715-281363/Greece--Same-tragedy-different-scripts).

Center for Responsive Politics. 2010. "Barack Obama: Top Contributors." Retrieved December 27, 2010 (http://www.opensecrets.org/pres08/contrib.php?cycle=2008&cid=N00009638).

Coughlan, Sean. 2010. "Student tuition fee protest ends with 153 arrests." *BBC.* Retrieved December 27, 2010 (http://www.bbc.co.uk/news/education-11877034).

DiMaggio, Anthony. 2010. "World in Revolt: The Global Backlash Against Budget Cuts." *truthout.* Retrieved September 27, 2010 (http://www.truth-out.org/world-revolt-the-global-backlash-against-budget-cuts63465).

Doyle, Dara. 2010. "Ireland Urged to Take Aid by Officials Amid Debt Crisis." *Bloomberg.* Retrieved November 15, 2010 (http://www.bloomberg.com/news/2010-11-14/ireland-resists-european-union-rescue-as-germany-pushes-aid-to-calm-market.html).

Egger, Pepe. 2011. "Remnants Of A Greek Past, Image From The Future." *Znet.* January 7, 2010 (http://www.zcommunications.org/remnants-of-a-greek-past-image-from-the-future-by-pepe-egger).

Epitropoulos, Mike-Frank. 2010. "Greece as a Demonstration Project: Will the Black Sheep Bite Back? Will the PIIGS? What about US?" *Dollars&Sense*, May/June 2010, pp. 9–11.

——. 2009. "B-Fest Synopsis." *Znet.* June 23, 2009 (http://www.zcommunications.org/b-fest-synopsis-by-mike-epitropoulos).

——. 2006. "Magic, Deception, and Stalemate in Greece." *Znet.* October 3, 2006 (http://www.zcommunications.org/magic-deception-and-stalemate-in-greece-by-mike-epitropoulos).

Fahy, Louisa and Emma Ross-Thomas. 2010. "Irish, Spanish, Greek Bonds Rise as Auctions Ease Debt Concern." *Bloomberg.* Retrieved September 21, 2010 (http://www.bloomberg.com/news/2010-09-20/german-bonds-fall-as-analysts-forecast-successful-eu-area-periphery-sales.html).

Forelle, Charles. 2010. "Greece, Germany Grapple Over Debt." *The Wall Street Journal.* Retrieved November 22, 2010 (http://online.wsj.com/article/SB10001424052748704584504575616033310586068.html).

Garofalo, Pat. 2010. "Before Bankruptcy, Conservatives Touted Ireland as Model for U.S." *ThinkProgress.* Retrieved December 11, 2010 (http://thinkprogress.org/2010/12/02/celtic-tiger-flip/).

Gordon, Greg. 2010. "How Goldman secretly bet on the U.S. housing crash." *McClatchy.* Retrieved December 27, 2010 (http://www.mcclatchydc.com/2009/11/01/77791/how-goldman-secretly-bet-on-the.html).

Hahnel, Robin and Alex Doherty. 2010. "Digging in a Hole." *New Left Project via Znet.* December 5, 2010 (http://www.zcommunications.org/digging-in-a-hole-by-robin-hahnel).

Hudson, Michael. 2010. "'Drop Dead Economics': The Financial Crisis in Greece and the European Union: The Wealthy Won't Pay Their Taxes, So Labor Must Do So." *GlobalResearch.ca: Center for Research on Globalization.* Retrieved September 18, 2010 (http://www.globalresearch.ca/index.php?context=va&aid=19107).

Irish Times. 2010. "Greece seeks activization of €45 billion aid package." *Irish Times.* Retrieved April 23, 2010 (http://www.irishtimes.com/newspaper/breaking/2010/0423/breaking28.html).

Jessen, Corinna. 2010. "Entering a Death Spiral?: Tensions Rise in Greece as Austerity Measures Backfire." *Der Spiegel.* Retrieved September 2, 2010 (http://www.spiegel.de/international/europe/0,1518,712511,00.html).

Klein, Naomi. 2008. *Shock Doctrine: The Rise of Disaster Capitalism.* New York, NY: Metropolitan Books.

Korten, David C. 2009. *Agenda for a New Economy: From Phantom Wealth to Real Wealth.* San Francisco, CA: Berrett-Koehler Publishers.

Krugman, Paul. 2010a. "US Spending Plan Is Too Little, and Perhaps Too Late." *truthout.* Retrieved October 6, 2010 (http://www.truth-out.org/krugman-frustrated63920).

——. 2010b. "Our Acute Case of Fiscal Madness." *truthout.* Retrieved October 1, 2010 (http://www.truth-out.org/our-acute-case-fiscal-madness63692).

Kushlis, Patricia. 2010. "The Greek Financial Crisis through a Political Lens Darkly." *Whirled View.* Retrieved September 10, 2010. (http://whirledview.typepad.com/whirledview/2010/03/the-greek-financial-crisis-through-a-political-lens-darkly.html).

Lewis, Michael. 2010. "Beware of Greeks Bearing Bonds." *Vanity Fair.* Retrieved October 10, 2010 (http://www.vanityfair.com/business/features/2010/10/greeks-bearing-bonds-201010).

Marsden, Chris. 2010. "Greece: What is behind the right wing-split from SYRIZA?" World Socialist Web Site. Retrieved September 18, 2010 (http://www.wsws.org/articles/2010/jul2010/syri-j12.shtml).

Matich, Alen. 2010. "Trust Greece ... To Default." *The Wall Street Journal,* September 17, 2010. Retrieved September 18, 2010 (http://blogs.wsj.com/source/2010/09/17/trust-greeceto-default/).

Mavroudeas, Stavros. 2010. "The Greek External Debt and Imperialist Rivalries: 'One Thief Stealing from Another.'" *MRZine, A Project of the Monthly Review Foundation.* Retrieved December 20, 2010 (http://mrzine.monthlyreview.org/2010/mavroudeas200210.html) .

Melander, Ingrid. 2010. "Greek parliament passes austerity bill." *Reuters.* Retrieved April 23, 2010 (http://in.reuters.com/article/idINIndia-46690820100305).

Newmark, Evan. 2010. "Mean Street: What Leon Trotsky Teaches Us About the Greek Crisis." *The Wall Street Journal.* Retrieved September 11, 2010. (http://

blogs.wsj.com/deals/2010/02/11/mean-street-what-leon-trotsky-teaches-us-about-the-greek-crisis/).

Omadeon Worldpress. 2010. "Max Keiser on the Greek Debt Crisis – Video 1." *Al-Jazeera news segment translation and subtitle (English).* Retrieved May 5, 2010 (http://www.youtube.com/watch?v=AbH1JsOTInk).

Petras, James. 2010a. "Greece: The Curse of Three Generations of Papandreou's." the James Petras website. Retrieved September 18, 2010 (http://lahaine.org/petras/articulo.php?p=1800&more=1&c=1) .

——. 2010b. "Crisis, What Crisis? Profits Soar!" *Pravda Online.* Retrieved September 18, 2010 (http://engforum.pravda.ru/showthread.php?293375-Crisis.-What-Crisis-Profits-Soar!-by-james-petras).

Prasch, Robert E. 2010. "'Disaster Capitalism' Comes to Ireland." *CommonDreams.org.* Retrieved December 3, 2010 (http://www.zcommunications.org/disaster-capitalism-comes-to-ireland-by-robert-e-prasch).

Quinn, Ben. 2010a. "Amid Greek debt crisis, Iceland still recovering from its own collapse." *The Christian Science Monitor.* Retrieved September 18, 2010 (http://www.csmonitor.com/World/Europe/2010/0217/Amid-Greek-debt-crisis-Iceland-still-recovering-from-its-own-collapse).

——. 2010b. "Iceland financial crisis: Voters reject debt repayment plan." *The Christian Science Monitor.* Retrieved September 18, 2010 (http://www.csmonitor.com/World/Europe/2010/0307/Iceland-financial-crisis-Voters-reject-debt-repayment-plan).

Stiglitz, Joseph. 2010. "A principled Europe would not leave Greece to bleed." *The Guardian.* Retrieved December 11, 2010 (http://www.guardian.co.uk/commentisfree/2010/jan/25/principled-europe-not-let-greece-bleed).

The Economist. 2010. "A very European crisis: The sorry state of Greece's public finances is a test not only for the country's policymakers but also for Europe's." *The Economist* February 4, 2010. Retrieved October 11, 2010 (http://www.economist.com/node/15452594). TheRealNews. 2010. "Greece, a crisis born of neo-liberal madness." theREALnews.com. Retrieved September 18, 2010 (http://www.youtube.com/watch?v=kFrMwXRwksk&feature=related).

Trabanco, Jose Miguel Alonso. 2009. "Civil Unrest in America?" *GlobalResearch.ca: Center for Research on Globalization.* Retrieved March 18, 2010 (http://www.globalresearch.ca/index.php?context=va&aid=12619).

Wachman, Richard and Nick Fletcher. 2010. "Standard & Poor's downgrade Greek credit rating to junk status: Fears that financial crisis may spread to other eurozone countries." *The Guardian.* Retrieved December 27, 2010 (http://www.guardian.co.uk/business/2010/apr/27/greece-credit-rating-downgraded).

Watson, Paul. 2008. "CIA Preparing to Install Military Government in Greece?" *PrisonPlanet.* Retrieved March 18, 2010 (http://www.prisonplanet.com/cia-preparing-to-install-military-government-in-greece.html).

Wolff, Richard D. 2010a. "Class Struggles and National Debts." *Rethinking Marxism: a journal of economics, culture, & society*. Retrieved September 18, 2010 (http://rethinkingmarxism.org/cms/node/1370).

——. 2010b. "Economic Crisis, Greek Theater, Our Drama." *Rethinking Marxism: a journal of economics, culture, & society*. Retrieved September 18, 2010 (http://blogs.wsj.com/source/2010/09/17/trust-greeceto-default/).

——. 2010c. "Why France Matters Here Too." *MRZine*. Retrieved October 27, 2010 (http://zcommunications.org/why-france-matters-here-too-by-richard-d-wolff).

Znet, Many Authors. 2010. "Italian Students Protest Against Education Changes." *Znet*. Retrieved December 1, 2010 (zcommunications.org/Italian-students-protest-against-education-changes-by-many-authors.pdf).

Chapter 6

The Global Capitalist Crisis and Latin America[1]

Henry Veltmeyer

This chapter provides a critical perspective on the current global capitalist crisis from the standpoint of its dynamics in Latin America. The past two years has seen the publication of various books and articles, many of which converge on a common theme: the lack of financial regulation and the resulting acceleration of irresponsible speculation. The general argument advanced in these publications is that the global economic crisis, precipitated by the sub-prime debacle, together with misguided policies, has allowed financial speculation to proceed unchecked, giving unscrupulous lenders and traders free rein to exploit the lack of regulatory oversight. Essentially, it is argued that the crisis is neither systemic nor even structural but financial, and thus correctable with the right monetary policy fix, the construction of a new and more effective financial architecture and global governance.

In this chapter I argue that the current global capitalist crisis is but the latest and most virulent manifestation of an endemic propensity of the system to develop into a crisis. However, this particular crisis, which has quickly transformed from a financial into a production crisis of global scope and multiple dimensions, is not uniform in its regional dynamics. I argue that in Latin America diverse popular and non- or anti-capitalist responses are indicating a possible way out of the crisis that goes *beyond* out-of-control markets, greedy and corrupt bankers, and ineffective regulation, and challenging the institutional structure and the pillars of the *capitalist system*.

This argument is constructed in four parts. First, the premise of my argument is established—that capitalism has an inherent propensity towards crisis. Then the recent literature on the crisis is reviewed to identify two basic strands: monetary and structural. It is argued that the latter gets closer to the real world—*the roots of the crisis*. The chapter then turns to the dynamics of the crisis as it has been

1   This chapter is a revised and edited version of an earlier article published in Spanish as "La crisis global y América Latina" for Problemas del Desarrollo in *Revista latinoamericana de economia*, Vol. 41, Num. 160 (Enero-Marzo, 2010). Reprinted with permission (all rights reserved, not for reproduction). The editor, Berch Berberoglu, edited various sections of the article which is published here with the approval of the author and the publisher.

unfolding in Latin America. The focus here is on the impact of the crisis on the economy and the diverse responses to it. In this context, I examine some of the popular alternative responses to the crisis that are emerging in the region, drawing some conclusions that are summarized at the end of the chapter. One conclusion I draw is that neither definancialization, the reregulation of global capital in its speculative form, new checks on the excesses and the "forces of economic freedom" unleashed in the "new world order" of neoliberal globalization, nor a counter-cyclical approach to the crisis with the restoration of credit or a production stimulus plan will suffice to stave off the crisis.[2] Another conclusion is that this is the moment for moving *beyond capitalism* to socialism in some form. And a final conclusion is that the agency for this development—the way out of the crisis—is the active mobilization of the forces of change in the popular sector of society. Developments in Latin America, precisely those in the popular sector, are pointing the way forward.

Propensity of the Global Capitalist System Toward Crisis

Notwithstanding the diversity of perspectives on what has emerged as a global financial and economic crisis,[3] the most significant patterns of economic and

---

2   The International Labor Office (ILO) has compiled a comprehensive survey of stimulus plans and finds that the majority of G-20 countries have put together some sort of stimulus package that total roughly US$2 trillion. By definition, all of these plans are expansionary in nature ("counter-cyclical" according to some)—meaning that they are designed to increase spending so as to stimulate demand. With the exception of most Latin American countries, the majority of these plans originate in developed or large developing countries. The U.S. stimulus package of US$787 billion consists largely of tax cuts and support for infrastructure, with some funding for healthcare and green energy. China's stimulus plan of US$586 billion (much larger than the U.S. plan in terms of GDP) goes into infrastructure, disaster protection and programs for auto-makers, shipbuilders and electronics factories. As mentioned above, it is estimated that over the past year up to US$2 trillion has been injected into the economies of the G-8 to buoy up the markets and to replace the $US50 trillion wiped off world financial assets over the course of the crisis in 2008–09. It is probable that this estimate will have to be revised upwards, perhaps by a factor of two or three, but that even so bankers will continue to withhold credit, i.e. put their capital at risk, the stock markets will likely sputter and fail to recover for at least one or two years, and the system as a whole will continue to suffer the effects of a global production crisis.

3   Ironically it was Alan Greenspan in 2007, recently "retired" from his close to life-time "service" as a president of the U.S. Central Bank (the Federal Reserve or Fed), who first warned of an impending economic recession in the U.S. with possibly momentous global repercussions. The irony consists in the fact that Greenspan played an important role in creating the system that made the global financial crisis inevitable. Under the leadership of Robert Rubin and Lawrence Summers, the U.S. Treasury cooperated with the Federal Reserve under Alan Greenspan to substantially deregulate the U.S. financial system. This deregulation gave rise to a whole new set of financial instruments. The basic innovation

political development over the past four decades derive from a fundamental built-in propensity of the world capitalist system towards crisis. Prior to the 1990s there were two competing operating systems, capitalist and socialist, and three worlds of development based on these systems (Worsley 1984). But for a number of as yet un- or not well-explained reasons, socialism succumbed to a crisis of its own which led to an economic and political restructuring process in which a number of "actually existing" forms of socialism collapsed—in the USSR and Eastern Europe, but also in China and other parts of Asia. As it turned out, socialism in Africa never was more than an idea; the conditions for its implementation were simply not available. Cuba, a victim of the forces deriving from this collapse, managed to survive a momentous production crisis by means of a radical restructuring of the socialist model, a restructuring that threatened the survival of socialism in this one island state, but that resulted in a slow but steady recovery that has been sustained over a decade of on-going economic reform.

Other countries in the region and other parts of the world which remain under the sway of a restructured world capitalist system have been subject to the diverse destructive forces generated by a process of capitalist development and neoliberal globalization. As for the dynamics of the systemic crisis that currently holds economies across the world in its grip, as Walden Bello (2009) has argued, they can best be traced back to the system-wide crisis of overproduction in the early 1970s that ended the "golden age of capitalism"—what French historians have dubbed the "thirty glorious years" (1945–75). Notwithstanding the accelerated rhythm of crisis—increasing in number if not duration from the 1970s to the 1990s—this involution in the system of global capitalist production (a crisis of overproduction manifest in a tendency towards stagnation) unleashed a lengthy and as yet ongoing restructuring process in the form of:

- the technological conversion of the global production apparatus, leading to a process of "productive transformation" (ECLAC 1990);
- the global spatial or geographical displacement of capital and production, resulting in the appearance of a succession of newly industrializing countries in the global south and a new international division of labor (Fröbel, Heinrichs and Kreye 1980);
- a restructuring of macroeconomic policy designed to renovate the institutional structure of the world capitalist system and reconfigure decision-making power regarding the allocation of reproductive resources, thereby releasing forces of economic freedom from the regulatory constraints of the welfare-developmental state (Petras and Veltmeyer, 2001, 2005);
- a corresponding political restructuring in a neoconservative counter-revolution that diminished the power of the centralised state and

---

involved was the ability to bundle risky assets together, combine them with various forms of risk insurance and re-package them as safe investment vehicles.

destroyed that of organised labor *vis-à-vis* capital, resulting in a process of decentralization and redemocratization designed to share the responsibility of governance with a broadly reconstructed system of "civil society" organizations (Veltmeyer 2007); and, since the late 1980s,

- a process of *financialization*, leading to the appearance of an enormous disjunction between the real economy and a financial superstructure, and, in 2008, to a major crisis of the financial system, a financial implosion and meltdown of global investment capital that has overgrown and is threatening to overwhelm the already troubled real economy and shake the very foundations of global capitalist production with a sharp contraction in the "real economy" at the center of the system and powerful reverberations in the periphery (Bellamy Foster and Magdoff 2009).

As Walden Bello conceives of this process, the economic and political adjustment to the requirements of a "new world order" in the 1980s had three major dimensions, each associated with an attempt to escape what was essentially a crisis of overproduction: *neoliberal restructuring, globalization* and *financialization*.

[1] *Neoliberal restructuring*, in Bello's account, took the form of Reaganism and Thatcherism in the North and "structural adjustment" in the South. The aim, as he sees it, was to "invigorate capital accumulation" by (a) "removing state constraints on the growth, use and flow of capital and wealth" and (b) "redistributing income from the poor and middle classes to the rich on the theory that the rich would then be motivated to invest and reignite economic growth" (Bello 2008). The problem with this formula, Bello continues, "was that in redistributing income to the rich … the incomes of the poor and middle classes [were gutted], thus restricting demand while not necessarily inducing the rich to invest more in production" (Bello 2008).[4] As a result, neoliberal restructuring, generalized in the North and the South during the eighties and nineties, had a poor record in terms of growth: "Global growth averaged 1.1 percent in the 1990s and 1.4 percent in the 1980s, compared with 3.5 percent in the 1960s and 2.4 percent in the 1970s when state interventionist policies were dominant" (Bello 2008).

[2] The second "escape route" taken by global capital was "extensive accumulation" or *globalization*—"the rapid integration of semi-capitalist, non-

---

4   By "the rich" Bello has in mind the bankers and financiers, the finance capitalists, who, as well-explained by Bellamy Foster and Magdoff (2009), following Sweezy and Magdoff in 1998, are reluctant or unwilling to lend money or invest in a "crisis of insolvency" in which "the balance sheet capital of the … financial institutions … has been wiped out" and the likelihood that even the most creditworthy borrowers and investors will be unable to settle their debts at prevailing real interest rates. The macro-level problem here, as Bellamy Foster and Magdoff (2009: 8) note, is the sheer size of the total debt on invested capital, which over the last decade (most of it speculatively) has ballooned to a totally unsustainable level under current conditions—in the U.S. alone from around 150% of GDP in 1960 to an astronomical 373% in 2007 (US$51.3 trillion).

capitalist, or pre-capitalist areas into the global market economy" (Bello 2008). The aim, as Bello reconstructs it, was for capital to gain access to cheap labor, emerging markets and new sources of cheap agricultural and raw material products. Integration is accomplished via trade liberalization, removing barriers to the mobility of global capital, and abolishing barriers to foreign investment—policies of financial and trade liberalization, a major plank in the program of neoliberal policies instituted under the Washington Consensus.

The problem with this escape route is that it exacerbates the problem of overproduction because it adds to productive capacity. For example, "a tremendous amount of manufacturing capacity has been added in China over the past 25 years, with a depressing effect on [capital accumulation,] prices and profits elsewhere in the system" (Bello 2008). Not surprisingly, Bello notes, by around 1997 the profits of U.S. corporations stopped growing.[5] According to one calculation cited by Bello (2008), "the profit rate of the *Fortune 500* went from 7.2 in 1960–69 to 5.3 in 1980–90 to 2.3 in 1990–99 to 1.3 in 2000–2002". By the end of the 1990s, with excess capacity in almost every industry, the gap between productive capacity and sales was comparable to the Great Depression.

[3] Given the limited gains in countering the depressive impact of overproduction via neoliberal restructuring and globalization, the third escape route—*financialization*—became very critical for maintaining and raising profitability. With investment in industry and agriculture yielding low profits owing to overcapacity, large amounts of surplus funds have been circulating, being invested and reinvested, in the financial sector.

The result, all too evident in a spate of recent accounts, is an increased bifurcation between a hyperactive financial economy and a stagnant real economy. As noted by one financial executive in the *Financial Times*: "there has been an increasing disconnection between the real and financial economies in the last few years. The real economy has grown ... but nothing like that of the financial economy—until it imploded" (cited in Bello 2009; but see Bellamy Foster and Magdoff 2009 for an extended analysis of the dynamics of this "financial implosion").

This multi-dimensional restructuring can be traced out in close to four decades of capitalist development, a process dominated by a decisive turn from a welfare-developmental state to a neoliberal state: a "short history of neoliberalism" in the conception of David Harvey (2005) and others. This short history can be traced out in four development cycles (Petras and Veltmeyer, 2009): (i) in the policies engineered in the 1970s by a new generation of Chicago-trained economists and implemented under the military regime of Augusto Pinochet; (ii) in the response,

---

5   If this is the case, then the general stagnation of corporate profit that Bello points to relates only to productive investments in the real economy; for system-wide, the rate of profit continued to climb well past 1997 and at least into 2005 if not beyond (Bellamy Foster and Magdoff, 2009). As Bellamy Foster and Magdoff construct and interpret the data, the global rate of "financial profit" literally skyrocketed from 1997 to 2005 as the index of profit growth rose from around 1,300 (1970 = 100) to well over 3,000.

in the early 1980s, to a call for a "New World Order" in which Thatcher, Reagan and other neoconservatives turned to a program of "structural reforms" in national policy designed by the economists at the World Bank on the model of the Pinochet regime, under a Washington Consensus and conditions of a major external debt crisis; (iii) a third round of neoliberal reform in the 1990s under a post-Washington Consensus regarding the need for a more socially inclusive, sustainable and governable form of neoliberalism, together with a better balance between the state and the market in the development process (on this see, in particular, Ocampo, 2006, 2007); and (iv) in the new millennium, under conditions of an enormous financial bubble (more of a balloon) that exceeded many times the growth of the real world economy, and a global primary commodities boom (2003–08) led by the demand in China and India for energy and natural resources (on these developments in the Latin American context see Petras and Veltmeyer, 2009).

Rethinking the Global Capitalist Crisis

At one level, the dynamics and the root causes of capitalist crises are clear enough, having been elaborated by a long line of scholars who have followed Marx in his conception of the inherent propensity of capitalism toward crisis (Magdoff and Sweezy, 1988; Bellamy Foster and Magdoff, 2009). What is different and somewhat new about the current global capitalist crisis is not its depth or global scope, but its multiple dimensions and forms—financial, real estate, overproduction, labor regulation (Fordism), food and energy, environmental, social and political. It is evident that this multiple crisis is deeply rooted in the economic and social structure of the global capitalist system, and in this regard can be deciphered with reference to Marxist theory of the dynamics of capitalist development. In terms of this theory, capitalism is clearly advancing into a new phase and the diverse indications of crisis prefigure a restructuring of the conditions of the capital accumulation process. It is certainly possible that these conditions can lead to either the collapse or the overthrow of the system. But it is more likely, given the resilience of the system and the diverse mechanisms of response to the situation, that the current crisis, notwithstanding its depth and global scope, will lead to a renewed process of capital accumulation via an effective restructuring of the system which, like the crisis itself, is likely to be multi-dimensional in form—economic (neoliberal reform, globalization, financialization, technological conversion) and even political.

As for the political dimension, restructuring is the likely outcome of a system that is fast approaching its political limits in expanding production on a capitalist basis: the concentration of decision-making as to the allocation of productive resources and the resulting social distribution of wealth and income. In a previous phase of crisis-restructuring (the 1970–1990s) these *political* limits to the capitalist development of the productive forces were overcome via a process of state-led development of these forces and the institution of a social-democratic form of the welfare state (Glynn, Hughes, Lipietz and Singh, 1990).

In the current context of neoliberal globalization, these same limits have given rise to a post-Washington consensus on the need for a more socially inclusive form of neoliberalism, new more democratic forms of local and global governance, the re-emergence of social democracy as a global social movement, and a more pragmatic way of balancing the state and market in the process of capitalist development. Whether this new political form (pragmatic neoliberalism or what some term "post-liberalism"), and the underlying configuration of social and political forces, can be used to harness the forces of resistance and re-establish "order" remains to be seen.

The Dynamics of the Global Capitalist Crisis in Latin America

Between 2003 and 2008 Latin America generally, and South America in particular, managed a way out of the production crisis that beset many countries at the turn of the new millennium. More than a few of these countries rode a short five-year wave of a primary commodities boom fuelled by the explosively growing demand in Asia—China in particular (on this see Bowles, 2009)—for energy, minerals and other industrial inputs, as well as middle class consumer goods. Over the course of this boom, the rate of economic growth increased from an average regional rate of 0.6 percent in 1996 and a bare 1 percent in 2002 to a regional average of 6.2 percent in 2004, 5.5 percent in 2005 and 5.6 percent in 2006. In the South American countries that led the boom, the rate of recovery and sustained growth from 2003 to 2007 was even greater, ranging from 8.3 percent in Argentina and 8.0 percent in Venezuela to 6.3 percent in Peru and 3.9 percent in Bolivia—and, in a different systemic context, 9.0 percent in Cuba.

In 2008, however, this primary commodities boom was caught up in the vortex of the current economic crisis. The first response to this crisis, at the level of government, was to deny it — as in the case of Mexico's President Felipe Calderón, who argued (at Davos, to an assembly of world capitalism's most illustrious representatives) that Latin America was more or less insulated from this particular crisis and that it could ride out the storm easily enough. Ironically, Calderón heads the most vulnerable economy in the region *vis-à-vis* the U.S. economy at the epicenter of the crisis. As for Mexico itself, even at the time of Calderón's public statement that did nothing to soothe the tempers back home, economists in Mexico were predicting the loss of upwards of at least 500,000 jobs in a contracting economy—at least 175,000 in the first half of 2009. By mid-March, the estimate of Mexico's GNP growth for 2009 was reduced from -1.5 percent to -3 percent (*La Jornada*, March 17, 2009).

Other Latin American governments were not so quick to discount the effects of the crisis on the regional and local economies, even though the initial response of many, in the last quarter of 2008 and even into 2009, as Petras (2009) notes, was "self-delusion": the belief that their country could ride out the crisis on the basis of relatively high reserves of foreign currency and relatively healthy (reduced) levels of short-term debt. This was particularly so for those countries in South America that had ridden the wave of the primary commodities boom on the world market, a boom that has largely gone bust to the consternation of both the agro-elites and the governments who had substantially benefited from the boom in the form of higher prices, windfall profits and increased fiscal revenues (Petras and Veltmeyer, 2009). Nevertheless, many of the countries in the region continued to register high rates of growth, including some that even surpassed the levels obtained in the pre-crisis period. Uruguay, for example, weathered the storm well by tacking with the winds of change so as to post a surprisingly robust growth rate of 11 percent in 2008. In Argentina, GDP growth in 2008 was down to 6.8 percent (from 8.7 percent in 2007); in Bolivia it was 5.8 percent (actually up from 4.6 percent); in Ecuador the GDP grew from 2.5 percent to 6.5 percent; in Brazil, it was 5.9 percent (also up—from 5.7 percent); in Chile it was 3.8 percent (down from 5.1 percent); and in Mexico—the country most affected by the crisis because of its openly neoliberal policies as a signatory to the North American Free Trade Agreement (NAFTA), the GDP growth fell from 4.8 in 2006 and 3.2 percent in 2007 to 1.8 percent in 2008 (ECLAC, 2009: 37ff.). But if the economists at ECLAC (2009) and participants in the January 19–21, 2009 international symposium on the "Global Crisis and Latin America" held in Mexico are correct in their assessment and prognosis, the leaders of the other countries in the Southern Cone have no reason to be sanguine in the face of the apparent failure of the G-8 to solve the crisis at the epicenter of the system, and the possibility, nay the likelihood, that they will have to seriously contend with its spread-effects in both the financial markets and the real economy.

No country, according to a recent study of Latin American government responses to the crisis by ECLAC (2009), is immune to the crisis, not even those that, in the context of the primary commodities boom, were careful not to over-spend or cut short-term debt on the global market and build up reserves. The Latin American economists who gathered recently in Mexico City to analyse what the crisis might mean for the region established that no country is safe from the maelstrom of the global capitalist crisis, notwithstanding what the *Economist* sees as Latin America's "valiant efforts" thus far to manage, if not elude, the crisis. The *Economist* puts Mexico, Brazil, Argentina, and Venezuela among the nations most likely to fall, although it is the private sector that is facing the greatest challenges, rather than the governments in these countries. Governments and the capitalists in the private sector in these countries, it turns out, either still have a high amount of short-term debt as a percentage of their total reserves, or their bank loans as a percentage of total deposits are at risk with the impending credit squeeze, or both (Bustillo and Helloso, 2009: 35ff; ECLAC 2009).

In any case, Latin America, according to the Washington Office of ECLAC, has already (since October 2008) felt the effects of the crisis, primarily at the level of the market with the credit crunch, a slowdown in capital inflows and a dramatic decline in portfolio investment flows, large declines in stock price indexes, significant currency adjustments and an increase in debt spreads. Latin America's GDP projected growth for 2009 declined from 3.6 percent in September 2008 to 1.4 percent in December 2008 (*Financial Times*, January 9, 2009). More recent projections estimate Latin America's GDP per capita falling to -2 percent. As a result, bankruptcies are expected to proliferate and state spending on social services will undoubtedly decline. State credit and subsidies to big banks and businesses will increase. Unemployment will expand, especially in the agromineral and transport (automobile) export sectors. Public employees will be discharged and experience a sharp decline in wages. Latin America's external financial flows will also suffer the loss of billions of dollars and euros from declining remittances from overseas workers. Foreign speculators are withdrawing tens of billions of investment dollars to cover their losses in the U.S. and Europe. Foreign disinvestment will replace "new foreign investment", eliminating a major source of financing for any major joint ventures.

According to the IMF, 40 percent of Latin America's financial assets (US$22 billion) were lost in 2008 with the decline of the stock market and other asset markets, and through currency depreciation. This decline reduced domestic spending by 5 percent in 2009. Latin America's terms of trade have deteriorated as sharply as commodity prices have fallen, making imports more expensive and raising the specter of growing trade deficits (*Financial Times*, January 9, 2009: 7). The onset of the recession in Latin America is evident in the 6.2 percent fall in Brazil's industrial output in November 2008 and its accelerating negative momentum (*Financial Times*, January 7, 2009: 5). As a result of these developments, governments in the region that are heavily dependent on the flow of foreign direct investment—particularly Chile, Peru, and Colombia—took defensive action to protect these markets and to minimize their exposure to the crisis by means of diverse "countercyclical policies to buffer the impact of the crisis" (*CEPAL News*, XXIV, No. 2, February 2009).[6] But thus far to little avail.

In retrospect, it can be concluded from the available evidence that these measures succeeded in restoring stability to the financial system but at the expense of the working class in its multitudinous and variegated forms—public and private sector wage laborers and employees, an urban proletariat of informal sector street workers, and a rural proletariat of landless and near-landless direct producers. ECLAC estimates that the crisis resulted in an increase of 90,000 in the number of the poor. At the same time it is evident that the financial sector, the rich and the well-to-do generally have rebounded from the crisis, while the popular sector remains awash with the detritus. For example, *Forbes* (2011) reports that Carlos Slim, Mexico's wealthiest and most renowned capitalist and the world's richest

---

6   The initial response of the "center-left" political regimes to the deepening recession/ depression has largely focused on: 1) financial support for the banking sector (Lula) and lower taxes for the agro-mineral export elite (Kirchner/Lula); 2) cheap credit for consumers to stimulate car purchases (Kirchner); and 3) temporary unemployment benefits for workers laid off from closed small- and medium-size mines (Morales).

man, experienced a 38 percent increase in the value of his assets and his personal fortune since 2009, while Mexico's workers and the poor, officially estimated at 44 percent of the population, have not been so fortunate, having to bear the brunt of the production crisis in the form of lost jobs, fewer income-generating assets and opportunities, increased economic insecurity, and impoverishment. One manifestation of this is in youth unemployment, already high but seriously compounded by the crisis. In the wake of the crisis, a survey of 15- to 24-year-old Mexicans, who are estimated to make up at least a quarter of the working poor, revealed that up to 60 percent saw the employment opportunities provided by the narco-trafficking druglords (and associated lumpen-capitalists) as the only pathway out of poverty.

Governments, the Left and the People Respond

Governments in the region are not the only entities responding to the crisis. Sectors of the Left and a number of popular organizations that bring together unions, diverse class-based organizations, and social movements throughout the region have conducted their own analysis of what the global crisis means for them and the region. As they see it—and there is a virtual consensus at this level— although production and the crisis have been financialized, the crisis reflects the decline of neoliberalism (*el agotamiento de la ideologia neoliberal*) as well as conditions of capitalist development that are endogenous to the region. Further, it is recognised that although the crisis has assumed multiple and diverse forms, it is primarily a crisis of production: a massive loss of jobs, the erosion of incomes and of pensions wrapped up in capitalist financial institutions, the cutback of essential government services, and the lack of access (affordability) to food—all problems that are reaching crisis proportions with disastrous social effects.

In the absence of a nationally organized revolutionary force, the recession by itself will not lead to a social transformation. At least in the initial phase of response to the crisis, most mass pressure and struggles will be in the direction of conserving jobs, blocking mass layoffs, and even some defensive factory occupations. This may be accompanied by demands for greater state involvement, either through subsidies to failed enterprises or selective nationalizations. The demise of neoliberal ideology is inevitable, but its initial replacement will most likely be "state capitalism" or a muted, more socially inclusive, pragmatic form of neoliberalism parading as democratic socialism or social democracy à la Chile as per the post-Washington Consensus, achieved in an alliance between the center-left in state-power with "civil society".

The most radical response and popular demands, according to Petras (2009), will likely occur in those countries most dependent on primary product exports and world demand, and in those countries integrated into the depressed markets of the U.S. and the E.U. These countries and regions include Mexico, Central America, Ecuador, Peru, Venezuela and Bolivia. Chile, Argentina, Brazil, and Colombia, with more diversified exports and a larger internal market, will also be impacted by global and regional recession, but not as severely or abruptly. The recession will likely proceed in phases, cushioned initially by large foreign reserves. By mid-2009, the recession deepened under conditions of capital flight and the loss of credit, investment markets and remittances. Local producers and capital markets were hit hard.

James Petras (2009), an astute analyst of Latin American political and development dynamics, in the context of the capitalist crisis argued that radicalization of the Left could well take hold if the counter-cyclical economic stimulus plans and public works programs fail to stimulate the economy, and if the recession were to deepen. The key to the growth of revolutionary movements, he argued, is their location in the socioeconomic centers of the crisis with organized cadre and leaders capable of articulating and linking local discontent with a national plan of struggle, informed by a clearly anti-imperialist socialist program (Petras, 2009). In effect, he argued that the recession might well lead to the re-emergence of mass movements, which would provide conditions for a revival and renewal of a socialist movement. The global capitalist crisis, Petras argued, "not only undermines even further what remains of the legitimacy of neoliberalism but challenges the entire capitalist class configuration" (2009). The threat of economic collapse and the failure of the banks and the financial system to expand and sustain production would also revive the spectre of "statist nationalism" as a prelude to a radically changed and unbalanced relation between the state and the market, favoring the former. Under these conditions in the context of capitalism, which is unable to operate through weakened market mechanisms and growing protectionism, severe strains in U.S.-Latin American relations are inevitable and promising for a possible revival of the socialist project. Unfortunately, the prognosis of a deepening of the crisis turned out to be premature and, as of the time of writing (March 2011), there is little or no sign of a revival of the socialist project. Except for some advances in Chávez's Venezuela, the concerns—or hopes—related to a turning of the political tide (the materialization of a "red tide" in national and regional politics), so far appear to be misplaced.[7]

Although the process of crisis and response is on-going and some of the offered solutions are poorly defined, there is an emerging trend for both the academic and political Left in the region, along with popular sector organizations, to discuss or negotiate their ideas and actions with some of the progressive or quasi-socialist governments in the region (Hugo Chávez, Rafael Correa, Evo Morales, even Ignacio [Lula] Da Silva, Cristina Kirchner and Michelle Bachelet, pragmatic

---

7   On the concerns on the Right and the illusions of the Left regarding this red tide of regime change in the context of a widespread disenchantment with neoliberalism, and a veritable legitimation crisis, see Petras and Veltmeyer (2009). A subsequent publication of the state-social movement relation in the context of the recent so-called global financial crisis (Petras and Veltmeyer, 2011) documented a general decline of the social movements on the Left in the region associated with, if not directly brought about by, the taking of state-power by the center-left.

or social neoliberals all, who cannot by any stretch of political imagination be accused of being "socialist")—governments formed in the wake of a region-wide wave of anti-neoliberalism (Petras and Veltmeyer 2006, 2009). These proposals have included:

- an increase in social spending and infrastructure investment, and a reorientation of Central Bank policy away from stabilization and towards a priority concern for employment generation (the first recommendation of the structuralist—and institutionalist—economists gathered in Mexico City in January);
- an extension of regional banking and development finance institutions such as the Bank of the South (a consensus proposal from all sectors);
- the extension and deepening of ALBA, an alternative regional trade mechanism originally proposed by Venezuela (Chávez) and now including a supportive popular regional trade alliance of Bolivia and Ecuador with Cuba and Venezuela, as well as Nicaragua and Honduras—and possibly even El Salvador after the recent victory of the FSLN (another consensus position on the Left);[8]
- an alternative model of local food production and food security based on the sustainable livelihoods of small-scale peasant producers (advanced by *Via Campesina*); and
- socialism in one form or another (state centralised or, as in some proposals, decentralised to allow for popular power in public decision-making), socializing both the means of social production and consumption. This proposal—also advanced by elements of the labor movement such as the Union of Electrical Workers of Mexico, which emphasises the fact that the workers had nothing to do with causing the crisis but everything to do with ending it—presupposes an engaged public agency based on the active social mobilization of all sectors of the Left, including: the state, in the case of Venezuela—and perhaps Bolivia and Ecuador; the intellectual and political Left and supportive elements of civil society critical of neoliberalism; organized labor where possible; and the social movements as well as regional alliances

8   One of the major policy responses recommended by this group was to "change the dominant paradigm" of externally-oriented growth towards production for the domestic market and intra-regional (south–south) trade. In this connection, several "progressive" or centre-of-left governments, including Argentina, having probably the lowest level of external "opening" to the global economy of any major country in the region, have increased their intra-regional trade—in the case of Argentina even with Cuba, outside the context of ALBA. In January 2009 Kirchner signed a trade agreement with Cuba in the areas of health, energy and commerce. On the basis of such regional trade mechanisms and agreements the government proposes to lessen the country's integration into the circuits of global capital and to strengthen intra-regional trade, insulating the economy somewhat from the vicissitudes of global capital and the financial crisis.

and coordinating bodies (*Coordinadores*) such as the *Coordinadora de movimientos Sociales* (CMS) in Ecuador.

As for the counter-cyclical policies recommended by the structuralist (and Keynesian welfare state) economists at the Mexico City Symposium, policies that are consistent with those recommended by other groups of economists in the region on the social democratic Left, it turns out that many of the governments in the region have already taken or begun to take precisely these policies. For example, in a summary of counter-crisis policy measures taken by different governments in the region, a study by ECLAC (2009) notes that 16 out of 21 countries in the region over the past year did in fact increase spending on infrastructure. Five also promoted job creation (including Argentina, the country with the lowest external "openness" index) and as many as 14 either maintained or even increased their public social program spending. Nevertheless, the predominant response of these governments reflects their understanding of the crisis as essentially a financial market and monetary/fiscal policy issue.[9] In the policy response of the major countries in the region to the crisis there was a predominance of monetary, financial, fiscal and exchange rate measures. Six governments reduced their hard currency reserve requirements and, in a similar move to that taken by the G-8 governments, 15 of them increased liquidity in national currency and eight of them in foreign currency (ECLAC, 2009).

Two structural (as opposed to monetary or fiscal) policy measures of particular relevance were implemented or acted upon by a number of progressive governments in the region, most notably Venezuela, the pivotal center of the Latin American Left since 1999 and a new axis of center-left governments, together with Cuba, Bolivia, and Ecuador. However, this axis and these measures—including the construction of a new axis for intra-regional trade (ALBA), a new institutional mechanism for promoting national economic development (The Bank of the South), and the renationalization of natural resources and economic enterprises in strategic sectors—predated or were coincident with rather than in response to the crisis. They represented a response to both U.S. imperialism and the model of neoliberal globalization in place throughout the region since the 1980s but now in serious decline. Like the timid moves in the U.S. and the U.K. toward an ownership stake in the country's major banks and financial institutions (in exchange for a financial

---

9 The most widespread policy response to the crisis was in recognition of the importance of maintaining financial liquidity in the face of a global credit crunch. To this end, central bank interest rates were lowered while domestic, but also especially USD, credits were made available. These efforts were designed to maintain the smooth functioning of domestic credit markets, although the availability of credit does not guarantee that it will be used to increase consumption or guarantee a medium-term stimulus to the economy. Nevertheless there is a virtual consensus among policymakers in the region that the main tool for stimulating the economy is counter-cyclical fiscal policy. The idea is that in the face of an economic downturn the state is to increase spending as a buffer against the worst effects of the crisis while keeping productive resources in use.

bailout)—and calls for outright nationalization—they also point to the "need for a systemic alternative to capitalism" (Panitch and Gindin 2009), conceived by Hugo Chávez as "socialism of the 21st century". As to the form that socialism "in the new conditions" will or might take there is no consensus, or as Chávez insists, no model—just an agreement in principle for the need of a new and "fully human" society, a "society of equals", a "new world of justice, dignity, and equality" that is only possible with socialism (Chávez 2007: 247).

Indications are that these and other such "structural" changes in the organization of national and regional development can help insulate the countries and the people in the region from the anticipated ravages of the restructuring process, which has already destroyed up to US$50 trillion of capital in the world economy, with seriously negative consequences for the livelihoods of those having to work or make a living in the real economy, not only at the center of the system but on its periphery. Often, if not normally, such a capital restructuring process always hits hardest those who are on the margins and the furthest away from the "center", unable to protect themselves from the restructuring strategies pursued at their expense by the guardians of the world capitalist system and the neoliberal world order. The only way for working peoples to defend themselves from this restructuring process is to disconnect where and how they can from the system— and to actively mobilize not only for a change of direction but for "another world", i.e. systemic change.

Strategic and Policy Responses to the Crisis in the Popular Sector

We can distinguish several types of strategic response to the crisis in the popular sector, particularly in the social movements made up of indigenous peoples, peasants and rural landless workers that dominated the political landscape in the 1990s (Petras and Veltmeyer 2005). At the moment these strategies exist primarily in the form of ideas, but there is in formation an active debate on how to proceed in acting on these ideas. This debate is largely internal to the popular movement, but in the context of the global financial and production crisis there has emerged a series of conversations and discussions between social movement leaders and other sectors of the political left, elements of which in recent years (1989–2008) have, in fact, captured state power in a number of South American countries (Venezuela, Argentina, Brazil, Bolivia, Ecuador, Chile, Uruguay and Paraguay), establishing in the process a number of center left or left-of-center regimes.

A Shift Toward the Left at the Level of Macro-economic and Social Policy

Generally, the Left that had managed to capture state power in the pre-crisis period in 1989 (in the context of a wave of anti-neoliberal sentiment and a primary commodities boom) did not see socialism as the abolition of private property in capitalist form or the socialization of the means of production, but rather as (i) the nationalization of the country's natural resources (as in Bolivia) and capitalist enterprises in the strategic sectors of the economy, or (as in Venezuela) the proprietors or CEOs not fulfilling their assigned social responsibilities; (ii) regulation of the market and economic activity in the "private sector" in order to place a ceiling on the ability of capitalists to exploit labor and for investors to enrich themselves at the expense of other social sectors; and (iii) a more just or equitable distribution of the social product in the form of national income.

The problem is that, with the exception of Venezuela, none of the center-left regimes that had come to power took advantage of the highly favorable economic and political conditions of the pre-crisis years (2002–2008) so as to change policy in this "socialist" or even in a "progressive" direction. In this regard, with the exception of Venezuela it is not possible to observe any significant difference between the policies regarding the allocation of fiscal resources (and the social distribution of these resources) adopted by these Left-leaning regimes and those with a pragmatic or even dogmatic neoliberal orientation (Chile, Peru, Colombia, and Mexico).

In any case, as explained above, under the conditions of the current crisis it will be much more difficult for these regimes, regardless of their ideological orientation, to reorient national policy and tax expenditures in a progressive direction. Even so, in this changed context of the financial crisis (with a capital loss in the region of up to US$220 billion over six months), virtually all of the governments in the region have adopted counter-cyclical policies designed to pump-prime demand, prevent massive unemployment and minimize the negative socioeconomic impact of the crisis, and, at the same time, contain the forces of social discontent and political opposition that will undoubtedly be generated by these conditions. In anticipation of such developments, virtually every country in the region has sought not only to maintain liquidity at the level of financial markets but to invest in and increase fiscal expenditures on both economic and social infrastructure, and on social programs designed to redistribute income and alleviate poverty (on these policy dynamics see Petras and Veltmeyer 2009).

Nationalization of Resources in the Commons

Nothing is more important to the social movements than respect for the territorial rights of indigenous peoples in relation to communal resources, in particular water, the struggle over which has replaced "land" as a, perhaps *the*, major concern of the popular movement. With reference to water as a "fundamental human right" and a public good that should in no case be turned into a commodity (major demands of the social movements), one of the very first legislative actions of the government of Evo Morales in Bolivia was to renationalize ownership of natural resources such as oil and gas, and to prevent a commercial encroachment on the global commons, the heritage of humankind (Abya Yala, 2009).

With this reversion of the neoliberal policy to privatize these resources together with other means of production, and a more extended policy in this direction in Venezuela to nationalize companies in the strategic sectors of the economy, nationalization is understood as a transitional form of "socialism"—the "socialism of the XXI century", according to Hugo Chávez. Thus, "socialism" in this context takes the form of nationalization combined with a policy of regulation regarding markets and private enterprises in its capitalist form, capping the ability of the owners of these enterprises to exploit labor and enrich themselves, and a more equitable distribution of social product by means of the instrument of fiscal expenditures.

However, within the popular movement a different conception of socialism as an alternative to neoliberalism prevails. Within the movement "socialism" is understood in a similar way as the utopian socialists of the nineteenth century understood it: as "communalism", "our political practice" in the words of Evo Morales (2003), leader of the Movement Towards Socialism (MAS). As constructed within the social movement and understood by Morales this "practice" is rooted in a culture of solidarity, i.e. in "relations of reciprocity, complementarity and equity" (Abya Yala 2009). As for socializing the means of production, a country's natural resources are common property of the people and cannot be privatized. They are under the stewardship of "the people" in their communities in a social relationship of solidarity and "respect and harmony with Mother Earth" (Abya Yala 2009). In terms of peoples' "territorial rights," socialism does not mean and should not take the form of state control. Rather, it implies a decentralized state allowing the people in their local communities to exercise their collective responsibility in protecting and sustaining the heritage of humankind, to allow people to live well (*vivir bien*), in harmony with nature and in solidarity with each other.

An Agrarian Reform Based on a New Model of Agricultural Production

The principal problem of the countryside and rural poverty is land—the separation of peasants from the land, forcing them to migrate to the cities or be transformed into a proletariat (so as to provide capitalist or big landowners with a source of cheap labor) or a class of capitalist entrepreneurs (to improve their access to markets, capital, and modern technology). To reverse this process and ensure the sustainability of their livelihoods, peasant movements are demanding land reform—not "market assisted" as the World Bank conceives of it, but "state-led" (i.e. the distribution not of idle public land, but of land concentrated in the hands of large landowners and capitalists in the sector). Another demand of the movement, with reference here to the *Via Campesina*, is to change the model that governs agricultural production—an agro-export model that only benefits the large landowners (the oligarchs) and capitalist corporations—in favor of small producers and the peasant economy oriented towards the local and national markets, to provide for food sovereignty and security, and to meet the needs of the people at affordable prices.

A Minga of Resistance and Popular Action

On February 29, 2010, a Bolivia-based regional alliance of indigenous, peasant and social movements convoked a "Minga of Resistance" in association with "other peoples and processes" in the region (Abya Yala 2009). *Minga* is a Quechua word meaning "collective action" and having wide currency among the indigenous poor, both indigenous and mestizo, in the Andes. The call to join in a *Minga* that is at once local and global, gains force from both its cultural and historical references to a shared experience of subjugation. By calling their movement a *Minga*, the indigenous participants call attention to both the work that must go into politics and the need for collective action.

Thought and action in this direction—in the search for an alternative that goes beyond capitalist development and neoliberalism, the undoubted source of the current global capitalist crisis as it happens and is wisely understood—is underway in the popular sector of different countries in the region (see for example the Convocation on January 20, 2009 of the Social Movements of America at the World Social Forum in Belém). Starting with a diagnosis of the profound crisis of capitalism in the current conjuncture, the representation of a broad regional coalition of American social movements announced the need, and its intention (*un "proyecto de vida de los pueblos" frente al "proyecto del imperialismo"*) to create a popular form of regional integration "from below"—social solidarity in the face of imperialism." (alba@movimientos.org)

From this popular perspective the global crisis is not a matter of financial markets but rather a production and social issue—a matter of sustainable livelihoods, employment and the price of food, which is rapidly escalating under the conditions of the global and local crisis. In this connection ECLAC Executive Secretary José Luis Machinea has noted that the steep and persistent rise in international food prices is hitting particularly hard the poorest in Latin America and the Caribbean, worsening income distribution. If urgent measures are not taken to reduce the effects of these price rises, nearly ten million people would become destitute, and a similar number would increase the ranks of the poor. This does not even take into consideration the aggravating social situation of those who were already poor or destitute prior to the price rises and the global economic crisis.

Another example of popular action against the production and food crisis is the peasant–worker alliance recently formed in Mexico to make available affordable food to workers in the cities (*La Jornada* On Line, February 24, 2009). In regard to the staple *tortilla*, the prices of which have literally hit the roof over the past year (see the analysis of the price dynamics by Bello, 2008), spokespersons for the alliance at a Press Conference announced that the producers in the alliance would deliver goods to workers and their families at cost or at prices at least 20 percent below those of commercial enterprises—and there would be no taxes charged. Efraín García Bello, Director of the *Confederación Nacional de Productores Agrícolas de Maíz de México* (CNPAMM), a signatory to the production alliance, noted that actions of this sort would support both the workers in the urban areas and the inhabitants in the countryside.

Along the same lines, and supportive of this popular action against the crisis, different organizations in Mexico's peasant movement, including those set up by or close to the government, proposed that the government's anti-crisis plan include a policy of local production in corn and rice, milk, vegetable oil, pork products, etc., ending the policy of free agricultural imports under NAFTA which, as the EZLN (the Zapatista Movement) had predicted, has been the cause of a major production crisis in agriculture if not its "death knell". In regard to the local production and imports of vegetable oil, the President of the Senate's Rural Development Commission pointed out that in just this one case (elimination of import duties) government policy put at risk the livelihoods and direct employment of up to 10,000 people in the sector, plus an additional 30,000 that would have been employed indirectly (Pérez 2009).

At issue in this and other such actions in the popular sector is whether the political and intellectual Left are up to the challenge levelled by Abya Yala of being able and willing to actively support if not lead the forces of revolutionary change that are being formed in the popular sector.

As for the government, it responded as have other governments in the region by attempting to head off the possible political spread-effects of a growing crisis-generated social discontent via fiscal expenditures on a program of social and development assistance. In the case of Mexico, the basic mechanism of this anti-crisis response is "*Oportunidades*" (Opportunity), a program designed to assist those with scarce resources most directly affected by the global economic crisis. With a negotiated World Bank loan of US$500 million this program was expected in 2009 to pump US$4 billion into the countryside and the local economy, continuing the time-honored tradition (at least since the 1960s) of using rural development as a means of demobilizing the social movement and defusing revolutionary ferment in the countryside.

Conclusion

The global capitalist crisis in substance is not a financial crisis but rather a crisis of capital—of the system governing global production. To ensure that the usual victims of this crisis, the people in the popular sector of the less-developed societies on the periphery of the system, are able to resist and cope with the forces released in the capital restructuring process, it is essential that the people actively mobilize and resist the neoliberal capitalist model and determine their own solution based on the unification of all anti-capitalist forces. This mobilization of movements and forces in the popular sector, as well as their political representatives outside of the movement, must resist any proposal for a solution to the crisis that includes the existing capitalist system. The various "solutions" to the crisis proposed by the Left in its "actually existing" forms in power generally presume the institutional framework of capitalism, seeking only to mitigate the effects of the crisis, but the challenge in a post-crisis environment is to ensure the more sustainable, socially inclusive, equitable, participatory, and humane society beyond capitalism that is possible only under socialism.

References

Abya Yala—Movimientos Indígenas, Campesinos y Sociales. 2009. "Diálogo de Alternativas y Alianzas," *Minga Informativa de Movimientos Sociales*, La Paz, 26 de Febrero.

Bárcena, A. 2009. *Preliminary Overview of the Economies of Latin America and the Caribbean.* Santiago: ECLAC.

Beinstein, Jorge. 2009. "Acople Depresivo Global (radicalización de la crisis)," *Servicio Informativo Alai-Amlatina*, 13/0409, Buenos Aires.

Bellamy Foster, John and Fred Magdoff. 2009. "Financial Implosion and Stagnation: Back to the Real Economy," *Monthly Review*, 60 (6) (December): 1–10.

Bello, Walden. 2008. "A Primer on the Wall Street Meltdown," *Links* (September 25). http://links.org.au/node/657

———. 2009. "The Global Collapse: A Non-Orthodox View," *Z Net*, February 22. [http://www.zmag.org/znet/viewArticle/20638]

Bernanke, Ben. 2000. *Essays on the Great Depression.* Princeton University Press.

Bulmer-Thomas, Victor. 1996. *The Economic Model in Latin America and its Impact on Income Distribution and Poverty.* New York: St. Martin's Press

Bustillo Inés and Helvia Helloso. 2009. *The Global Financial Crisis: What Happened and What's Next.* Washington DC: ECLAC, Washington Office, February.

Chávez, Hugo R. 2007. "El Socialismo del Siglo XXI," in Néstor Kohan, (ed.), *Introducción al pensamiento socialista.* Bogotá: Ocean Sur.

ECLAC—Economic Commission for Latin America and the Caribbean. 1990. *Productive Transformation with Equity.* Santiago: United Nations.

———. 2009. *The Reactions of Latin American and Caribbean Governments to the International Crisis: An Overview of Policy Measures up to 30 January 2009.* Santiago: United Nations [LC/L.3000, 30 January].

George, Susan. 1999. *The Lugano Report: On Preserving Capitalism in the 21st Century.* London: Pluto Press.

Glynn, A., A. Hughes, A. Lipietz and A. Singh. 1990. "The rise and fall of the Golden Age," in Stephen Marglin and Juliet Schor (eds), *The Golden Age of Capitalism: Re-interpreting the Post-War Experience.* Oxford: Clarendon Press.

Harvey, David. 2005. *A Brief History of Neoliberalism.* Oxford: Oxford University Press

Lipietz, Alain. 1987. *Mirages and Miracles: The Crisis in Global Fordism.* London: Verso.

Liviera, Francisco de and Leida Maria Paulini. 2007. "Financialization and Barbarism: A Perspective from Brazil," in P. Bowles et al. (eds), *National Perspectives on Globalization: A Critical Reader.* London: Palgrave Macmillan.

Magdoff, Harry and Paul Sweezy. 1988. *The Irreversible Crisis.* New York: Monthly Review Press.

Morales, Evo. 2003. "La Hoja de Coca, una Bandera de Lucha," Interview with *Punto Final* [Santiago], May.

Ocampo, Jose Antonio. 2006. "Latin America and the World Economy in the Long Twentieth Century," in K. S. Jomo (ed.), *The Great Divergence: Hegemony, Uneven Development, and Global Inequality.* New York: Oxford University Press.

——. 2007. "The Macroeconomics of the Latin American Economic Boom," *CEPAL Review* 93.

Ocampo, José, J.S. Jomo and Sarbuland Khan (eds) 2007. *Policy Matters: Economic and Social Policies to Sustain Equitable Development.* London: Orient Longman; New York and Penang: Third World Network.

Ortega, Eduardo. 2008. "Lanza Felipe Calderón Cinco Medidas para Enfrentar la Crisis, "*El Financiero*, 9 de Octubre.

Panitch, Leo and Sam Gindin. 2009. "From Global Finance to the Nationalization of the Banks: Eight Theses on the Economic Crisis," Socialist Project The Bullet (February 25) http://www.socialistproject.ca/bullet.

Pérez Caldentey, Esteban and Matías Verneng. 2008. *Back to the Future: Latin America's Current Development Strategy.* New York: Monthly Review Press.

Petras, James. 2009. *Global Depression and Regional Wars*. Atlanta: Clarity Press.

Petras, James and Henry Veltmeyer. 2001. *Globalization Unmasked: Imperialism in the 21st Century*. Halifax: Fernwood Books and London: Zed Books.

——. 2005. *Empire With Imperialism*. London: Zed Books.

——. 2009. *What's Left in Latin America*. Surrey: Ashgate.

——. 2011. *Social Movements in Latin America: Neoliberalism and Popular Resistance.* New York: Palgrave Macmillan.

World Bank. 2008. *Latin America and the Global Crisis*. Washington DC.

Worsley, Peter. 1984. *The Three Worlds: Culture and World Development.* Chicago: The University of Chicago Press.

Chapter 7

The Global Capitalist Crisis and the Rise of China to the World Scene

Alvin Y. So

In 2008, the subprime mortgage crisis in the United States has grown into the deepest economic crisis since the Great Depression. The crisis is no longer simply confined to the financial sector, but has spread to the larger global economy. The crisis is still in the process of unfolding and the high-profile bankruptcies of investment banks like Lehman Brothers and insurers like AIG only marked the beginning of the broader capitalist crisis. The 2008 crisis not only marked the end of the golden era of unbridled free-market economics in the United States, but could also serve as the turning point of the capitalist world economy.

At the onset of the crisis in 2008 there was speculation as to whether China might seize upon the crisis as an opportunity to rise up to become a dominant player in the capitalist world economy (Hung 2009). However, since China's economic growth is mostly export-driven, China could face very serious economic problems and social protests triggered by the global financial crisis. At the onset of the economic crisis in fall 2008, China's exports suffered a sharp slowdown, down more than 20 percent from the previous year (Barboza 2009). In China's Pearl River Delta, many toy export processing companies are closing their doors or going bankrupt because of order reductions from the United States and Europe (*China Stakes* 2008). China may be on its way to a hard landing, with the data showing a sharp deceleration of economic growth, sharply falling spending on consumer durables, falling home sales, and a sharp fall in construction activity. Yardley and Bradsher (2008) reported that China's domestic stock exchanges have lost 65 percent of their value, and real estate sales have plummeted. As a result, unemployment became a growing concern in the urban areas in late 2008. China needed a growth rate of at least 5 percent to absorb about 24 million people joining the labor force each year. The sharp decline of export trade left millions without work and set off a wave of social instability. The *Sunday Times* reported on Feb 1, 2009 that social unrest among unemployed workers spread more widely in China than was officially reported.

In the light of the above gloomy data, researchers began to speculate whether China is heading toward collapse. Javers (2009) argues that the Chinese economic miracle was nothing but a paper dragon: "the Chinese have dangerously overheated their economy, building malls, luxury stores and infrastructure for which there is almost no demand, and that the entire system is teetering toward collapse."

Ho-fung Hung also doubts that China could challenge the United States after the crisis. Hung argues that the crisis has deepened China's market dependency and financial dependence on the United States, and China will remain "Americans' head servant" in the near future (Hung 2009: 5). Because China is so dependent on foreign technology, production, and markets, Martin Hart-Landsberg (2010: 28) similarly contends that "the current world crisis has had, at best, minor effects on current Chinese economic strategies and could not possibly lead to the rise of China as a global economic power."

Contrary to the above interpretations, I would argue that China emerged from the global economic crisis considerably strengthened. The crisis provided not only a golden opportunity for China to strengthen its state-developmental model, but also a chance to expand its power in the inter-state system. The crisis has increased the probability of the rise of China as a global power, as well as a shift of the center of global capital accumulation from the West to the East in the twenty-first century.

In the following sections, I will first discuss China's state-developmentalist model. After that, I will explain how this model has successfully helped China to take advantage of the global economic crisis, leading to the industrial upgrading of the economy, the strengthening of state capacity, and the realignment of social forces in society. Finally, I will discuss the prospects for the rise of China, as well as the challenges that it will face when it becomes a global economic power in the twenty-first century.

State-Developmentalism in China

China's path of development is actually more similar to that of the East Asian developmental state than to the neoliberal state in the West. China's state-developmentalism has the following characteristics.

First, it has a strong state machinery with a high degree of state autonomy and a strong capacity to carry out its goals. Although a cadre-capitalist class has emerged at the local level when the state managers were asked to promote local development—so-called local state corporatism (Oi 1992)—this cadre-capitalist class has failed to capture the central party-state. Thus, the state can still uphold the moral high ground of state socialism, going after the capitalists for tax evasion and the breaking of environmental laws, standing on the side of the workers by strengthening the labor laws, and standing on the side of peasants by cutting rural taxes and relocating more resources to the countryside. The party-state at the center blames corrupt officials for causing social unrest at the local level. Although many local states are captured by business interests, the central state is highly autonomous in the sense that it is not "captured" by vested economic interests at the local level. The old generation of capitalists was largely destroyed in the Communist Revolution and later in the Cultural Revolution. The nascent capitalist class that has just emerged in the market reforms of the 1980s and 1990s is too weak and too dependent on the state to pose any challenge.

In addition, the Chinese state has the capacity to carry out its developmental plans. Since it owns the banks and controls the financial sector it has powerful policy tools at its disposal that makes the cooperation of indigenous business more likely: access to cheap credit, protection from external competition, and assisted access to export markets are all levers that the Chinese state can use to ensure business compliance with governmental goals. Since the Chinese corporations have a high debt/equity ratio, even the threat of withdrawal of state loans would be serious.

Second, like other developmentalist states in East Asia, the Chinese state has actively intervened in the economy. The state has become the engine powering capital accumulation. Aside from debt finance and infrastructure construction, the Chinese central state also develops plans for strategic development, decrees prices, regulates the movement of capital, shares risks and underwrites research and development.

Third, like other developmentalist states in East Asia, the Chinese state has actively mobilized the ideology of nationalism and defines itself as carrying out a national project to make China strong and powerful. In the post-reform era, China was experiencing an ideological vacuum since the state could no longer be legitimized by Marxism or communism. Thus, nationalism became the state's only hope to get the support of the Chinese masses. The Chinese state seems to believe that the best response is to build a strong sense of national cohesiveness based on cultural heritage and tradition rather than to develop a nationalism based solely on hostility toward the outside world. Nationalism, however, can cut both ways. The Chinese state knows well that excessive nationalism might not only undercut the Communist Party's ability to rule but also disrupt China's paramount foreign policy objective of creating a long-term peaceful environment for its modernization program. The Chinese state's concern is reflected in its rejection of a more radical nationalism, such as that advocated by the authors of *The China that Can Say No*, as well as in its efforts to control anti-Japanese sentiment. Indeed, China's response to the provocation caused by the Japanese leader's visit to their controversial war shrine was far more restrained than it was in Taiwan and Hong Kong. The Chinese state's concern that nationalism had to be controlled was also evident in its efforts to restrain anti-Americanism in the aftermath of the NATO bombing of the Chinese embassy in Yugoslavia (Ogden 2003).

Fourth, like other developmentalist states in East Asia, China's communist party-state adopts authoritarian policies to discipline labor, suppress labor protests, and to pacify civil society in order to maintain a favorable environment to attract foreign investment and to facilitate capital accumulation. It seems authoritarianism is unavoidable in export-led industrialization because labor subordination is an important means to cheapen labor and to make the working class docile. Otherwise, the exports of the East Asian developmentalist states would not be competitive in the world economy, and transnational corporations would not relocate their labor-intensive production to East Asia. It is ironic that the Chinese state, with its tightly organized party-state machinery, has proven to be very effective in co-opting labor activists, dividing the working class, and silencing labor protests.

In the 1980s, when China first started to re-enter the capitalist world economy, the communist party-state pursued the path of neoliberalism, with policies such as market liberalization, downsizing the state bureaucracy, loosening its regulations, cutting back its social welfare commitment, privatizing its state economy, etc. However, at the turn of the twenty-first century, when the communist party-state's survival was threatened by the growing number of labor protests in the cities and peasant protests in the countryside, China changed from neoliberal capitalism to state-developmentalism in order to preempt the further intensification of class conflict (So 2010b).

In the first decade of the twenty-first century, the Chinese communist party-state slowed down, stopped, or reversed the pro-market neoliberal policy. Under the policy of "building a new socialist countryside" and a "harmonious society", the Hu/Wen regime tried to move towards a greater balance between economic growth and social development. State-developmentalism advocates a transfer of resources from the state to strengthen the fiscal foundation of the countryside. Not only was the agricultural tax abolished to help relieve the burden on peasants, but the state increased its rural expenditure by 15 percent (to $15 billion) to bankroll guaranteed minimum living allowances for peasants, and provided an 87 percent hike (to $4 billion) in the health-care budget (Liu 2007).

Before the arrival of the global economic crisis in 2008, China was already in the process of transition from neoliberalism to state-developmentalism. As such, what was the reaction of China's state-developmentalism towards the global economic crisis?

China's Response to the Global Economic Crisis in 2008

State-developmentalism enabled China to respond quickly to the crisis. Beijing announced a massive stimulus program in early November 2008—only seven weeks after the Lehman Brothers collapse. China's stimulus package was budgeted at 4 trillion yuan (US$586 billion), which is equivalent to 13.3 percent of China's 2008 GDP. It is one of the largest economic stimulus packages (both in spending levels and as a percentage of GDP) that were announced by the world's major economies to date. The package included the following key items (Morrison 2009: 6):

- *Public transport infrastructure* (37.5 percent), including railways, highways, airports, and ports
- *Rebuilding areas hit by disasters* (25 percent), including areas hit by an earthquake in Sichuan province in May 2008
- *Affordable public housing* (10 percent)
- *Rural infrastructure* (9.3 percent), including irrigation, drinking water, electricity, and transport

- *Technological innovation* (9.3 percent), including research, development and structural change
- *Health care and education* (3.8 percent)
- *Environmental projects* (5.3 percent)

China's stimulus program was intended both to promote capital accumulation and to soften the acute social contradictions that had emerged in Chinese society over the previous few decades.

In order to promote capital accumulation, the state targeted 10 strategic industries (i.e. industries deemed by the state to be vital to China's economic growth) to promote their long-term competitiveness. Those industries include autos, steel, shipbuilding, textiles, machinery, electronics and information, non-ferrous metals, and logistics. State support policies for the 10 industries include tax cuts and incentives (such as tax rebates), industry subsidies, and consumer subsidies for certain products (such as consumer goods and autos), fiscal support, directives to banks to provide financing, direct funds to support technology upgrades and the development of domestic brands, government procurement policies, and funding to help firms invest overseas (Morrison 2009: 7).

In addition, the stimulus program was aimed at the rising gap between city and countryside, and the growing inequalities and conflict among different sectors of Chinese society. Thus, on April 7, 2009 the state announced plans to spend an additional US$124 billion over the next three years to create a universal health care system. The health plan would attempt to extend basic coverage to most of the population by 2011, and would invest in public hospitals and training for village and community doctors. A number of efforts have been made to boost rural incomes and spending levels, and to narrow the gap in living standards between rural and urban citizens. For example, since February 2009 an estimated 900 million Chinese rural residents have been eligible to receive a 13 percent rebate for purchase of home appliances; and public housing projects, education, and infrastructure projects are largely targeted to rural areas (Morrison 2009: 7).

In short, the stimulus program was aimed at encouraging consumer spending and bolstering the domestic economy. The state wants to promote domestic consumption and to improve collective consumption and social insurance. The assumption is that unless the social safety net and social insurance are expanded, Chinese consumers will be more inclined to save than to spend, and the enlarged domestic market will not be able to absorb the slack in the export market caused by the global economic crisis of 2008–09.

In retrospect, China's stimulus package has worked very well. Whereas the United States, Japan, and the "big four" European countries of Germany, France, Britain, and Italy suffered a contraction of up to 4 percent in their economies in 2009, China still managed to have a GDP growth rate of 9 percent in 2009 (Hiro 2010). By 2010, newspapers were reporting that China's economy is roaring ahead:

- *New York Times*: "China surged past the United States to become the world's largest automobile market—in units, if not in dollars" (Wines 2010a)
- *USA Today*: "China is on track to overtake Japan as the second-largest economy behind the USA this year, cementing its status as one of the world's most formidable superpowers" (Chu 2010)
- *New York Times*: "China is also on track to make nearly half of the world's wind turbines this year, ... and the country passed the United States last year as the world's largest wind turbine market" (Bradsher 2010a)
- *New York Times*: "Just a year after the layoff of millions of factory workers, China is facing an increasing labor shortage ... Thanks to a half-trillion-dollar government stimulus program, jobs are being created in the interior" (Bradsher 2010b).

What is the impact of the stimulus program on China? How did it affect China's economy, polity, and society? I would argue that the stimulus program has made a significant impact on China, leading to the restructuring of the Chinese economy, the strengthening of state capacity, and the realignment of social forces in society.

Restructuring the Economy

"Guo Jin, Min Tui."

There was a huge expansion of the state sector at the expense of the private sector, aptly expressed in the catchphrase "*guo jin, min tui*" or "the state advances, the private sector retreats". During 2008-09, investment by state-controlled companies skyrocketed, driven by hundreds of billions of dollars of government spending and state bank lending to combat the global financial crisis.

There are no comprehensive statistics to catalog the expansion of the state's influence on the economy, so the shift is partly inferred from such coarse measures as the share of financing in the economy provided by state banks (which sharply rose during the financial crisis); the list of the 100 largest publicly listed Chinese companies, all but one of which are majority state-owned; and the growing political and financial influence of China's state-owned giants—"129 huge conglomerates that answer directly to the central government, and thousands of smaller ones run by the provinces and cities" (Wines 2010b).

While no public breakdown exists, most experts say the vast bulk of the four trillion renminbi (US$586 billion) stimulus package that China pumped out for new highways, railroads, and other big projects went to state-owned companies. Some of the largest state companies used the flood of money to strengthen their dominance in their current market or to enter new ones. Wines (2010b) reports that "some of the upstream state-owned enterprises are now expanding downstream, organizing themselves as vertical units. They are just operating on a much larger scale."

At the local level, Wines (2010b) further reports that "the government set up 8,000 state-owned investment companies in 2009 alone to channel government dollars into business and industrial ventures." A publicized case is the Zhejiang Geely Holding Group, a Chinese automaker which "made worldwide headlines in March 2010 when it agreed to buy Sweden's Volvo marque from Ford. Much of the $1.5 billion purchase price came not from Geely's relatively modest profits, but from local governments in northeast China and the Shanghai area."

When China's state-run companies were on the march, there were news stories that privatization of the state companies had been blocked. In August 2009, for example, when thousands of workers came out in protests in Linzhou, Henan Province, the provincial government quickly halted the privatization of a state-owned steel mill (Bradsher 2009a).

Upgrading and Relocating

The global economic crisis has deepened the fear that the low-cost manufacturing industry that helped propel China's rapid economic growth was becoming obsolete because of the rising cost of production. Government efforts to improve conditions in the interior provinces through the stimulus program have lifted growth in those regions and persuaded many young workers to find jobs closer to home in interior provinces, leading to labor shortages in coastal provinces. Because of labor shortages, the growing intensity of labor unrest, and government efforts to raise the minimum wage to improve the livelihood of migrant workers, pay rates in the Pearl River Delta have nearly doubled over the last five years (Barboza 2010b).

As a result, manufacturing costs have risen rapidly in China in response to nagging labor shortages and worker demands for higher wages to help offset soaring food and property prices. Those pressures were evident in mid-2010, when a series of big labor strikes in southern China disrupted several Japanese auto factories and resulted in hefty pay raises. There is also the looming prospect that China's currency, the renminbi, will strengthen against other world currencies in the near future; that would make goods produced in China even more expensive to export, and further erode what manufacturers say are already thin profit margins.

Subsequently, in seeking lower costs, manufacturers responded by relocating to poor inland regions of China where wages are as much as 30 percent lower than in coastal provinces. For example, Dell, the PC maker, planned to open a manufacturing, sales, and service center in Chengdu, Western China, in 2011 that could eventually employ more than 3,000 workers. *China Daily* also reported that rising labor cost had triggered industrial relocation from coastal areas to interior provinces. For example, global computer maker Hewlett Packard (HP) and manufacturer of electronic products Foxconn International Holdings planned to jointly invest US$3 billion to build a manufacturing plant for laptops in Chongqing in Southwestern China; the world's largest pharmaceutical firm, Pfizer

Inc., planned to set up a new research and development (R&D) center in Wuhan in Central China to support Pfizer's global R&D projects (*China Daily* 2010).

In addition to relocation, companies also felt the need to upgrade and to revamp their labor-intensive industries so as to embark on the higher level of development that is encouraged by the government's stimulus program. For instance, Kwonnie Electrical Company, after years of assembling vacuum cleaners and rechargeable toothbrushes for Philips, wanted to do more original design and build its own brand. The TAL group, which operated an immense garment-making plant, was expanding into supply-chain management for J.C.Penny, one of its big shirt-buyers. Through an extensive computerized system, TAL could stock and restock shirt shelves in all 1,100 of Penney's retail stores in the United States as demand warranted (Barboza 2010b).

In order to provide technicians, scientists, researchers, and a highly skilled workforce to upgrade China's industries, *China Daily* (2010) reported that the Chinese state issued a Medium and Long-term Talent Development Plan (2010–2020) which aimed at increasing the ratio of citizens with a higher education background in the work force from 9.2 percent in 2008 to 20 percent by 2020.

Developing Green Industry

During the global economic crisis, China had stepped on the gas in an effort to become the dominant player in green energy, including wind, solar, and geothermal power. Of the US$31.6 billion from the stimulus program allocated to green industries, 51 percent went to solar firms, while the remaining 49 percent went to a diverse cross-section of the economy—materials science, agriculture, water and waste management, energy efficiency, and energy storage (Goswami 2010).

Bradsher (2009b) reported that "Chinese governments at the national, provincial, and even local level have been competing with one another to offer solar companies even more generous subsidies, including free land, and cash for research and development. State-owned banks were flooding the solar industry with loans at considerably lower interest rates than were available in Europe or the United States." For example, Suntech, based in Wuxi, was on track in 2009 to pass Q-Cells of Germany to become the world's second largest supplier of photovoltaic cells. In order to reduce shipping costs and to bypass WTO rules, Suntech planned to go overseas and build a solar panel assembly plant in the United States.

As a result, China has become the world's leading producer of wind turbines and solar panels, and has already begun exporting its technology to the United States (Klare 2010). In the area of green energy, China is rapidly catching up with the core states.

Consolidating the Developmental State

Facing sharp economic downturn and growing social unrest, the Chinese communist state had abundant reasons to move away from neoliberal capitalism to state-developmentalism. The advantages of a developmental state, as Prime Minister Wen Jiabo explained in a March 2010 address, "enable [China] to make decisions efficiently, organize effectively, and concentrate resources to accomplish large undertakings" (Wines 2010b).

The Chinese developmental state was well-equipped to deal with the global economic crisis during 2008–2009 because it had gained considerable experience with designing and implementing stimulus projects a decade earlier in the 1997/1998 Asian financial crisis. Harushiko Kuroda, the President of Asian Development Bank, explained that "China today is more resilient to external shocks than it was a decade ago when the Asian crisis hit the region. After years of prudent economic policy making, the country has achieved commendable fiscal consolidation and a strong external position" (Kuroda 2009).

In addition, after 10 years of intensive financial reform, Chinese banks were in relatively good shape and had ample liquidity to help fund the government-mandated lending. Unlike the United States (the largest debtor nation in the world), China has substantial reserves of foreign currency, sovereign investments, and domestic savings, enabling it to fund its deficits and stimulus spending without requiring external sources of capital. China had $2.2 trillion in reserves (Friedman 2009), so it had a very strong fiscal position; the Chinese developmental state could spend its way out of the global economic crisis for as long as it wishes.

The Chinese developmental state's legitimacy was not undermined by the growing protests during the economic downturn because most of the protests in the countryside and in the city were directed against the local governments, not against the central state. However, in order to prepare for potential social unrest during the global economic crisis, the central state took no chances and had further strengthened its repressive apparatus.

When Hu Jintao, the leader of the Chinese Communist Party (CCP), gave a speech in December 2008 pointing out that "China should continue to hoist high the great flag of socialism with Chinese characteristics and push forward the significance of Marxism." In several CCP meetings in late 2008, President Hu also called on the armed forces and police to pull out the stops to uphold social stability by putting down disturbances and assorted conspiracies spearheaded by anti-China forces. Willy Lam (2009) labeled the above policies as "The Great Leap Backward" because they signaled a sharp U-turn from the neoliberal policies of the late 1990s.

In March 2009, Ching Chong further reported that the Chinese state had set up a special "6521 Group" (the numbers refer to the 60th anniversary of the founding of communist China, the 50th anniversary of the Tibetan uprising, the 20th anniversary of the Tiananmen crackdown, and 10th anniversary of the crackdown on the Falungong movement) and issued a notice detailing 33 measures that governments at every level must take to protect public order when they are dealing with such economic threats as the "highly dangerous mob events" triggered by land grabs, massive urban and rural unemployment, labor disputes, and public discontent over the sale of fake or unsafe goods.

The Chinese state further consolidated its power when it successfully hosted the Olympic games in Beijing in summer 2008 and actively participated as "G2" in the inter-state arena.

Realignment of Social Forces

From the 1970s onwards, China pursued a neoliberal policy to promote export-led industrialization. The state actively promoted decollectivization, proletarianization and marketization, downsized the state sector, and opened its coastal areas for foreign investment. Although these neoliberal policies had led to very rapid economic growth, they had also induced numerous social protests and political movements in the 1980s and 1990s. Despite all this social resistance, Hung (2009: 24) argues that the state refused to re-orient its neoliberal policy because it was captured by a powerful "elitist faction" which consisted of "officials and entrepreneurs from the coastal provinces".

However, I would argue that at the turn of the twenty-first century, under the new Hu/Wen leadership, China began to adopt a state-developmental model, moving toward a more balanced development between economic growth and social development. The state would play a more active role in moderating the negative impacts of marketization, and it included "the people and environment" in its development plan, not just focusing narrowly on GNP indicators and economic growth (So 2010b: 142). What then is the impact of the global economic crisis on the social forces behind the Chinese developmental state?

Intensifying the Conflict Between the State and the Transnationals

Both Hung (2009) and Hart-Landsberg (2010) contend that China would be more dependent on the transnationals after the global economic crisis, i.e. China might remain as "America's head servant" because of China's trade dependency, export dependency, and financial dependency on the United States. This chapter, however, points to a different path of Chinese development during the crisis.

To start with, the global economic crisis has led to a growing conflict between the Chinese state and the global capitalist class. In August 2009, the Chinese government arrested and prosecuted several executives of a foreign mining giant, the Anglo-Australian Rio Tinto, as spies accused of stealing state secrets. Although the spy charges were later dropped, the Rio Tinto executives still faced lesser charges of bribery and theft of trade secrets. This espionage threat stirred broad unease among the transnational companies operating in China, which feared they could face persecution and closed-door trials for engaging in what much of the business world would regard as bare-knuckle business tactics. As James Feinerman, an expert on Chinese law, commented, "China had undergone 'a real pushback' in the last five years on some fronts, reasserting political dogma in some areas where commercial norms and the rule of law had begun to have more sway" (Wines 2009).

In early 2010, Google threatened to shut down its search engine in China on the grounds that the Chinese state had maintained a tight control over its sites. However, Barboza (2010c) reported that Google had to leave China because Google, like other American internet companies including Yahoo and eBay, failed to gain significant traction in the China market and could not compete against Chinese companies like Baidu, Tencent and Alibaba.

By late 2010, foreign businesses in China were voicing frustration over China's heavily regulated market—a bureaucratic maze many transnational capitalists say is designed deliberately to hamstring non-Chinese players to the advantage of their local competitors (Ford 2010). The European Union Chamber of Commerce in China also issued a position paper listing hundreds of market-access problems reported by foreign companies across a range of industries.

Transnationals' concerns have been sharpened in recent years by a series of regulatory changes in China that appear directly intended to shut out foreigners. For example, a proposal known as "Indigenous Innovation Accreditation" caused alarm among foreign high-tech companies because it set up a complicated licensing system that required companies to register their IPR (Intellectual Property Rights) in China before registering elsewhere in order to qualify (Jiang 2010). Christian Murck, the president of the American Chamber of Commerce in China, voiced his "concern about the operating environment in the future, because of the regulatory-policy changes and narrowing of market access" (Jiang 2010). Reuters reported that "the European Union pressed China to amend its trade practices to stop technology theft, counterfeiting and discriminating against foreign companies" (Reuters 2010).

Foreign companies also complained loudly that they are being shut out of much of the lucrative government procurement sector. For example, not one of the 25 valuable contracts awarded to companies under the Chinese government's US$586 billion stimulus program went to a foreign-owned company (Jiang 2010).

Adopting a Stronger Pro-Worker Stand

If the global economic crisis had induced the state to take more aggressive action to protect Chinese industries from the transnationals, the crisis had also induced the state to take a stronger stand to protect Chinese workers from exploitation in the export sector. The new labor contract law took effect in 2008 despite the transnational business community—as represented by the American Chamber of Commerce in Shanghai, the U.S.-China Business Council, and the European Union Chamber of Commerce in China—putting up a strong battle to oppose the labor law (So 2010a).

When a series of wildcat strikes broke out against Honda and Toyota in several cities in South and Central China in the summer of 2010, the state allowed the Chinese mass media to cover the strikes in detail. The tacit approval of coverage of the strikes seems to reflect a genuine desire of the Chinese state to see higher wages for the workers so as to increase domestic consumption during the global economic crisis. The above speculation is confirmed by the fact that soon after the strike wave in the summer of 2010, various local governments in Shenzhen, Nanhai, and Beijing quickly announced that they would raise the minimum wage by 10–20 percent in the following months (Insurgent Notes, 2010).

In August 2010, Chinese Premier Wen Jiabao further bluntly warned "Japan that its companies operating in China should raise pay for the workers" during a high-level Japan-China meeting. Wen told the Japanese officials that behind the labor unrest was the relatively low level of pay at some foreign companies (Browne and Shirouzu 2010).

Adopting a Stronger Pro-Peasant Stand

The decline of exports at the onset of the global economic crisis in fall 2008 also induced the state to engineer a rural prosperity policy as part of its effort to shift the driver of economic growth from export-led industrialization to domestic consumption.

The economic stimulus program included many allocations aimed at promoting collective consumption and social protection in the countryside so as to reduce social inequalities and narrow the gap between city and countryside. For example, as mentioned earlier, US$124 billion was allocated to a health care plan which would extend basic coverage and would invest in public hospitals and training for village and community doctors; US$59 billion was allocated to improve rural infrastructure such as drinking water, electricity, and transport; another US$59 billion was allocated to affordable public housing for rural areas; and hundreds of millions of rural residents have been offered hefty rebates for the purchase of home appliances. These massive allocations to the peasants should cut down the social grievances in the countryside, arrest rural decline, and prevent the rural areas becoming centers of protest as in the 1980s and the 1990s.

Adopting a More Pro-State Sector Stand

In the high tide of neoliberalism in the 1990s, pundits predicted that China's state sector would gradually disappear because it was highly inefficient and state enterprises were losing money. On the other hand, China's private sector was expanding very rapidly because private enterprises were said to be highly efficient and profitable.

During the global economic crisis, however, there was a major expansion of the state sector at the expense of the private sector in China. The bulk of the Chinese stimulus program funds went into the state sector, i.e. into the state banks and the state enterprises. The state also strengthened environmental regulations and tightened the tax loopholes on private business, leading to an avalanche of complaints from private enterprises in the export sector. For example, many Hong Kong companies said they had to close down their factories in the Pearl River Delta because of the worsening of the business environment due to new regulations and taxation.

Challenges Ahead

Despite having a robust economy during the global economic crisis in 2008/2009, China does face a number of internal and external challenges in the near future.

First of all, China's rapid recovery from the global economic crisis has been fueled by its domestic investment growth, which accounted for more than 90 percent of its total growth in 2009. This kind of domestic growth, which was catalyzed by China's massive US$586 billion stimulus program, is clearly not sustainable. Will China experience economic decline when it exits from the stimulus program?

Second, there is the concern of an overheated economy. Much of China's recovery has been fueled by aggressive lending and soaring property prices. Lending by state-run banks was one of China's most aggressive forms of stimulus in 2009, but analysts constantly warned that banks could face the risk of overbuilding, overcapacity, and nonperforming loans (Barboza 2010a).

Third, with urban housing prices rising around 10 percent monthly in early 2010, analysts are warning of the formation of a residential property bubble, which could lead to serious political consequences. "There was massive overcapacity in housing, with one Chinese electric company reporting 60 million units connected and not using any electricity, so presumably empty. If another 20 to 30 million units under construction are added, China's excess capacity could house the entire U.S. population" (Dapice 2010). A public opinion poll showed that housing affordability is rated to be a top domestic problem in China. Rising housing prices would exclude low-income urban residents and rural migrant workers from the housing market, making China more polarized and divided (Yao and Luo 2010).

Finally, there is a concern as to whether China can boost its domestic consumption and reduce its reliance on exports and on foreign investment. Although there are signs to show that the gaps between rural–urban and between coastal–interior provinces are narrowing as a result of rising wages, industrial relocation, and rural investment, domestic consumption may not grow as fast as necessary to absorb the decline in the export market.

Nevertheless, given the fact that the Chinese developmental state has strong state capacity and a high degree of autonomy, there is a good possibility that the state will be able to meet the above challenges. For example, the state has recently put up new regulations to tame housing prices, rein in overly aggressive lending, and stop banks from shifting loans off their books. It also tightened requirements for mortgage loans used to finance non-owner-occupied property; this has slowed market turnover and price inflation at the high-end of the market significantly. At the same time, the state is quickly increasing affordable public housing capacity in order to meet the demand at the low-end of the market (Bottelier 2010).

At the inter-state level, there are growing tensions between China and other core states. The United States, in Paul Krugman's (2010) words, is increasingly "taking on China", accusing China of currency manipulation and wanting the U.S. Congress to pass a bill that would sanction China over its currency policy. Krugman remarks that although the bill was mild, "there was dire warning of a trade war and global economic disruption" (Krugman 2010). At the time of writing, Chinese exports still continue to surge and China's foreign exchange reserves have ballooned to US$2.65 trillion (Barboza 2010d).

On the currency issue, Timothy Geithner, U.S. Treasury Secretary, complained to the U.S. Congress that China had substantially undervalued its currency to gain an unfair trade advantage, tolerated theft of foreign technology, and created unreasonable barriers to American imports. In fall 2010, the United States put pressure on the International Monetary Fund to hold China accountable for rebalancing the global economy. However, Wen Jiabao, China's premier, said that China could not let the Chinese renminbi appreciate because "many of our factories will shut down and society will be in turmoil" (Chan 2010).

Christine O'Donnell, a Republican Senate nominee and a Tea Party-backed hopeful, said in a 2006 debate that "China was plotting to take over America" (Evans 2010). Perhaps O'Donnell's statement is influenced by news reports that "China will overtake the United States as the world's largest economy as early as 2030" (Becker 2010).

Rising frictions between China and its neighbors in fall 2010 over security issues, however, have given the United States an opportunity to assert its power over China. U.S.–China tensions can be seen from the following disputes over China's territorial boundary: the Chinese government voiced its disagreement over President Obama's meeting with the Dalai Lama, the Tibetan religious leader, and Washington's approval of a $6.7 billion arms sale to Taiwan, which China regards as its territory (Wines 2010c); in summer 2010, Washington leapt into the middle of heated territorial disputes between China and Southeast Asian nations despite stern Chinese warnings that the United States should mind its own business; in September 2010, the United States carried out war games with South Korea in the Yellow Sea in order to help Seoul rebuff threats from North Korea even though China denounced these naval exercises, saying that they intruded on areas where the Chinese military operates (Wines 2010c); and in late September 2010, China's increasingly tense standoff with Japan over a Chinese fishing trawler captured by Japanese ships in disputed waters was pushing Japan back under the American security umbrella.

Conclusion: The Global Economic Crisis and the Rise of China

The global economic crisis is a period of turbulence, upheaval, political vacuums, and prolonged conflict; it is a period where states, classes, and ethnic groups try to re-define their relationships, to re-align their configuration, and to re-set the rules governing their access to key resources in the capitalist world economy. As such, how did the global economic crisis affect China's position in the capitalist world economy?

This chapter shows that unlike the Western advanced capitalist economies which have experienced negative growth and a very high unemployment rate during the global economic crisis, China still managed to grow at a fast rate of around 10 percent and experienced labor shortages in its export zones. Indeed, this chapter argues that the global economic crisis has presented a golden opportunity for China to consolidate its state-developmentalist model. At the onset of the crisis in fall 2008, the Chinese state quickly put up a massive stimulus program of US$586 billion. The stimulus program invested heavily in infrastructure, agriculture, science and technology, environment, education, healthcare, and affordable public housing.

As a result, the stimulus program led to a major expansion of the state sector at the expense of the private sector, industrial relocation from coastal provinces to interior provinces, industrial upgrading of labor-intensive industries, and the rapid development of green industries. Although conflict was intensified between the Chinese state and the Western transnationals, there was little social protest from workers and peasants because the state had adopted a pro-worker and pro-peasant stand: the state warned Japan that its companies operating in China should raise the wages of workers, and the state's massive stimulus program pumped enormous resources into the countryside.

However, despite its expanding economy and political stability, China still faces internal problems of an overheated economy, the formation of a residential property bubble, and difficulties in creating a large domestic economy to balance its export economy. In addition, there are external challenges because the United States and other Western states keep pressuring China to raise the value of its currency, keep stirring trouble for China over territorial disputes with its neighbors like Vietnam and Japan, and keep formulating the discourse of "the China threat" in order to slow down the rise of China. However, since the Chinese state has a track record of managing crisis and resolving social and political problems, and since the state has not been weakened during the global economic crisis, it should be able to handle these internal and external challenges.

If China emerged strong from the global economic crisis, would this indicate the rise of China? Before answering this question, we need first to clarify what does "the rise of China" mean? It means China has become a strong core state in the inter-state system and is ready to challenge the hegemonic power of the United States. The rise of China can be examined through the following dimensions: economic, political, and cultural.

The Rise of China: Economic

China is now a major economic power and holds the largest foreign exchange reserves (US$2.65 trillion) in the world (Barboza 2010d). Thus China's fiscal policies could have a major impact on the global economy. If China's economic growth is strong, this could boost its demand for export and serve as the growth engine of the world economy. Stephen Roach, Morgan Stanley's analyst, thus asked the question "Can China save us?" because economists hope that the resurgent economy of China will act as a catalyst to help the still-shaky Western economies to recover from the deepest recession since World War II (Schwartz 2009).

Having accumulated so large a currency reserve, China has made good use of it during the global economic crisis to acquire oil fields, natural gas reserves, mines, pipelines, refineries, and other resource assets in a global buying spree of almost unprecedented proportions. The rapid economic growth of China has generated a rising demand for oil, steel, copper, and other primary materials.

Since 2008, Western firms have been reluctant to make major investments in foreign oil ventures, fearing a prolonged downturn in global sales. The Chinese state-owned companies on the other hand accelerated their buying efforts because they saw the crisis as a perfect opportunity for acquiring critical resources for a potentially energy-starved future at bargain-basement prices. "'The international financial crisis ... is equally a challenge and an opportunity,' insisted Zhang Guobao, head of [China's] National Energy Administration [in] 2009. 'The slowdown ... has reduced the price of international energy resources and assets and favors our search for overseas resources'" (Klare 2010).

As a policy matter, the Chinese state has worked hard to facilitate the accelerating rush to control foreign energy resources. Among other things, it has provided low-interest, long-term loans to major Chinese resource firms in the hunt for foreign properties. Michael Klare (2010) reports that "[i]n 2009, for example, the China Development Bank (CDB) agreed to lend CNPC [China National Petroleum Corp] [US]$30 billion over a five-year period to support its efforts to acquire assets abroad. Similarly, CDB has loaned [US]$10 billion to Petrobras, Brazil's state-controlled oil company, to develop deep offshore fields in return for a promise to supply China with up to 160,000 barrels of Brazilian crude oil per day."

In December 2009, "CNPC signed an agreement with the government of Myanmar (Burma) to build and operate an oil pipeline that will run from [Burma to the] Chinese province of Yunnan. The 460-mile pipeline will permit China-bound tankers from Africa and the Middle East to unload their cargo in [Burma] on the Indian Ocean, thereby avoiding the long voyage to China's eastern coast via the Strait of Malacca and the South China Sea, [an area] dominated by the U.S. Navy" (Klare 2010).

Other acquisitions in 2009 included Sinopec's US$7.5 billion purchase of the Canadian oil company Addax in August 2009 and Mineral's US$1.38 billion purchase of Australia's O.Z. Minerals in June 2009 (Yao 2009).

In 2010, Saudi Arabia announced that it had sold more oil to China the previous year than to the U.S. "Energy and mineral producers that once directed their production – and often their political allegiance – to the U.S., Japan, and to Western Europe now view China as a major customer and patron." Therefore, when Western capitalist states finally recover from the global economic crisis, they will soon "discover that the global resource chessboard has been tilted strongly in China's favor" (Klare 2010).

In early 2010, Ford Motor sold its Volvo subsidiary to a Chinese conglomerate, in the clearest confirmation yet of China's global ambitions in the auto industry. Bradsher (2010c) remarks that the sale of one of Europe's most storied brands shows how China has emerged not just as the world's largest auto market in the past year, but also as a country determined to capture a large share of the global market.

The Rise of China: Political

On the political front, Shambaugh (2009) points out that China is more and more actively engaging in global affairs. Shambaugh lists the following activities that may indicate the rising power of China in the international arena:

- China has played a particularly vital role in the Six-Party Talks process concerning North Korea's nascent nuclear program.
- China has participated in the "5+1" United Nations Security Council "quintet" concerning Iran's nuclear program.
- China has also ramped up its contributions to UN peacekeeping operations, making China the fourteenth largest contributor in the world but first among Security Council members.
- China has become a major contributor of aid to poor African and other developing countries.

Thus, American leaders now talk about "strategic dialogues," "strategic and economic dialogues," and "strategic reassurance" when they are dealing with Chinese leaders. The world press now starts to speak of the G-2 (the United States and China) who, in effect, wield world power. Wallerstein (2010) remarks "how different this is from the late 1960s when China spoke of the United States and the Soviet Union as the 'two superpowers' against whom everyone else should unite."

The Rise of China: Cultural

In the cultural sphere, Wasserstrom (2010) points out that China is engaging in an ongoing "re-branding" drive. It is aiming to foster an image of China as a place that combines humanistic traditions (represented by Confucius) with impressive strides toward economic modernity. The re-branding drive can be seen in the image presented in the opening ceremonies of the Olympics and the establishment of government-funded "Confucius Institutes" around the world. All these re-branding efforts strive to demonstrate how dramatically China has changed and that it is again a central player in world affairs. These re-branding drives are also aimed at differentiating today's China from the China of Mao's day, the Communism of the Soviet Union, and from nakedly repressive neighbors like Burma and North Korea.

Commenting on a recent dialogue between Confucian and African thinkers funded by China's Confucius Institute, Bell (2010) remarks that such dialogues are relatively new. Now that China has more wealth, it can afford to fund dialogues that develop China's "soft power" and explore political alternatives to Western values and Western models of development.

During the global economic crisis, the mass media and policy circles began to talk about "The China Model" of development in order to celebrate China's fast-paced development, and especially China's fast-paced recovery from the economic crisis. Before the crisis, the "China Model" was used to represent an alternative economic development model to the "Washington Consensus", which was a U.S.-led plan for reforming and developing the economies of small, less-developed countries (Ramo 2004).

In the 2010s, when China is making inroads in Africa, the Middle East, and Latin America for raw materials and minerals, as Chinese state enterprises are encouraged to extend their investments in other parts of the world, the "China Model" is put forward to provide an ideological foundation for the above-mentioned overseas adventures of the Chinese state and the Chinese transnationals. As Dirlik (2004: 2) remarks, the China Model "appears, more than anything, to be a sales gimmick—selling China to the world, while selling certain ideas of development to the Chinese leadership."

Developing and post-socialist countries are buying into this China Model because they are highly dissatisfied with neoliberalism's Washington Consensus, the shock therapy, and Structural Adjustment Programs. The Brazilian leader Lula da Silva, for example, expressed his admiration for China and its ability to globalize without giving up its autonomy and sovereignty (Dirlik 2004).

In short, the above discussions show that China's developmental state was able to seize the opportunity of the global economic crisis to strengthen not only its economy, but also to expand its political power in the inter-state system and to begin to articulate a new set of values and a new model of development to challenge the United States.

What then is the future prospect for the rise of China? Would it suffer from a premature death like that experienced by Japan in the 1980s? Japan was a very promising global power in the 1980s, but its rapid economic growth came to a halt when it failed to resist U.S. pressure to raise its currency at the Plaza Accord in 1985. After Japan raised its currency by a wide margin in the late 1980s, it went into a decade-long recession and its economy could no longer serve as an engine to power the global capitalist economy forward.

Trying to avoid Japan's mistake in the 1980s, China has been very reluctant to raise its currency despite the strong pressure from the United States and European states; the global mass media and pundits are suggesting that a currency war is looming in 2010.

Since global economic crisis is a period of uncertainty, it is hard to predict whether China will succeed in its rise to be an economic superpower. What is certain, however, is that the rise of China will trigger more conflict and chaos in the global economy of the twenty-first century.

References

Bacani, Cesar. 2009. "China's Economic Recovery: Miracle or Mirage?" *Time* November 16, 2009.

Barboza, David. 2009. "Obama Begins First Visit to China." *The New York Times* November 16, 2010.

——. 2010a. "Report Warns of Risks to China's Bank System." *The New York Times* July 14, 2010.

——. 2010b. "China Shift Away from Low-Cost Factories." *The New York Times* September 16, 2010.Access at http://www.ndtv.com/article/world/china-shifts-away-from-low-cost-factories-52638 on November 2010.

——. 2010c. "China's Booming Internet Giants May be Stuck There." *The New York Times* March 23, 2010.

Becker, Antoaneta. 2010. "China: Second Richest Plays Poor." *Global Issues* September 20, 2010.

Bell, Daniel A. 2010. "Developing China's Soft Power." *The New York Times* September 23, 2010.

Bottelier, Peter. 2010. "China; Is the Recovery Too Strong?" *International Economic Bulletin* March 2010.

Bradsher, Keith. 2009a. "Bowing to Protests, China Halts Sale of Steel Mill." *The New York Times* August 16, 2009. Access at http://www.nytimes.com/2009/08/17/business/global/17yuan.html on November 2, 2010.

——. 2009b. "China Racing Ahead to U.S. in the Drive to Go Solar." *The New York Times* August 24, 2010. Access at http://www.nytimes.com/2009/08/25/business/energy-environment/25solar.html?_r=1 on November 2, 2010.

——. 2010a. "China Takes Lead in Clean Energy with Aggressive State Aid." *The New York Times* September 8, 2010. Access at http://www.nytimes.com/2010/09/09/business/global/09trade.html on November 2, 2010.

——. 2010b. "China, Defying Global Slump, Faces a Labor Shortage." *The New York Times* February 26, 2010. Access at http://www.nytimes.com/2010/02/27/business/global/27yuan.html?ref=business on November 2, 2010.

——. 2010c. "Chinese Company Geely to Buy Volvo." *The New York Times* March 28, 2010.

——. 2010d. "Exports of Chinese Goods Continued to Surge in September." *The New York Times* October 13, 2010.

Browne, Andrew and Norihiko Shirouzu. 2010. "Beijing Pressures Japanese on Wages." *The Wall Street Journal* August 29, 2010.

Chan, Sewell. 2010b. "Geithner Calls for Global Cooperation on Currency" *The New York Times* October 6, 2010. Access at http://www.nytimes.com/2010/10/07/business/global/07imf.html on November 2, 2010.

China Daily. 2010. "Rising Labor Costs Trigger Industrial Relocation." *China Daily* July 6, 2010.

China Stakes. 2008. "Bankruptcies and Closures: 'toy stories' in the Pearl River Delta." *China Stakes* October 29, 2008.

Chu, Kathy. 2010. "China Posed to Replace Japan as World's No. 2 Economy." *USA Today* August 16, 2010. Access at http://www.usatoday.com/money/world/2010-08-16-china-japan-gdp_N.htm on November 2, 2010.

Dapice, David. 2010. "Once a Winner, China Sees Globalization's Downsize — Part II." Yale Global Online, October 11, 2010. Access at http://yaleglobal.yale.edu on October 15, 2010.

Ding Xueliang. 2000. "Systemic Irregularity and Spontaneous Property Transformation in the Chinese Financial System." *China Quarterly* 163: 655–676.

Dirlik, Arif. 2004. "Beijing Consensus: Beijing 'Gongshi': Who Recognizes Whom and to What End?" Access at http://www.en.chinaelections.org/uploadfile/200909/20090918025246335.pdf

Evans, Ben. 2010. "O'Donnell said China Plotting to take over U.S." *The Associated Press* October 4, 2010.

Ford, Peter. 2010 "Foreigners Doing Business in China Feel Boxed Out: Report." *The Christian Science Monitor* June 29, 2010.

Friedman, Thomas. 2009. "Lost There, Felt Here." *The New York Times* November 15, 2009.

Goswami, Rahul. 2010. "A Pearl River Tale, Power and Pride in China." *Energy Bulletin*, August 28, 2010.

Hart-Landsberg, Martin. 2010. "The U.S. Economy and China: Capitalism, Class, and Crisis." *Monthly Review* 61 (#9): 14–31.

Hiro, Dilip. 2010. "America Is Suffering a Power Outage." *Huffington Post* September 23, 2010. Access at http://www.huffingtonpost.com/dilip-hiro/america-is-suffering-a-po_b_736567.html on October 10, 2010.

Hung, Ho-Fung. 2009. "America's Head Servant? The PRC's Dilemma in the Global Crisis." *New Left Review* 60: 5–25.

Insurgent Notes. 2010. "Wildcat Strikes in China." *Insurgent Notes* June 17, 2010. Access at http://insurgentnotes.com/2010/06/wildcat-strikes-in-china/ on October 10, 2010.

Javers, Eamon. 2009. "Is China Headed Toward Collapse?" *Politico* November 10, 2009.

Jiang Chengcheng. 2010. "Why Foreign Businesses in China Are Getting Mad" *Time* September 9, 2010.

Klare, Michael. 2010. "China's Global Shopping Spree: Is the World's Future Resource Map Tilting East?" *TomDispatch.Com* April 1, 2010. Access at "http://www.tomdispatch.com/blog/175226/tomgram%3A_michael_klare,_ shopaholic_china" on October 11, 2010.

Krugman, Paul. 2010. "Taking on China." *The New York Times* September 30, 2010. Access at http://www.nytimes.com/2010/10/01/opinion/01krugman. html on November 2, 2010.

Lam, Willy. 2009. "Hu Jintao's Great Leap Backward." *Far Eastern Economic Review* January/February 2009: 19–22.

Liu, Melinda. 2007. "Beijing's New Deal." *Newsweek* March 26, 20007.

Nonini, Donald M. 2008. "Is China Becoming NeoLiberal" *Critique of Anthropology* 28, 2: 145–176

Ogden, Suzanne. 2003. "Chinese Nationalism: The Precedence of Community and Identity over Individual Rights" in *China's Developmental Miracle: Origins, Transformations, and Challenges*, edited by Alvin Y. So. Armonk, NY: M.E. Sharpe.

Oi, Jean. 1992. "Fiscal Reform and the Economic Foundations of Local State Corporatism in China." *World Politics* 45: 99–126.

Ramo, Joshua Cooper. 2004. "The Beijing Consensus." *The Foreign Policy Center*. Access at http://219.143.73.108/bookscollection/reports/200909/ P020090921313163521955.pdf on March 7, 2010.

Reuters. 2010. "Europe Presses China to Alter Trade Practices." *The New York Times* October 6, 2010. Access at http://www.nytimes.com/2010/10/07/ business/07eutrade.html on November 2, 2010.

Roubini, Nouriel. 2008. "The Rising Risk of Hard Landing in China," *Japan Focus*, November 4.

Scherer, Michael. 2009. "Should Obama Get around China's 'Great Firewall'?" *Times* November 16, 2009.

Schwartz, Nelson. 2009. "Asia's Recovery Highlights China's Ascendance." *The New York Times,* August 23, 2009.

Shambaugh, David. 2009. "Is China ready to be a global power?" *Global Times* November 11, 2009.

So, Alvin. 2010a. "Post-Socialist State, Transnational Corporations, and the Battle for Labor Rights in China at the turn of the 21st Century." *Development and Society* 39: 97–118.

——. 2010b. "Globalization and China: From Neoliberal Capitalism to State Developmentalism in East Asia." Pp. 133–154 in *Globalization in the 21st Century: Labor, Capital, and the State on a World Scale*, edited by Berch Berberoglu. Palgrave Macmillan.

Wallerstein, Immanuel. 2010. "How to Think about China." *Commentary* No. 273. (January 15).

Wasserstrom, Jeffrey. 2010a. "Power in a Symbol: Commentary on China's Unwanted Nobel Prize." *The New York Times* October 9, 2010.

Wines, Michael. 2009. "China Warms to New Credo: Business First." *The New York Times* August 13, 2009. Access at http://www.nytimes.com/2009/08/14/world/asia/14china.html on November 2, 2010.

———. 2010a. "As China Rises, Fears Grow on Whether Boom can endure." *The New York Times* January 11, 2010. Access at http://www.nytimes.com/2010/01/12/world/asia/12china.html on November 2, 2010.

———. 2010b. "China Fortifies State Businesses to Fuel Growth." *The New York Times* August 29, 2010. Access at http://www.nytimes.com/2010/08/30/world/asia/30china.html on November 2, 2010.

———. 2010c. "U.S. Alarmed by Harsh Tone of China's Military." *The New York Times* October 11, 2010.

Yao Shujie. 2009. "China Emerges as a Global Power on 60th Birthday." The University of Nottingham China Policy Institute Briefing Series—Issue 55.

Yao Shujie and Dan Luo. 2010. "Chinese Economy 2009: Leading the World Economy out of Crisis." The University of Nottingham, China Policy Institute, *Briefing Series*—Issue 59.

Yardley, Jim and Keith Bradsher. 2008. "China, an Engine of Growth, Faces a Global Slump." *The New York Times* October 23, 2008.

Chapter 8

The Global Capitalist Crisis and the End of Neoliberal Capitalist Globalization

Martin Orr

The "Great Recession" is not just another economic downturn from which we are "recovering." Instead, we are experiencing a profound transformation of global proportions that will prove more significant than the collapse of the Soviet Union. In the aftermath of the Cold War, more than any other power in history, the United States enjoyed something approaching world hegemony. At that time, the U.S. sought to perpetuate its domination of the world economy through neoliberal globalization. Although many "free trade" agreements were reached that have served to protect corporations from political regulation —to make people less able to defend themselves from corporate predation—that effort stalled due to global opposition. Neoconservative unilateralism emerged in the attempt to achieve the same end with regard to the most fundamental commodity in industrial society— oil. This attempt even more quickly failed as a result of the growing opposition around the world. Now, with the rise of China over the last decade and the growing Russian influence, the United States has lost the status of "lone superpower." With the economic collapse, the United States has been fully unmasked as a nation with a "crony capitalist" polity supported by a crumbling infrastructure and living beyond its means through the goodwill of other nations. Whether the United States becomes one power among many, a junior partner of a more solvent nation, or fully degenerates into an unviable society is uncertain, but the "New American Century" that the neoconservatives tried to impose on the world, in large part thanks to their efforts, lasted less than a decade.

This chapter offers an analytical history of the rise and fall of the U.S. Empire. The rise of U.S. capital to world dominance was the direct result of its ability to supply, at a profit, the oil that fueled the Allied war machines. Victorious, the United States imposed on both vanquished and allies alike an international financial and trade system that was protected by its unrivaled military, and legitimized by a United Nations responding impotently to the effects of neocolonialism. As long as the nation was able to supply its own energy needs, the United States was able to expand its economy while also responding to popular demand to reduce inequalities in several areas. But in the early 1970s, domestic oil production peaked. Less than 30 years in ascendance, the empire began to decay—rising budget and trade deficits, rapid inflation, rising inequality, capital flight, neglect of public services and infrastructure characterize the 1970s and 1980s. The disintegration of the

Soviet Union enabled the United States to reassert its leadership through neoliberal trade policy and neoconservative foreign and domestic policies. In response to popular opposition, both of these failed. As U.S. capital lost its ability to dominate workers in other nations, it facilitated ever greater exploitation of the U.S. working class, with growing indebtedness masking stagnant wages. The bursting of the real estate bubble amid rapid energy inflation prevented further indebtedness, destroyed demand, and the economy collapsed. The "Great Recession" marks a transition in many ways, as nations increasingly ignore neoliberal dogma for nationalist, populist and socialist alternatives, and as the leadership of other nations, most notably China and Russia, show increasing contempt for the United States. What shape the emerging global order will take is far from clear, but one thing is certain—it won't be dominated by the United States. Having paid for its military machine on installments, having demonstrated its inability to control world events, and having provoked a global financial meltdown, soon the United States will likely have to focus attention on maintaining domestic order.

The Origins, Development, and Decline of the U.S. Empire

Imperialism is the organizing theme of United States history. A collection of mostly English colonies freed in the first modern war of national liberation, the United States quickly adopted its own colonial enterprise, displacing natives, buying territory from other colonial powers and instigating war to seize the territory of sovereign nations. By 1850 it had conquered the continent, and with its defeat of Spain not only dominated the Western Hemisphere but established footholds in the Pacific and Asia. The United States emerged from World War I rivaling the economic and military might of any nation in Europe, and in the aftermath of World War II it supplanted the U.K. as the dominant capitalist power, checked from establishing a world empire only by the existence of the Soviet Union. Its supremacy among capitalist nations was cemented both by its preeminent military power as well as by the financial and trade protocols established by the Bretton Woods agreements, which established the World Bank and the International Monetary Fund (IMF). Almost immediately, the United States began to engage in imperial overreach and to squander its wealth, and by the early 1970s it was in every respect a nation in decline. The collapse of the Soviet Union briefly gave the United States an opening to make U.S. domination global and permanent—a "New World Order" and a "New American Century" were promised, not without megalomania, by advocates of "nation building," "humanitarian interventions," and "free trade." Absent the pretext of defending against the "Soviet menace," neoliberal and neoconservative policies intended to advance U.S. hegemony were quickly and successfully challenged.

The rise of the United States is generally attributed to some ideal force. "Manifest Destiny," "American Exceptionalism," the character or ingenuity of the "American People," or the putative advantages of the uniquely libertarian nature of U.S. capitalism have all been offered as explanations for the ascendance of the United States in the twentieth century. Material forces are of course more significant—most especially a huge resource base (and superexploited slave, indentured and immigrant labor). Although land, iron and coal were the basis for many fortunes, a single resource—oil—has been at the center of wealth and political power from J.D. Rockefeller to Halliburton. Vast oil wealth forced the West to accept U.S. leadership. The World Wars that led to the high-water mark of U.S. Empire were fought over oil and with oil. The victors were those who could deprive the enemy of oil.

The inter-imperialist oil wars from which the United States emerged triumphant can be traced to 1912, when First Lord of the Admiralty Winston Churchill ordered the transition of his battleships from coal to oil—soon thereafter, in part to fuel its navy, the British government bought a majority share of the Anglo-Persian Oil Company, now BP (Klare 2001: 30). The United Kingdom's desire to block Germany's access to oil through the Berlin to Baghdad railway set the stage for World War I (Engdahl 2004), and 80 percent of the Allies' petroleum was supplied by the U.S.—"The Allied cause [floated] to victory on a wave of oil" (Yeomans 2004: 9–10). The United States quickly joined Europe in the scramble for Middle Eastern oil. Saudi Arabia granted oil concessions to Standard Oil of California in 1933, and in 1943 the U.S. government began providing military aid to the Saudis. In World War II, Hitler's inability to reach the oilfields of Baku contributed to the German defeat, the United States' blockade of Japanese oil and steel imports precipitated the attack on Pearl Harbor, and destroying their oil tankers cut off the islands from the one material essential for an industrial war economy (Klare 2001: 31). Months before the end of the war in Europe, President Franklin Delano Roosevelt met with King Abdul Aziz ibn Saud in February 1945 aboard the USS *Quincy* to at least implicitly link U.S. protection of the Saudi regime with access to Saudi oil. With President Truman's subsequent letter to King ibn Saud in 1948 there was no mistake as to the arrangement: "No threat to your Kingdom could occur that would not be a matter of immediate concern to the United States" (Yeomans 2004: 16). By the end of World War II the United States was producing two-thirds of the world's oil. As a result, it also had half of the world's manufacturing capacity and held 70 percent of the world's gold reserves. The United States used its wealth and power to make Europe and its former colonies economically and militarily dependent.

The relationships and institutions that would characterize the period of U.S. ascendancy following World War II began with negotiations between bankers and industrialists in the United States, the United Kingdom, and Germany in the 1930s regarding how to prevent the approaching war from interfering with trade (Seldes 1943). Following the U.S. victory the modern international order took shape. The United Nations (UN) and the North Atlantic Treaty Organization (NATO), both by design dominated by the United States, remain central to this system of political and military control. The basis of U.S. financial control was established by Bretton Woods institutions—the World Bank, the International Monetary Fund, and the

General Agreement on Tariffs and Trade (GATT). U.S. capital was checked only by the need to compete with the Soviet Union for the "hearts and minds" of people in other nations, and to demonstrate to domestic audiences the advantages for working people of capitalism. As long as there was a material basis for its power, this system served U.S. capital well.

But this material basis was being extracted and consumed at accelerating rates. In 1970, with the United States already importing a third of its oil, the annual rate of domestic production of crude peaked. The following year, President Richard Nixon took the U.S Dollar off of the gold standard, abrogating the central tenant of the Bretton Woods agreements. World governments quickly followed suit, and "market confidence" (i.e., the interests of wealthy investors) has subsequently determined the value of a nation's currency. At roughly the same time, the Organization of Petroleum Exporting Countries (OPEC) emerged to challenge the major oil corporations, and demonstrated its economic power to protest U.S. support for Israel during the 1973 Arab-Israeli War. Also before mid-decade, it was clear that the war in Vietnam was lost, that Nixon was indeed a crook, and that, despite some meaningful social reforms and levels of inequality lower than any point since the Great Depression, the movements of the previous decades would not fundamentally rein in a self-destructive corporate capitalism.

Reagan's campaign promise to restore "Morning in America" reflected the unconscious realization that in the 1970s the U.S. was in decline. Under his administration, the levels of inequality began the upward climb that has continued for three decades. Taxes on the wealthy were reduced, military boondoggles like the "Star Wars" anti-missile defense program were promoted, the social safety net was systematically underfunded, and deficit spending exploded. During the twelve years of Reagan-Bush, the national debt rose from a third of GDP to nearly two-thirds (U.S. Census Bureau 2010). Capital flight was encouraged, and industry relocated from unionized labor markets in the "Rust Belt" to the U.S. South, to Maquiladoras in Mexico, and to "Free Trade Zones" in the Philippines. In the 1980s, due to lingering domestic and foreign opposition to the Vietnam War, the U.S. faced increasing obstacles to its ability to project power. Iran had been lost, our favored dictator in Nicaragua had been overthrown, and attempts to bring these and other nations into line failed despite the illegalities that came to be known as "Iran-Contra." The best Reagan could do is to topple an already unstable government on the tiny Caribbean island of Granada. Although George H.W. Bush was able to invade Panama and remove Manuel Noriega from power, his war against Iraq ended only in containment and the imposition of economic sanctions. The only major foreign policy "success" of the Reagan-Bush era was helping Afghani warlords stalemate the Soviet Union. Although it contributed to the dissolution of the "Evil Empire," it also set the stage for the dissolution of the U.S. Empire.

Neoliberalism and Anti-Globalization, Neoconservatism and the Crisis of Empire

The collapse of the Soviet Union and the restoration of capitalism in the Warsaw Pact nations gave the remaining "lone superpower" the opportunity to reassert global leadership, but absent the pretext of the "red menace" the U.S. was compelled to take a less belligerent and more multilateral approach. "Free trade," neoliberalism and globalization became the centerpiece of an international order that, although premised on putative consensus and mutual benefit, was no less intended to provide Western capital with unfettered access to markets abroad than was direct colonialism. The 1994 North American Free Trade Agreement (NAFTA) was the most significant early effort toward this end, and in 1995, linked to the Bretton Woods institutions and the culmination of GATT negotiations, a suitably authoritarian international body was established to enforce global trade agreements.

The World Trade Organization (WTO) is nominally charged with administration of trade agreements, arbitration of trade disputes, and facilitating continuing negotiations. In practice, the WTO serves to penalize governments that impede "free trade" through tariffs, bans on imports and exports, and other "trade restrictive" laws that protect workers, consumers, and the environment. Laws that limit the length of the workweek or prohibit child labor, equal pay, minimum wage and workplace safety provisions, consumer safety, product labeling and environmental protection requirements, and public services including education and health care can be challenged as "distorting markets" and impeding trade. IMF "structural adjustment" policies, which also serve to dictate governments' control of domestic economic policy, have come under attack. These policies have had such direct and immediate impacts on communities that an anti-globalization movement has quickly gathered momentum around the world. A central starting point has been the efforts of the Zapatista movement in Chiapas, Mexico, who staged an uprising to protest the implementation of NAFTA. Their pioneering use of the internet and other media led to incredibly effective outreach, to well-organized solidarity efforts in the United States, and served as inspiration for the anti-globalization movement. By the end of the decade, these and many other efforts culminated in the "Battle in Seattle".

On November 30, 1999, over 40,000 people gathered in opposition to neoliberal globalization. Demonstrators blocked intersections and off-ramps leading to the Seattle Convention Center, where the WTO was to meet. Attempts to clear the streets using batons and pepper spray initially failed, and later there was a standoff in which hundreds of protestors occupied the intersection of 4th and Pike Streets. A curfew was imposed, and the following day Seattle Mayor Paul Schell prohibited anti-globalization speech and assembly in downtown Seattle. Police from around the area, as well as hundreds of National Guard troops, were deployed as reinforcements. Violations of Schell's suspension of the U.S. Constitution led to over 500 arrests, to continued attacks upon nonviolent demonstrators, and to several assaults against bystanders.

In retrospect, the demonstrations were wildly successful. Because access had been denied to the delegates, the opening sessions of the WTO were delayed. Delegates representing less-developed governments, many of whom were opposed to WTO proposals, were emboldened by the support for their positions in the streets (Weissman 1999). The following year, the 133 members of the G77 group of developing nations expressed support for the anti-globalization movement and, in what one observer called the "Seattle effect," the meetings of the IMF in Prague the following year "turned into a contest over which fat cat could show the most contrition for capitalism's shortcomings and evince the greatest sympathy for the poor" (Zachary 2000). Seattle also gave momentum to the movement—over the next years similar demonstrations were held against the IMF and the World Bank in Washington, D.C. and in Prague, against meetings in Miami devoted to a proposed Central American Free Trade Agreement, against meetings of the G-8 group of major industrial economies, and against the conventions of both the Republican and Democratic Parties in the summer of 2000. The response to the anti-globalization movement by the state and the media served to only to radicalize opposition. Comparing the escalating violence and subterfuge of the state to the media whitewash of both the issues and the treatment of protesters led to the development of a broader agenda, to more sophisticated analyses of class power, and to more effective strategies and tactics.

After Seattle, state repression of opposition to globalization in the U.S. and Europe escalated, becoming increasingly violent and preemptive. Apart from the truncheons and chemicals in the streets, tactics have included surveillance and infiltration, raids of offices and staging areas, preemptive arrests and detention of movement organizers, compilation of lists of activists subsequently shared by governments, seizure of literature, mass arrests, police brutality in custody, live ammunition, and deadly force. The level of state surveillance was immediately compared to the "red squads" and the FBI's COINTELPROs of decades past (Scher 2001). Demonstrations against the institutions of global power have become routine to the point that any meeting of the Bretton Woods institutions or their political enablers requires a militarized perimeter around the site.

Corporate media, which devoted little attention to the WTO prior to Seattle, have since served to ignore the consequences of neoliberalism, vilify those who oppose globalization, and cover up state repression. Mergers, acquisitions and deregulation have led to a media system that is increasingly corporatized and concentrated (Bagdikian 2004). Major media are now owned by a handful of private interests like General Electric, Disney/ABC, AOL/Time Warner and News Corporation—multinationals that, along with their advertisers, are beneficiaries of neoliberal policy. As a result, critical analysis of the human toll of global inequality is effectively self-censored, and discussion of child labor, sweatshops, environmental degradation and human rights violations that result from globalization is all but absent (Baker 2000). In the absence of media coverage of the costs of neoliberalism, activists' demands seem ill-informed, and they become legitimate targets of police violence (Ackerman 2000).

The responses of the state and corporate media have only served to radicalize opposition, strengthen coalitions, broaden their demands, and force the development of new strategies and tactics. State and ideological repression has served to foster the creation of a more organizationally diverse and internationalist movement, employing a wide range of tactics. The rallies and pickets, the guerrilla street theater and the direct disruption of public meetings have been supplemented with third party election campaigns and legal challenges to repression, as with the successful suits against the City of Seattle. Central to their continuing success, alternative and more participatory media outlets have been established. The Indymedia network, inspired by the Zapatista's use of the internet and intended to coordinate the efforts of activists, became the source for breaking news in Seattle and at subsequent demonstrations. It and many other participatory forms of journalism have been essential in bypassing corporate media, and have contributed to the development of community among activists.

The anti-globalization movement remains an extremely broad-based coalition— labor, students, environmentalists, religious communities, and small business and farming interests from around the world continue to exhibit tremendous solidarity in the struggle against neoliberalism. Sophisticated analyses of power, innovative uses of the media, and growing support from publics worldwide could not be ignored. The anti-globalization movement helped derail neoliberalism, forced "public" meetings behind increasingly militarized police lines, and compelled the WTO and international capital more generally to concede legitimacy to other nations and to global publics. Although negotiations continue, little progress has been made in expanding the WTO agenda, and the United States has been prevented from normalizing its dominance through the ostensibly peaceful means of trade policy.

However, the attacks on the World Trade Center and the Pentagon shifted world attention from neoliberalism and the anti-globalization movement. It provided the "evildoers" that, like the Soviet Union, could be employed to justify neoconservative and unilateralist policies. Amidst the catastrophic consequences of neoliberalism, and with U.S. dominance challenged by an international movement calling into question these policies, September 11 offered the Bush administration the perfect pretext to launch a final bid to dominate the distribution of oil and natural gas from the Middle East and South Asia, and to clamp down on domestic dissent in the process. The attacks constituted the "new Pearl Harbor" that the neoconservative Project for a New American Century had hoped would rally the U.S. public to support their agenda.

The invasion of Afghanistan was accepted as a legitimate response to the attacks by most, but its place in energy politics was clear. Afghanistan lies in the path of a proposed pipeline to transport natural gas from the Caspian Sea Basin. The Taliban government was apparently unwilling to accept the terms offered, and plans for an October 2001 invasion were prepared months before 9/11

(Brisard and Dasquie 2002). The halfhearted search for bin Laden, the installation of former Unocal consultant Hamed Karzai as president, and the acceptance of the corruption and election fraud that has kept him in power has confirmed that the invasion and occupation of Afghanistan had little to do with bringing people to justice, preventing additional attacks, promoting democratic sovereignty, or protecting human rights.

The invasion of Afghanistan, which has only led to destabilization of what has become a wider war in the "AfPak theater," was followed by a massive international public relations effort to draw the Bush Administration's preferred target of Iraq into the "War on Terror" (Rampton and Stauber 2003). The invasion and occupation of Iraq was no more successful. From the already miserly conditions that resulted from a decade of U.S.-imposed sanctions and isolation, life under occupation quickly degenerated (Parenti 2004). Approximately 650,000 Iraqis died in the first three years of the occupation (Burnham et al., 2006), and the United Nations High Commission for Refugees estimated that 2 million Iraqis were internally displaced and 2.2 million left Iraq altogether (Cockburn 2007). For the Iraqi people, the motives behind this aggression were unmistakable (Bacon, 2007). In October 2000, the Iraqi government had demanded compensation for its oil in Euros—one of the first consequences of the occupation was to return to the U.S. dollar for oil transactions. Although the Bush Administration, with the eager help of corporate media, was able to convince most Americans that Iraq was a front in the "War on Terror," the war was condemned by most European allies, and tens of millions of people demonstrated against the war in cities all over the world. Revelations of torture and other atrocities at Guantanamo and Abu Ghraib, the claims of Iraqi chemical and biological weapons capabilities proven false by their absence, and the wholesale carnage let loose upon the Iraqi people made the nature of this war glaringly obvious, the world became increasingly united in opposition to U.S. foreign policy.

By 2007, 32 percent of those surveyed in five major European countries responded that the United States government is the greatest threat to world peace. This belief is not foreign to the United States. About 11 percent of Americans— and 35 percent of Americans age 16 to 24—also believed that the United States threatened global stability more than any other nation (Dombey and Pignal 2007). In addition, 78 percent of Americans said they opposed the war against Iraq, 45 percent of Americans reported that they wanted the U.S. House of Representatives to begin impeachment proceedings against George W. Bush, and 54 percent favored the impeachment of Vice-president Dick Cheney (Agence France-Presse 2007). For several years, the majority of Americans has favored withdrawal from Afghanistan. Neoconservativism proved a disaster. It led only to genocide, torture and other war crimes abroad, to media propaganda, governmental secrecy and heightened surveillance domestically, to neoliberalism without the pretense of consensus or democracy. It was ultimately rejected by its victims, U.S. allies, and the American people.

The "Great Recession," Class War, and the End of Empire

Although the United States retains its nuclear deterrent, it is now acting from a position of economic, political, and military impotence. Both neoliberalism and neoconservatism were born of the attempt to project a faltering American "leadership" into the distant future, but in the face of opposition both failed to achieve that result. The "Great Recession" was the consequence. Domestic inequalities were exacerbated by neoliberal capital flight and transfer of public wealth required by the neoconservative militarism. Class polarization led to the workers' increasing reliance upon debt, monopoly power in the financial sector exploited this fact and encouraged this trend, and the rapid rise in oil prices over the preceding several years finally destroyed demand. The resultant liquidity crisis on Wall Street quickly spread to Europe. Rather than embrace reform, Western capital has demanded more austerity for the many in order to allow the few to return to business as usual, a program that popular opposition may well come to block. Regardless of the ability of publics to challenge the domestic policies of their own governments, other world powers are asserting their right to be heard. The U.S. government is bankrupt, and the global order it championed has clearly collapsed.

The "Great Recession" refers to the most significant global economic crisis since the Great Depression. The Business Cycle Dating Committee of the National Bureau of Economic Research dates the downturn from the fourth quarter of 2007 (Business Cycle Dating Committee 2008), but the Great Recession will probably be remembered as beginning with the liquidity crisis on Wall Street that culminated in the crash of October 2008. Although an international crisis of capitalism, the epicenter of the recession was the United States.

The basis for the Great Recession is the growing gap between the fortunes of capital and labor in the United States. Neoliberalism encouraged the transfer of unionized manufacturing jobs to repressive labor markets, the off-shoring of service and professional work, and the superexploitation of migrants fleeing the ravages of NAFTA upon rural Mexico. Real wages have been stagnant since the mid-1970s as the percentage of income accruing to the best paid five percent of households increased from 14.8 percent in 1974 to 22.6 percent in 2006 (U.S. Census Bureau 2009). Inflation has further eroded the purchasing power of workers, as "inflation-adjusted dollars" fail to account for the fact that the prices of the basic needs upon which most people spend almost the entirety of their income—food, energy, health care and education—have increased at several times the general rate of inflation. In addition, effective tax rates on the rich and their estates have been dramatically reduced, regressive taxes and "user fees" on working people have been increased, and social services have been slashed. Finally, the skyrocketing cost of the neoconservatives' preemptive wars has contributed to deteriorating public services. But since technological developments continue to increase the productivity of U.S. workers, there is a widening chasm between the value of the commodities produced by labor and the purchasing power of workers. Over the last three decades, this gap has been closed by the growing indebtedness of households (Foster 2006; Wolff 2009). Since 1975, the ratio of household debt to income has more than doubled.

With the manufacturing sector largely dismantled, U.S. capital touted the emergence of an "information economy," and investment flowed toward internet startup firms. Although a few of these went on to become giants in retail and media, most had no tangible assets and no prospect for profitability. When the dot-com bubble burst in 2000, many investors turned to the more lucrative real estate market, driving up prices. This housing bubble was facilitated by the 1999 repeal of the Glass-Steagall Act, lifting the separation of commercial and investment banking. This encouraged the development of "exotic investment instruments," and especially "collateralized debt obligations" (CDOs) that bundled and sold homeowners' debt to investors. As the value of their homes rose in this market, many workers took advantage of the opportunity to borrow against their home equity to finance home improvements, pay medical bills, or simply maintain their standard of living in the midst of stagnant wages. Beginning in 2005, as real estate values began to fall, workers lost equity to borrow against to pay for unanticipated expenses, and the rate of foreclosure began to increase. Adding to the crisis, many buyers had agreed to "sub-prime mortgages" with initially low "teaser rates" offered by "predatory lenders"—often subsidiaries of the major banks. Often these borrowers lacked sufficient income to justify the mortgage, and as their adjustable rates rose they found themselves unable to make the higher payments. In addition to the systemic problem of class polarization, widespread corruption among mortgage lenders on Wall Street contributed to the collapse (Petras 2009; Taibbi 2009).

Rising inequality, the real estate bubble and the Ponzi-scheme capitalism of Wall Street had assembled a house of cards. The final blow came in the form of energy inflation. Spikes in oil prices have routinely triggered recessions—as with those following the 1973 Israeli-Arab War, the 1979 Iranian Revolution, and Iraq's invasion of Kuwait in 1990. Between 1988 and 2003, the inflation-adjusted, annual average price of oil didn't quite double (and it was at the same price it was in 1983). Between 2003 and 2008 the annual average price quadrupled, and spiked in the summer of 2008, six times higher than the 1988 average, at nearly $147 per barrel. In order to keep pace with rising global demand, stagnant production of light sweet crude has led to increasing reliance upon more expensive sources and technologies—heavy crudes, tar sands and deep-water drilling. As returns on real estate investment diminished, the more tangible energy market became more attractive, and speculators contributed to driving prices to their peak. Given the role of fossil fuels as central inputs for industrial agriculture, food prices followed energy prices closely, sparking food riots, rationing, and export bans around the world. Rising inequality and the collapse of the housing bubble had pushed workers to the brink, and then energy inflation pushed them over the edge, destroying consumer demand. As the foreclosure rate continued to soar, the CDOs based upon payment of mortgage interest became "toxic assets" with no market value. In October 2008 the U.S. economy collapsed, dragging the world economy with it.

European banks were heavily exposed to these toxic assets and were immediately drawn into the liquidity crisis. Caught up in their own housing bubble, contagion has led to several sovereign debt crises in Europe. Of greatest concern is the solvency of governments on the periphery of Europe, derisively called by bankers the "PIIGS"—Portugal, Ireland, Italy, Greece and Spain. Declining tax revenues and rising unemployment insurance and welfare costs have led to increasing budget deficits. But the monetary policies usually available to governments to manage a debt crisis—devaluation of the nation's currency and cutting interest rates—are in the hands of the European Union (EU) and the European Central Bank. As confidence in the ability of these governments to reduce their deficits waned (and as entire nations were effectively "shorted" by Wall Street), borrowing to service their debt became more difficult and more expensive, precipitating crisis. In April 2010, ratings agencies reduced Greek bonds to "junk" status, threatening the major European banks that held this debt. The EU and IMF lent Greece the funds to service its debt, but as always given neoliberalism conditional on "structural adjustment"—flattening taxes, reducing public spending, and liquidating government assets. This crisis led to the devaluation of the Euro by about 10 percent in a matter of weeks, and, despite the bailout, Greece remains at risk of default. Ireland has most recently been forced to accept an EU/IMF bailout on condition of structural adjustment, and attention is already turning to Portugal and (given the close ties between their economies) to Spain. If the contagion were to spread to Spain, the Eurozone's fourth-largest economy, it "would make the current crisis seem tame" (Marquand 2010). As a result of the Great Recession, the long-term viability of the Euro itself has been called into question, and should the sovereign credit defaults spread, even the most solvent nations in Europe will find it increasingly difficult to continue to borrow the money necessary to service their debt.

Facing huge budget and trade deficits itself, the ability of the United States to service its external debt may soon be called into question. Neoliberalism led to the export of the United States' manufacturing capacity, and the attempt to crush resistance requires the expenditure of over half of the federal government's discretionary budget on defense of empire, leading to massive deficit spending. Given the status of the U.S. dollar as the world's reserve currency and as the medium of exchange for oil transactions, other nations have been willing to finance these deficits. But central banks and investors worldwide are moving away from the dollar as support for U.S. fiscal and foreign policy erodes. Iran has proposed establishing an oil bourse that would compete with those of the U.S. and England, and in 2006 China opened its own petroleum exchange. Many oil exporters have proposed trading oil in Euros, Rubles, or through a "basket of currencies," and Russia and China have agreed to abandon the dollar for their bilateral trade (Qiang and Xiaokun 2010). The dollar has lost its monopoly status as the medium of international exchange, and will likely become increasingly valueless as a reserve currency. Like the rest of its economy, the opulence of the U.S. military machine is paid for by the rest of the world, but other nations will not be willing to prop up the United States government so that it can project military power indefinitely.

As the sun sets on the American Empire, other powers are on the rise. China has absorbed much of the United States' manufacturing base and is the largest foreign creditor to the federal government, holding over 26 percent of this debt (U.S. Department of the Treasury 2010). Although its export economy cannot remain stable in the absence of global demand, China has thus far been relatively immune from the Great Recession (IMF 2010)—while energy consumption in the U.S., Europe and Japan decreased between 2008 and 2009, China's petroleum consumption increased over 6 percent and its coal consumption increased by nearly 10 percent (BP 2010). Its growing economic power relative to the United States is leading to a flexing of its muscles. Japan's seizure of a Chinese fishing boat led to China blocking exports of rare earth elements—essential to the manufacture of electronics. When China's ally North Korea torpedoed a South Korean navy vessel, killing 46, and bombarded a disputed island, killing four, the U.S. was unable to even slap anyone's wrist. In response to the Federal Reserve Board's generation of $800 billion through "quantitative easing" designed to devalue the dollar, China—and Germany—did not hesitate to point out this currency manipulation as yet another example of U.S. hypocrisy.

Apart from China, a resurgent Russia was able to ignore hypocritical U.S. protestations of its alleged violation of the former Soviet republic of Georgia's sovereignty, continues to leverage Europe's dependence on its natural gas in its ongoing disputes with Belorus and Ukraine, and nearly outbid the U.S. out of a strategic base in Kyrgyzstan. In acquiescence to another emerging power, President Obama has supported India's bid to become a Permanent Member of the U.N. Security Council. In Latin America, once a relatively secure realm of empire, recent elections in Argentina, Bolivia, Brazil, Chile, Ecuador, Nicaragua, El Salvador, and of course Venezuela have been won by candidates who rejected neoliberal free-trade and who promised to use the wealth of their nations to eliminate the poverty imposed by the long history of U.S. intervention. Moreover, without the ability of the U.S. to force nations to the table, regional rivalries have become more intense—Pakistan's role in both Afghani and Indian terrorism becomes increasingly impossible to ignore, and Israel's continuing blockade of Gaza and "settlement" of the West Bank turns ever more brazen.

Despite the threat to capitalism, capitalists have become even more shortsighted and rapacious. As President Obama's former Chief of Staff Raum Emanuel put it, "Never let a serious crisis go to waste." Rather than closing deficits by raising taxes to preserve the consumer demand generated by the public sector, the bankers are imposing on their own people the IMF structural readjustment that before they were only able to impose upon the people of the less-developed countries. In Europe, Greece and Ireland were forced to accede to IMF demands. In the U.S., declining tax revenues have led to cuts in basic services, the devaluation of portfolios has contributed to deeper cuts in higher education, and declining donations to charitable foundations have made it increasingly difficult for them to meet increasing demand. The recent report of the National Commission on Fiscal Responsibility and Reform (2010) promises more of the same. Among its proposals are reducing the number of federal employees by 10 percent, reducing corporate taxes, reducing payments to Medicare, introducing copayments for Veteran's Administration medical care, privatizing public property, cutting funding for education and public broadcasting, and increasing the retirement age. For capital, on the other hand, public austerity has led to private fortune. The bankers and their bonuses were saved, preserving their ability to successfully lobby against meaningful financial reform, and U.S corporate profits have reached record highs (Rampell 2010).

Austerity—whether imposed by overtly political decisions or by what seems the anonymity of the market—has not gone unchallenged. Widespread cuts to social spending led to protests in Greece, a proposal to restrict pension benefits to protests in France, tuition increases to protests throughout Great Britain, and the Irish are now demanding early elections hoping to unseat those responsible for accepting the latest EU/IMF-imposed austerity program (Burns 2010). In the U.S., the most visible "movement" has been the misdirection of anger by the Koch-funded, Murdock-promoted Tea Party, but unions, students and community groups also continue to engage in protest, activism, and mutual assistance. Repeated releases of classified U.S military and State Department documents by the whistleblowers' outlet Wikileaks have contributed to eroding what remains of United States' reputation globally and domestically. And since young adults are often at the vanguard of any movement, the desperation visited upon them by this recession should give capital pause. In the United States, the unemployment rate for people aged 16–24 is about twice that of the general population, and studies demonstrate that entering the workforce during a recession leads to reductions in one's income over a lifetime (Ratner 2009). Despite voting in record numbers to protest the foreign and domestic policies of the Bush Administration in 2008 and tipping the election to Obama, the abstention of disgusted young people led to Republican victories in the mid-term elections of 2010. No attempt has been made to reverse the disasters of U.S. neoliberalism or neoconservativism. "Free trade" is still pursued, and the occupation of Iraq and Afghanistan continue. The surveillance of domestic opponents intensifies and the torture of foreign opponents continues. The architects of the economic crisis remain in the command posts of finance, the Federal Reserve and the U.S. Treasury. Although informed protests against austerity have not yet spread throughout the United States to the extent that they already have in Europe, economic privation amid a crisis of legitimacy remains a recipe for radical social change. The recent emergence, growth and popularity of the Occupy Wall Street movement could be an indication that this change is on the horizon.

Although the U.S. economy resumed modest growth in mid-2009, the economic crisis is far from over. The official unemployment rate in the United States continues to hover near 10 percent, and no one is predicting a return to pre-recession employment levels over the foreseeable future. As a result, consumer confidence remains exceptionally weak. Most important, the fundamentals of the U.S. political economy have not changed. The recession has only exacerbated inequality, "structural readjustment" will only increase the impact of poverty, and most people are being pushed out of the credit market that for a time facilitated this class polarization. In addition, the energy crisis that triggered the recession has and will only continue to grow worse. The rate of production of energy is set to peak—if it has not done so already (Campbell 2004; Heinberg 2003). Most ominous, Saudi Arabia, the world's "swing producer," recorded between 2005 and 2009 a decline in its rate of production of over 12 percent (BP 2010: 8). "The days of inexpensive, convenient, abundant energy sources are quickly drawing to a close ..." (U.S. Army Corp of Engineers 2005: 4), and access to oil is no longer simply a matter of seizing it militarily or through free trade. No matter how supplies are distributed, there is not enough energy to fuel even a stagnant economy indefinitely. Regardless of economic conditions in the U.S., continued growth in the emerging powers will inevitably generate new spikes in oil prices and destructions of demand. A "double-dip" recession seems almost certain, and compelling analyses from a wide range of perspectives should dispel naïve optimism regarding the future stability of the United States, much less its ability to dictate world affairs (Kunstler 2005; Orlov 2008; Osborn 2008). However we might collectively shape the future, U.S. capital will ultimately have no special role in that process.

Conclusion

Made possible by their seizure of the nation's oil wealth, the founding families of U.S. capital rose to a position of global supremacy within a century. For the three decades following World War II, the U.S. dominated the global financial system. Declining oil production, defeat in Vietnam, the challenge of OPEC, and the repression of a domestic dissent that might have revitalized the nation marked the onset of decline. Neoliberalism and neoconservatism constituted attempts to shore up U.S. capitalist hegemony, but both succumbed to domestic and international opposition. The "Great Recession," born of this failure—of inequality, debt, corruption and energy inflation—marks the end of U.S. dominance. Other major world powers are emerging, smaller nations are asserting their independence, and workers globally are increasingly unwilling to accept austerity as defined by the U.S., the EU, the IMF or subservient governments.

There is no basis for the delusion of "American exceptionalism." Domination was instead made possible by quirks of geophysics and geopolitics, and was prolonged only by the failed practices of neoliberalism and neoconservatism. As a result of these last ditch efforts, the United States remained at the head of the table until the end of the twentieth century. But attempting to dictate the affairs of other peoples and other nations, through either trade agreements or at the barrel of a gun, has inevitably led to opposition. The collapse of the global economy has exacerbated class warfare. Capital, at its own peril, is attacking the most fundamental aspects of the social contract, and a growing international movement continues to challenge a disastrous and unsustainable *status quo*. As never before, as a species, we are faced with a choice—save global capitalism, or save our planet's future.

References

Ackerman, Seth. 2000. "Prattle in Seattle: WTO Coverage Misrepresented Issues, Protests." *Extra!* (January/February): 13.

Agence France-Presse. 2007. "Much of US Favors Bush Impeachment: Poll," accessed online at *http://www.afp.com/english/news/stories/070706225930.sv6rw08w.html*.

Bacon, David. 2007. "Iraqi's Oil Should Stay in Public Hands." *Truthout.org*, accessed online at *http://www.truthout.org/docs_2006/071007C.shtml*.

Bagdikian, Ben. 2004. *The Media Monopoly*, Boston: Beacon Press.

Baker, Dean, 2000. "Free Trade Fables: Economic Misinformation in WTO Coverage." *Extra!* (January/February): 18.

Beaumont, Peter. 2008. "Food riots fear after rice price hits a high," *The Observer* (England), April 9: 33.

BP. 2010. "Statistical Review of World Energy," accessed online at *http://www.bp.com*.

Brisard, Jean Charles and Guillame Dasquie. 2002. *Forbidden Truth: U.S.-Taliban Secret Oil Diplomacy and the Failed Hunt for bin Laden*, translated by Lucy Rounds. New York: Thunder's Mouth Press.

Burnham, Gilbert, Riyadh Lafta, Shannon Doocy, and Les Roberts. 2006. "Mortality after the 2003 Invasion of Iraq: A Cross-sectional Cluster Sample Survey." *The Lancet*. 368(9545): 1421–1428.

Burns, John F. 2010. "Thousands in Dublin Protest Irish Austerity Plan." *The New York Times*, November 28: A13.

Business Cycle Dating Committee (2008) "Determination of the December 2007 peak in Economic Activity." National Bureau of Economic Research , accessed online at http://www.nber.org/cycles/dec2008.html.

Campbell, Colin. 2004. *The Coming Oil Crisis*. Brentwood, UK: Multi-Science Publishing Company, Ltd.

Chomsky, Naom. 2003. *Hegemony or Survival: The Imperialist Strategy of the United States*. New York: Metropolitan Books.

Cockburn, Patrick. 2007. "UN warns of five million Iraqi refugees." *The Independent*, (July 17), accessed online at *http://news.independent.co.uk/world/middle_east/article2640418.ece*.

Dombey, Daniel and Stanley Pignal. 2007. "Europeans see US as threat to peace." *The Financial Times*, July 1, accessed online at *http://www.ft.com/cms/s/70046760-27f0-11dc-80da-000b5df10621.html*.

Engdahl, F. William. 2004. *A Century of War: Anglo-American Oil Politics and the New World Order* London: Pluto Press.

Foster, John Bellamy. 2006. "The Household Debt Bubble." *Monthly Review*, 58(1): 1–11.

Heinberg, Richard. 2003. *The Party's Over: Oil, War, and the Fate of Industrial Societies*, Gabriola Island, British Columbia: New Societies Publishers.

International Monetary Fund. 2010. *World Economic Outlook: Rebalancing Growth.* The Washington, D.C.: International Monetary Fund.

Klare, Michael T. 2001. *Resource Wars: The New Landscape of Global Conflict.* New York: Henry Holt and Company.

Kunsler, James Howard. 2005. *The Long Emergency: Surviving the Converging Catastrophes of the Twenty-First Century.* New York: Atlantic Monthly Press.

Marquand, Robert. 2010. "Crisis in Ireland tests Eurozone Vision of Common Currency, Common Interests." *The Christian Science Monitor*, November 23: 1.

National Commission on Fiscal Responsibility and Reform. 2010. *Draft of CoChairs' Proposal.* accessed online at *http://www.fiscalcommission.gov/ sites/fiscalcommission.gov/files/documents/Illustrative_List_11.10.2010.pdf.*

Orlov, Dmitry. 2008. *Reinventing Collapse: The Soviet Example and American Prospects.* Gabriola Island, British Columbia: New Society Publishers.

Osborn, Andrew. 2008. "As if things weren't bad enough, Russian professor predicts end of U.S.: In Moscow, Igor Panarin's Forcasts are All the Rage; America 'Disintegrates' in 2010." *The Wall Street Journal,* December 29: A1.

Parenti, Christian. 2004. *The Freedom: Shadows and Hallucinations in Occupied Iraq.* New York: The New Press.

Petras, James. 2009. *Global Depression and Regional Wars.* Atlanta, GA: Clarity Press.

Qiang, Su and Li Xiaokun. 2010. "China, Russia quit dollar." *China Daily*, November 24, accessed online at http://www.chinadaily.com.cn/ china/2010-11/24/content_11599087.htm.

Rampell, Catherine. 2010. "3rd Quarter was Record for Profits in U.S. Firms." *The New York Times*, November 23: B2.

Rampton, Sheldon and John Stauber. 2003. *Weapons of Mass Deception: The Uses of Propaganda in Bush's War on Iraq.* New York: Tarcher/Penguin.

Ratner, Lizzy. 2009. "Generation Recession: young people have lost 2.5 million jobs to the crisis, making them the hardest-hit age group." *The Nation,* November 23: 23–26.

Scher, Abby. 2001. "The Crackdown on Dissent." *The Nation*, February 5: 23–24.

Seldes, George. 1943. *Facts and Fascism.* New York: In Fact, Inc.

Taibbi, Matt. 2009. "The Big Takeover." *Rolling Stone*, March 11: 66–97.

Trofimov, Yaroslav and Ian Johnson. 2001. "G-8 Protesters in Italy Describe Police Attack on Group in a School: In Interviews, They Say They Were Beaten, Deprived of Rights in Detention." *The Wall Street Journal*, August 6: A1, A6.

United States Army Corp of Engineers. 2005. "Energy Trends and Implications for U.S. Army Installations," accessed online at *www.peakoil.net/Articles2005/ Westervelt_ EnergyTrends__TN.pdf.*

U.S. Census Bureau. 2010. *Statistical Abstract of the United States*, 129th edition, accessed online at *http://www.census.gov/statab/www/*.

U.S. Department of the Treasury. 2010. "Major Foreign Holders of Treasury Securities," accessed online at *http://www.ustreas.gov/tic/mfh.txt*.

Weissman, Robert. 1999. "Welcome to Seattle: Ministerial Meeting Debates the World Trade Organization's Agenda for the 21st Century." *Multinational Monitor*, October/November: 9–13.

Wolff, Richard D. 2009. "Capitalism Hits the Fan." In *The Economic Crisis Reader*, ed. Gerald Friedman, Fred Moseley, Chris Sturr, et al. Boston, MA: Dollars and Sense.

Yeoman, Matthew. 2004. *Oil: A Concise Guide to the Most Important Product on Earth.* New York: The New Press.

Zachary, G. Pascal. 2000. "The New Imperialism: A Year After the 'Battle in Seattle,' the Rich are Embracing their Critics. Watch Out." *In These Times*, December 25: 30.

Chapter 9

The Collapse of Global Capitalism and the Movement Toward Socialism in the Twenty-first Century: New Beginnings

Walda Katz-Fishman and Jerome Scott

The current global economic crisis is a crisis of the entire global capitalist system, and thus it affects all of the system's components and institutions—i.e., capital, middle class, working class, and poor people in the United States and around the world, markets, governments, social institutions, civil society and political organizations, and the planet. Systemic crisis exacerbates and exposes the ever starker contradictions of society—of great abundance on a global scale of all the things people require, but of great want, deprivation, exploitation and oppression. Vanishing jobs, plummeting wages, soaring poverty, a broken social contract and neoliberal policies, growing militarism and police repression are a daily reality for U.S. workers and the vast majority of the world's peoples. Because of the historic legacy of white supremacy, black and indigenous peoples and immigrant communities are disproportionately affected by these multiple crises. In addition, patriarchy results in working class women and children being among the most impoverished and oppressed. At the same time wealth and power are being concentrated among an ever smaller class of global capitalists, who are using global institutions and their national governments to bailout capital's global financial institutions and corporations and to wage war to advance the latter's class interests (Amin 2003, Berberoglu 2009, Magdoff and Yates 2009).

In 2011, four years into the deepest structural crisis of capitalism the world has ever experienced, the question is how to secure the necessities of life for all humanity, protect the earth, and win the peace. Social movements and revolutionaries are in motion—responding to the economic crisis and "jobless recovery," massive social and ecological destruction, ongoing war and repression, and growing fascism on the part of capital and the state. These realities present new openings for movement organizing, analyzing, visioning, and strategizing (Gonzales and Katz-Fishman 2010, Harvey 2010a). Twenty-first century global capitalism requires a coordinated global movement from the bottom-up with working class leadership. As the mass movement develops and many forces are coming into play, the path forward leads toward socialism (Correa Leite 2005, Peery 2002, Santos 2006).

In the three sections of the chapter that follows we discuss: (1) What the systemic crisis of global capitalism means for capital, particularly finance capital, and its efforts to restructure the economy and the state in the interests of the capitalist class; (2) What the crisis means for labor—and the diversity of the working class—in relation to daily survival and struggle; (3) How the economic crisis informs the revolutionary process, consciousness, and political movement from below in the strategic direction toward socialism.

The Collapse of Global Capitalism: Systemic Economic Crisis

The twenty-first century "Great Recession" is vastly different from the Great Depression of the 1930s. Then the war economy and the enormous extension of credit drove the expansion of the capitalist market that brought the United States and the world out of the economic crisis and positioned the United States for global hegemony following World War II. In contrast, today's economic crisis is systemic and one of a dying capitalist global economy that has nowhere else to expand and is producing with less and less labor power—rupturing the essential social relation of production between capital and labor that holds the system together (Ford 2009, Gonzales and Katz-Fishman 2010, Robinson 2004).

Much has been written about the "Great Recession" and its continuing effects on global financial and industrial corporations, national governments and global political processes, working and poor people, and global struggles. It is critical to understand that today's struggles and movement toward a fundamentally new society are grounded in new objective conditions of global capitalism in the aftermath of the collapse of finance capital in 2007–2009 and beyond (Foster and Magdoff 2009). Wall Street came away from the financial meltdown with billions and even trillions of U.S. taxpayer dollars and renewed profitability, while official unemployment for U.S. workers remained near 10 percent at the beginning of 2011, millions lost their homes to foreclosure joining the ranks of the homeless, and millions more were hungry, and still without health care (Yang et al. 2010; Sklar 2010). This expresses the intensifying antagonism between the interests of the capitalist class and the needs and interests of the working class.

What stands between billions of working people worldwide and their basic needs—food, water, housing, education, health care, transportation, communication, etc.—and protection of the earth is global capitalism, the drive for maximum profit, and the commodification of virtually everything and of life itself for circulation in the market. The state system and global political forces are clearly aligned with capital to enforce and reproduce the global system of capitalist private property and accumulation, even as this is increasingly problematic for capital (Gonzales and Katz-Fishman 2010; Harvey 2010b; Katz-Fishman and Scott 2009).

The deep structural crisis is situated within the current stage of capitalism marked by extensive application of technology—information age and electronics—

and globalization. It is based in the closing decades of the twentieth century, beginning in the 1970s, with the hegemonic rise of the neoliberal policy agenda of the state and global financial institutions—the privatization, deregulation, downsizing, financialization and speculation, repression and militarism—resulting in a transnational world economy transformed into a truly global economy with globalized circuits of production, circulation, accumulation, labor markets, and crisis (Davis et al. 1997; Ford 2009; Robinson 2004).

By the 1980s and 1990s neoliberalism was well underway, creating the conditions for social disruption throughout the world, including the United States. The processes of neoliberal capitalist globalization and the widespread application of electronic-based technology—computers, robots, automation—to production, distribution, communication, and war resulted in massive job loss to both outsourcing and to technological redundancy. Electronic technology is labor-replacing, unlike the machine-based technology of the industrial era that was labor-enhancing. Huge gains in productivity and efficiency in all sectors of the economy and society from manufacturing to banking, to services were matched by loss of wages, loss of jobs, and increasing part-time and contingent work (Davis et al. 1997, Berberoglu 2002; Peery 2002; Halley 2010; Zakaria 2010). These new economic realities set the basis for the consolidation of the neoliberal policy agenda at the level of the nation-state, and at the global level of financial and political institutions and policies. The neoliberal regime eliminated social programs and imposed austerity measures throughout the developing world that eventually came to the United States, bringing with it new forms of social and political struggle and social movement organizing (Katz-Fishman and Scott 2009).

Thus, the technological revolution in the economic base of society gave rise to a qualitatively new environment within which capital, labor, and the system of global capitalism operate. The movement of capital from the "real economy" to the "speculative economy" is fueled by the drive for maximum profit (Foster and Magdoff 2009). The revolution in technology makes it impossible to realize maximum profit in the "real economy" since goods and services are produced with less and less labor, and contain less value. This process forces capital to financialization and speculation as the source of investment and profit (Gonzales and Katz-Fishman 2010; Harvey 2010a).

A succession of bubbles bursting—from the savings and loans crisis, to the dot.com crisis, to the mortgage crisis—set the stage for the current financial crisis. The meltdown of Wall Street and global corporations beginning in the closing months of 2007 continuing throughout 2008 and into 2009 was a long time in coming (Foster and Magdoff 2009). The global financial and economic crisis it sparked resulted, by mid-2009, in estimated losses of $55 trillion, according to the International Monetary Fund (IMF). Some projections suggest losses may rise to as high as $400 trillion (Harvey 2010b: 7).

The bailout from the U.S. government was almost immediate—negotiated by Treasury Secretary Hank Paulson at the end of the Bush Administration and continued by the Obama Administration's Treasury Secretary Tim Geithner. The

Troubled Asset Relief Program (TARP) for $700 billion was quickly followed by the stimulus package of roughly the same amount (Sklar 2010). Insurance giant American International Group (AIG) alone came in for $182 billion from the federal government (*The Washington Post* 2010b:A8). Recently it has been revealed that the Federal Reserve Board initiated an aid program for corporations and banks worldwide totaling $3.3 trillion (Yang at al. 2010:A17). By early 2009 estimates were that the U.S. government—the Treasury Department and the Federal Reserve Board—had put out $14 trillion for the bailout, and was guaranteeing over $200 trillion in assets (Ritholtz and Task 2009: 3; Harvey 2010b: 7). Meanwhile, with massive unemployment continuing, U.S. businesses were sitting on a record $2 trillion in cash reserves as 2010 came to a close (Sklar 2010).

Wall Street and the U.S. government are inextricably interconnected through personnel and policies. This is clear when a succession of Treasury Secretaries—from Robert Rubin during the Clinton years to Hank Paulson under Bush to Tim Geithner in the Obama Administration—come to government from Wall Street and often return there after their term in government office. And while the U.S. government is so generous in its bailout of Wall Street, middle income working people are losing their homes, their jobs, their food, and health care with little real relief. The reorganization of the economy and the government in the interests of the capitalist class, and especially global finance capital, makes the outlines of the developing fascist state in the United States more visible (Gonzales and Katz-Fishman 2010).

These processes of economic and political *systemic* crisis polarize and politicize society along class lines, and raise the stakes for working class leadership and open up new political directions. The economic crisis has ruptured the historic relationship between capital and labor at the very core of the global capitalist system. This constitutes an objective antagonism not resolvable within the existing system (Katz-Fishman and Scott 2009).

The capitalist class is moving to reorganize the state along fascist lines that entails an attack on the working class. This fascist movement may appear as a collection of Tea Party activists, racists, religious extremists, and reactionaries, but at its core are sophisticated political actors with a vision of a new social and economic order—one that protects private property and the wealth of capital and global corporations at the expense of the rest of society, especially the working class. The opposite pole is a coordinated social movement of all the exploited and oppressed with a vision of a cooperative, egalitarian, and peaceful society (Gonzales and Katz-Fishman 2010).

The Global Capitalist Crisis and the Working Class

Today's economic crisis is a cyclical crisis of overproduction and underconsumption within the structural crisis of global capitalism. But it is more than that. It marks a new round of struggle in this historic moment between capital seeking to expand markets and profit and working people seeking to secure the basic necessaries of life. The capitalists and their media trumpet the "new age of austerity" and tell the popular classes to get used to the "new normal" (Magdoff and Yates 2009; Sklar 2010).

The objective realities of capitalism today mean there is no recovery and there will be no recovery for working and poor people (Harvey 2010b). Crisis is a daily experience for the working class and is creating the political environment for new beginnings along the socialist path. New politics and policies in response to the new economic conditions are in place and being expanded all the time. Government attacks on education, health care, welfare, unions, and civil liberties demonstrate that the ruling class in the United States has made a calculated decision. It will not educate and care for a class of workers it no longer needs in the production process—a class of workers who can no longer expand its wealth (Berberoglu 2009; Peery 2002)

A fundamental problem is that a huge swath of the world's workers doesn't have the money to go into the market to purchase what they need to satisfy their basic human needs and realize their collective human rights. Three billion people live on less than US$2 a day (Amin 2003). Millions more working people, devastated by the global economic crisis, are caught up in the downward spiral of wages, are increasingly unemployed and underemployed, and are rendered redundant in the manufacturing and service sectors by the widespread use of electronic based technology—automation and robotics—that is labor replacing. This huge and growing section of humanity lacks the wages and income to buy what they need and often lacks access to credit or has maxed out on credit as an option (Davis et al. 1997; Robinson 2004).

While markets are not working for the masses of humanity, they are also not working for the capitalists and for the system as a whole—competition for markets is intense and market expansion to absorb all that is being produced cannot be sustained. This is because working people—as consumers—are three-quarters of the market; and when they are out of money and out of credit, they cannot buy and consume all the goods and services the corporations are trying to sell. The abundance produced with less and less labor cannot be sold in the market to workers who are losing their jobs and their wages (Ford 2009; Zakaria 2010).

Millions of apartments, condominiums, and houses sit vacant, while millions of people around the world are homeless, living on the streets, in slums and shacks. In the United States, with the subprime mortgage bubble burst, two million families lost their homes to foreclosure by early 2008. Another five million homes went into foreclosure with millions more vulnerable and in some stage of delinquency by 2010 (Ritholtz 2010). Thus, not surprisingly, consumer bankruptcies reached a high of 1.5 million in 2010—up 9 percent over 2009 (*The Washington Post* 2011: A9).

Tons of food in grocery stores and restaurants rot and are thrown away daily, while millions of children and families go hungry. World hunger soared to one billion in 2009 (International Food Policy Research Institute 2010).

Hunger in the United States grew to 50 million—16.6 percent—in 2009, up from 36 million in December 2007, when the "Great Recession" began. One in four children experienced hunger, as did 25 percent of black households, and 27 percent of Latino households (Feeding America 2010). Another essential of life—water—has been privatized and poisoned around the globe, and basic sewage and sanitation were beyond the grasp of 1.7 billion people worldwide in 2009 (Food and Water Watch 2010). From Cochabamba to Detroit water wars have begun over access to safe and affordable water (Barlow 2007; Miller and Alexander 2010). And so it goes.

The global economic crisis has wreaked havoc with the lives of people especially in the developing world, but in the developed world as well. Even in the United States, one of the wealthiest and most powerful nations in the world, the latest data released by the U.S. Census Bureau (2010) in September 2010 documents the disastrous effects of the crisis for the American people. Poverty rose from 12.5 percent in 2007 to 14.3 percent in 2009 overall. Multiple oppressions—based on class, gender, nationality, and race—have been central to the capitalist system. And poverty is a case in point, with over 25 percent of Blacks and Latinos living in poverty. This represents 43.6 million people living at or below the poverty line—a meager $21,954 for a family of four. Among youth, one in five children younger than 18 years of age must endure the ravages of poverty (U.S. Census Bureau 2010).

Because the United States lacks a national health care system, millions lack access to health care. The uninsured increased in 2009 to 16.7 percent or 50.7 million Americans with no health insurance, including 7.5 million children under 18 (U.S. Census Bureau 2010). Student struggles have broken out in the United States and across the globe over access to higher education. In the United States in June 2010, debt from financial aid to cover the soaring costs of college exceeded, for the first time on record, all credit card debt. At the end of 2010 it reached $879 billion (FinAid 2010).

Perhaps even more revealing is the "de-facto" unemployment rate calculated by the Center for Working-Class Studies at Youngstown State University (2010). They reported in September 2010 the "real" unemployment rate in the United States as 30.5 percent, up from 20 percent in December 2007. This included 14.9 million officially unemployed—9.6 percent; another 12 million underemployed, discouraged and marginally attached—for 8 percent; and 12.8 percent representing people on disability, receiving government support, in prison or jail, and in the military. By November 2010, official unemployment rose to 9.8 percent (U.S. Bureau of Labor Statistics 2010).

Today the new technology that is so very productive and requires so little labor is what makes the abundance of everything humanity needs possible. Most importantly the application of this technology is also what undermines market processes of exchange. It forms the very basis of the antagonism that the working class is facing in being permanently replaced by automation and robotics, while the wages of those still employed are plummeting, so they cannot afford to buy the very things they have produced or used to produce. Larger and larger sections of humanity are becoming dispossessed of what they once had, excluded from the markets, in debt, in poverty, and in need (Gonzales and Katz-Fishman 2010).

Political Struggle and Polarization: The Movement Toward Socialism

This raises the questions that activists, revolutionaries, and social movements around the world are grappling with: What is the vision of another world and another economy and society? What is the alternative to markets? Who are the forces that can bring about this much needed change?

For decades, and indeed for a century, revolutionaries have been struggling with the interrelationship between reform work in the mass movement and revolutionary work on the path toward socialism and communism. Today working class organizers and activists are again struggling with this issue. But they are doing so under very different objective economic conditions that offer new openings for development of a class conscious political force in the United States and globally (Berberoglu 2009; Harvey 2010b). History moves forward, not backward—there is no going back to the reform period of the welfare state; there is no recovery from the structural crisis of capitalism for the working class.

At the same time there are real lessons to be learned. The daily struggle for the necessities of life—housing, health care, food and water, education, energy and transportation, jobs and living wages—becomes a school for learning how capitalism, the state, and ideology move to crush working and poor people of all races and nationalities, across gender and sexuality, and intensify white supremacist inequality and oppression. And how, if we stay on course in holding to our demands for the satisfaction of our basic needs, we will come into direct confrontation with the state over whose class interests it serves (Katz-Fishman and Scott 2009).

The recent round of government assault on movement activists began on September 24, 2010—using new laws against so-called "terror" and vast networks of government organizations at all levels put in place after 9–11 (*The Washington Post* 2010a). The FBI raided the homes of fourteen activists in peace, labor, and solidarity struggles in Chicago, Minneapolis, and Michigan—seizing their computers and personal belongings, and serving them with Grand Jury subpoenas. Collectively they refused to participate in the Grand Jury's secret proceedings. In December, the FBI subpoenaed nine more activists to appear before the Grand Jury. The activists remained strong in their refusal to cooperate; and the movement has rallied in support and in defense of free speech, the right to organize, the right to oppose war and occupation (Committee to Stop FBI Repression 2010).

The government's expanding reach of intimidation and repression is intended for movement activists and organizers who envision and struggle for a cooperative society where human needs are satisfied. Not only the capitalist market, but also the capitalist state stands between humanity and our well being, peace, and prosperity.

It is a core task of revolutionaries from deep within the mass movement to use history and experience to raise class consciousness among the millions in motion. And that is happening. This is an essential step in the revolutionary process. It is from out of this struggle that political clarity about the systemic logic of capitalism is revealed, that political polarization intensifies, and *the formation of an independent working class political force takes shape.* The challenge is how to keep people engaged and help develop the necessary class-consciousness for the long haul in what still remains a "reform" period. Economic crisis and polarization, social destruction, massive migration flows, and ecological devastation are giving rise to a new politic—a politic that sees the path toward socialism as an objective necessity if humanity and the planet are to survive, not simply as a good and moral idea (Gonzales and Katz-Fishman 2010; Peery 2002).

Historical Context and New Beginnings

Globalization, the technological revolution, and economic crisis have gripped the world. History has entered a tumultuous period. The fall of the Berlin Wall and collapse of the Soviet Union left the socialist bloc and the political left of the twentieth century needing to regroup and assess their strategic direction. In the face of the new economic realities, organized labor is having to rethink its position (Correa Leite 2005; Harvey 2010b; Robinson 2004; Santos 2006). The decline of U.S. hegemony is much discussed and, regardless of one's position on this question, the reality of the emerging BRIC economies—Brazil, Russia, India, and China—is a power to be reckoned with.

The coming together of these forces has unleashed new actors and opened up new spaces. Social organizations and social movements grounded in the working class, and reflecting the broad diversity of the working class, have been and continue to organize and mobilize at the grassroots and community level around many fronts of struggle—from conditions for day laborers, to violence against women, to climate justice (Karides and Katz-Fishman et al. 2010, Smith and Karides et al. 2008). Social movement actors and intellectuals participating in and writing about this period argue that the "spirit of Porto Alegre" and the World Social Forum (WSF) expresses a new historic moment of social struggle and movement convergence—an alter-globalization from below—in opposition to the "the spirit of Davos" and the World Economic Forum (WEF)—and countering the crises of capitalist globalization and war (Correa Leite 2005; Katz-Fishman and Scott 2009; Santos 2006; Wallerstein 2010).

A key marker for the emergence of this moment is the Zapatista rebellion in Chiapas, Mexico which arose against implementation of the North American Free Trade Agreement (NAFTA) on January 1, 1994. The Zapatistas, with the First Intercontinental *Encuentro*—encounter—in 1996, inspired a movement "For Humanity and Against Neoliberalism." The Battle in Seattle in 1999 was a turning point that demonstrated the power and resilience of the growing global social justice movement in blocking a new round of World Trade Organization

(WTO) policies adversely affecting conditions of work, trade, investment, and environment within global capitalism. Various forces came together—organized labor, environmental justice and grassroots organizations, students and youth, NGOs, and revolutionaries—to create a counter-hegemonic movement dynamic for the twenty-first century that advocated the interests of workers against the interests of global capital and its current neoliberal regime (Karides and Katz-Fishman et al. 2010; Santos 2006).

In the new millennium various social movements across the world coalesced. The World Social Forum (WSF) convened in January 2001 in Porto Alegre, Brazil at the same time that the World Economic Forum (WEF) met in Davos, Switzerland to chart neoliberal global capitalism's path. Social movements gathered under the slogan "Another World is Possible" to vision the other world they are struggling to create in response to the assertion "There is No Alternative" (TINA) put forth by leading neoliberal architect, British Prime Minister Margaret Thatcher. The WSF, continuing in the spirit of the Zapatistas and Seattle, was initially located in Latin America where new socialist-leaning forces were reorganizing and in motion—including Lula in Brazil, Hugo Chavez in Venezuela, Evo Morales in Bolivia, and Rafael Correa in Ecuador, and the formation of ALBA (the Bolivarian Alternative) (Correa Leite 2005; Harvey 2010b; Santos 2006; Wallerstein 2010).

The first WSF in 2001 in Porto Alegre brought together 15,000 movement activists and organizers along the political spectrum from progressive to revolutionary and generated excitement and energy for an emerging socialist movement in the twenty-first century. The WSF gathered annually in Brazil until 2003, growing in size, diversity, and consciousness. In 2004 it moved to India and attracted 125,000 participants, the largest convergence. From 2004 onward the forum convened alternately in Asia, Africa, and Latin America. The WSF process encompasses local, national, regional, and continental social forums that are locally grounded, nationally organized, and globally interconnected. Thus, the WSF process expresses the growing bottom-up movement for social justice throughout the world (Correa Leite 2005; Mertes 2004; www.worldsocialforum.org).

Inside the United States, the U.S. Social Forum, convening for the first time in 2007, was a marker for U.S. social struggles and advancing an anti-capitalist mass movement connecting to global movements. It converged in Atlanta, Georgia, 15,000 strong and expressed the developing capacity and consciousness of a growing anti-hegemonic movement within the belly of the beast of the U.S. Empire. The forum pushed forward a collective leadership based on common political work that was bottom-up, grassroots, racially and gender diverse, and broadly based in the working class (Karides and Katz-Fishman et al. 2010; Smith and Karides 2008; www.ussf2010.org).

The U.S. Social Forum 2010 followed the logic of the anti-capitalist struggle—going from the U.S. South to Detroit, Michigan, the former automobile capital of the world that became the epicenter of the capitalist crisis. Twenty thousand organizers and participants representing over 2,000 organizations gathered in

Detroit at the USSF 2 in June 2010. The world was slipping into chaos and the effects of the Great Recession were intensifying—the global economy in turmoil, society falling apart, the environment and nature being privatized and destroyed, oppressed communities and peoples criminalized and under siege (www.ussf2010. org). Pushed forward by the systemic crisis, working people were resilient and social movements advanced.

Social forum leadership and participation continued to reflect the rich diversity of the working class across race, nationality, gender, sexuality, religion, age, and ability. Organized labor, e.g., the AFL-CIO, sat at the National Planning Committee (NPC) planning table in 2007, but was more engaged in 2010. Being in Detroit and the depth of the auto crisis generated significant United Auto Worker (UAW) participation, including among UAW retirees. Poor peoples' organizations—Poor Peoples Economic Human Rights Campaign (PPEHRC) and Michigan Welfare Rights Organization (MWRO)—stepped up their involvement as members of the NPC and MWRO as one of the Detroit anchor organizations. They were central to forming and leading the USSF Poverty Working Group, along with the Women's Economic Agenda Project (WEAP) (www.ussf2010.org; www.weap. org). Working class youth organized a youth space and the 2010 USSF Youth Social Forum. Revolutionaries from all tendencies—socialists, communists, anarchists—were there.

The USSF 2 brought together all the frontline struggles—from workers struggles to Indigenous sovereignty, from transformative justice and healing to environmental justice, from black liberation to poor peoples' economic human rights, from economic solidarity to anti-war movement and peace, from struggles for quality and liberatory public education to the health care movement for universal single payer, from immigrant rights to gender justice, from the right to housing and to the land to youth power (Guilloud 2010; www.ussf2010.org). The revolutionary potential of these very different struggles is the fact that what undergirds them all is systemic exploitation, oppression, and dispossession. The crisis of the system in its many forms is moving people to resist.

From the opening march to the National Peoples Movement Assembly (NPMA), movement organizers shared history, struggles, and culture, and grappled with the political path forward in over 1,000 workshops and fifty Peoples' Movement Assemblies (PMA). The PMAs represented collaboration and coordination among movement organizations and forces within the United States and globally. The forces of struggle that converged in the PMAs expressed the social responses to the multiple crises and embodied, in part, a left transformative project and socialist path (Katz-Fishman and Scott 2008; Santos 2006; Smith and Karides 2008).

The social actions undertaken at the many fronts of struggle that were reflected in the social forum are connected to the developing mass movement in the United States and to global struggles, forums, and movements. Movement organizations and activists affiliated with the forum have been part of the demonstrations against the banks, financial institutions, and government bailout policies sweeping the globe. Strikes have erupted around the world and in cities across Europe—from Greece to

France to England, as well as other regions to protest the increasingly intolerable conditions of the working class because of the financial crises and collapse. The uprisings in Tunisia, Egypt, Yemen, Bahrain, and elsewhere in the Middle East have inspired working people across the world to rise up against the forces of global capitalism and its local puppet regimes that collaborate with imperialism.

In the United States social movements demanding that the government "bail out the people, not the banks" were heard in the streets of Chicago, Washington, D.C., Atlanta, San Francisco, and on Wall Street itself (Sklar 2010). In the Occupy Wall Street movement that emerged in late 2011 workers and their unions, allied with other popular sectors of society including students, activists, and public employees, took to the streets in the tens of thousands and stormed state capitols in Wisconsin and other states across the United States to let their voices be heard. All of these are important actions in the movement toward socialism.

The Movement Toward Socialism

The financial collapse and "Great Recession," the irresolvable crises in people's lives are opening up new beginnings. The U.S. Social Forum 2010 made some history. The question many of the movement organizers and participants came with is: "Where is the U.S. movement in terms of its consciousness of systemic causes, its vision of alternatives and the future, and its articulation of a political strategy to realize a transformative and liberatory vision?"

The National Peoples Movement Assembly Preamble articulates that the demands of the social struggles are for basic needs to be met, the planet to be protected, self-determination and the cessation of all oppressions and wars against the world's peoples. Movement activists will build power through participation in popular and political education, sustained movement organization, infrastructure, and capacity, and through collective action. The motion and consciousness of the USSF 2 suggests that the movement is conscious of the global capitalist system as the cause of today's social, economic, political, and environmental crises. At the same time the growing movement is challenged to formulate a concrete vision of the world without capitalism, to declare its political independence from the ruling class, and to plan a winning strategy (http://pma2010.org/national-pma).

The day to day reform struggle is the school where revolutionaries connect theory and practice, consciousness and vision. It is where the movement develops strategic direction toward revolution in opposition to the harsh realities of state repression and policies, and the economic exploitation and poverty of the working class. Within the social forum and the Occupy Wall Street movement the task is to consolidate and coordinate across fronts of struggle. This will require building to a critical mass of people to have the political education and discussions necessary, and point the way forward along the strategic line of march. The social forum process in the United States became and continues to be a critical strategic tool for educating and coordinating a twenty-first century transformative movement from below. Movement builders and revolutionaries must seize the opportunity to deepen consciousness and vision, convergence and capacity, and strategy (Blau and Karides 2009, Karides and Katz-Fishman et al. 2010).

The social forum and the many fronts of struggle that converged on Wall Street and elsewhere express and are interconnected with the movement in society that is in opposition to the capitalist crisis and is part of the developing anti-systemic movement toward socialism in the United States and the world. The movement has to confront the enduring legacy of white supremacy that remains a block to keeping the struggle on track and to realizing working class unity. So the movement toward socialism must be not only anti-capitalist, but also anti-white supremacist and anti-patriarchy. All the various currents of struggle point in the same direction— the need for *independent working class politics* (Katz-Fishman and Scott 2009). History is on the side of the exploited, the oppressed, the impoverished, and the dispossessed.

The solution for the vast majority of humanity is the elimination of capitalist markets and profit; the distribution of goods and services on the basis of human need rather than ability to pay; and protection of the earth for future generations. The social forces and movements that can bring about this transformation come from the bottom up and are being pushed forward by the objective conditions— the social and ecological destruction and polarization of wealth and poverty in villages, communities, towns, and cities across the globe (Gonzales and Katz-Fishman 2010, Harvey 2010b, Karides and Katz-Fishman et al. 2010).

This socialist alternative and vision of a cooperative, egalitarian, and collectively organized society is possible given the realities of today's economy, and is grounded in the social struggles of U.S. and global movements converging and strategizing in many spaces and contexts. A future without global capitalism is a historical necessity. The struggle between the forces promoting capitalist globalization from above and the forces of alter-globalization from below—the popular movements of the world's working classes in all their diversity—has been joined in the twenty-first century.

References

Amin, Samir. 2003. *Obsolescent Capitalism: Contemporary Politics and Global Disorder*. New York: Zed Books.

Barlow, Maude. 2007. *Blue Covenant: The Global Water Crisis and the Coming Battle for the Right to Water*. New York: The New Press.

Berberboglu, Berch. ed. 2002. *Labor and Capital in the Age of Globalization*. Lanham, MD: Rowman and Littlefield.

——. 2009. *Class and Class Conflict in the Age of Globalization*. Lanham, MD: Lexington Books.

Blau, Judith and Marina Karides, eds. 2009. *The World and U.S. Social Forums*. Lanham, MD: Rowman & Littlefield Publishers, Inc.

Center for Working-Class Studies at Youngstown State University. September 10, 2010. "De-facto Unemployment Rate." http://cwcs.ysu.edu/resources/cwcsprojects/defacto.

Committee to Stop FBI Repression. 2010. "Palestine Solidarity Group Chicago Condemns New Subpoenas Issued to Palestine Solidarity Activists." December 20, 2010. (http://www.stopfbi.net/2010/12/20/palestine-solidarity-group-chicago-condemns-new-subpoenas-issued-palestine-solidarity-act).

Correa Leite, Jose. 2005. *The World Social Forum: Strategies of Resistance.* Chicago: Haymarket Books.

Davis, Jim, Thomas Hirschl and Michael Stack, eds 1997. *Cutting Edge: Technology, Information, Capitalism and Social Revolution.* New York: Verso.

Economic Policy Institute. 2010. Economic Policy Institute News. February 1, 2010 (www.epi.org).

Ford, Martin. 2009. *The Lights in the Tunnel: Automation, Accelerating Technology and the Economy of the Future.* United States: Acculant Publishing.

Foster, John Bellamy and Fred Magdoff. 2009. *The Great Financial Crisis: Causes and Consequences.* New York: Monthly Review Press.

Gonzales, Beth and Walda Katz-Fishman. 2010. "New openings for movement and consciousness in the U.S." *Interface: a journal for and about social movements* 2(1): 232–242 (May 2010). (http://groups.google.com/group/interface-articles/web/3GonzalesKatz-Fishman.pdf).

Guilloud, Stephanie. 2010. "US Social Forum II." *As the South Goes* 18(2): 8–9 (Fall). (www.projectsouth.org).

Halley. Drew. 2010. "A Robot Stole My Job: Automation in the Recession." *Singularity Hub.* (http://singularityhub.com/2010/12/15/a-robot-stole-my-job-automation-in-the-recession/).

Harvey, David. 2010a. *The Enigma of Capital and the Crises of Capitalism.* New York: Oxford University Press.

Harvey, David. 2010b. "Organizing for the Anti-capitalist Transition." *Radical Perspectives on the Crisis.* August 30, 2010.

International Food Policy Research Institute. 2010. "2010 Global Hunger Index." December 30, 2010 (http://www.ifpri.org/publication/2010-global-hunger-index).

Karides, Marina, Walda Katz-Fishman, Rose Brewer, Alice Lovelace and Jerome Scott, eds. 2010. *The United States Social Forum: Perspectives of a Movement.* Chicago: ChangeMaker Publications.

Katz-Fishman, Walda and Jerome Scott. 2009. "Another United States is Happening: Building Today's Movement from the Bottom-up – The United States Social Forum and Beyond." pp.57–70 in *The World and U.S. Social Forums* edited by J. Blau and M. Karides. Lanham, MD: Rowman & Littlefield Publishers, Inc.

Magdoff, Fred and Michael D. Yates. 2009. *The ABCs of the Economic Crisis: What Working People Need to Know.* New York: Monthly Review Press.

Mertes, Theodore. ed. 2004. *A Movement of Movements: Is Another World Really Possible?* New York: Verso.

Miller, Steve and Danny Alexander. 2010. *Water Wars – Coming Soon to Your Town*. Chicago: League of Revolutionaries for a New America.

Parker, Robert E. 2002. "The Global Economy and Changes in the Nature of Contingent Work." pp. 107–123 in *Labor and Capital in the Age of Globalization,* edited by Berch Berberoglu. Lanham, MD: Rowman and Littlefield.

Peery, Nelson. 2002. *The Future Is Up To Us: A Revolutionary Talking Politics With the American People*. Chicago: Speakers for a New America.

Ritholtz, Barry and Aaron Task. 2009. *Bailout Nation: How Greed and Easy Money Corrupted Wall Street and Shook the World Economy*. Hoboken, NJ: John Wiley & Sons, Inc.

Ritholtz, Barry. 2010. "Coming Soon: 5 Million More Foreclosures." *Roubini Global Economics.* February 16, 2010. (http://www.roubini.com/us-monitor/258411/coming_soon_5_million_more_foreclosures).

Robinson, William I. 2004. *A Theory of Global Capitalism: Production, Class, and State in a Transnational World*. Baltimore, MD: The Johns Hopkins University Press.

Santos, Bonaventura de Sousa. 2006. *The Rising of the Global Left: The World Social Forum and Beyond*. New York: Zed Books.

Sklar, Holly. 2010. "Wall Street Has Already Voted." *Common Dreams*. October 26, 2010. (http://www.commondreams.org/view/2010/10/26-6).

Smith, Jackie and Marina Karides, et al. 2008. *Global Democracy and the World Social Forums*. Boulder, CO: Paradigm Publishers.

The Washington Post. 2010a. "Monitoring America." (December 20, 2010) (http://projects.washingtonpost.com/top-secret-america/articles/monitoring-america/print/).

The Washington Post. 2010b. "AIG secures $4.3 billion in new credit lines." December 28, 2010: A8.

The Washington Post. 2011."Bankruptcy filings up 9 percent in 2010." January 4, 2011: A9.

U.S. Bureau of Labor Statistics. 2010. "Mass Layoffs Summary." December 22, 2010 (http://www.bls.gov/news.release/mmls.nr0.htm).

U.S. Census Bureau. September 16, 2010. "Income, Poverty and Health Insurance Coverage in the United States: 2009." (http://www.census.gov/newsroom/releases/archives/income_wealth/cb10-144.html).

United States Social Forum. 2010. (http://www.ussf2010.org).

USSF Peoples Movement Assembly. 2010. (http://pma2010.org/national-pma).

USSF Peoples Movement Assembly Working Group. 2010. (http://www.youtube.com/user/AstheSouthGoesTV).

Wallerstein, Immanuel. 2010. "Structural Crises." *New Left Review* 62:133-142.

World Social Forum. 2010. (www.worldsocialforum.org).

Yang, Jia Lynn, Neil Irwin and David Hilzenrath. 2010. "Fed's crisis aid benefited firms beyond Wall St." *The Washington Post*. December 2, 2010. A1, A17.

Zakaria, Fareed. 2010. "How to Restore the American Dream." *Time* (November 1, 2010). Vol. 176, No. 18: 30–35.

Chapter 10

Conclusion:
Beyond the Global Capitalist Crisis

Berch Berberoglu

The authors of the chapters included in this book have gone to great lengths to examine the extent and depth of the global capitalist crisis—a systemic crisis that is permanent and irreversible, notwithstanding the fact that there have been periods of recovery and expansion within the broader framework of overall epochal decline of the global capitalist system. The authors have done an excellent job of explaining the nature, extent, and intensity of the global economic crisis, arguing that this predicament is an inherent characteristic of the system itself, is endemic to it, and cannot be changed within the framework of the capitalist system.

Tracing the evolution of the capitalist economy and the capitalist business cycle historically, it becomes clear that the ups and downs—"booms and busts"—of the capitalist economy is the result of the "normal" process of evolution of the capitalist system, and that economic crises (i.e., recessions and depressions) are a recurrent aspect of capitalism at the national and now the global level. Thus, the crisis-ridden business cycle of capitalism—one that is to be found *only under capitalism*—is the life-blood of the capitalist system in that capitalism cannot grow and prosper without such a "correction" (crisis) in the economy every few years. And this can be seen as part of the process of capitalist expansion and contraction over its life-course.

The current global capitalist crisis that culminated in the Great Recession of 2007–2009 and beyond is just one serious crisis in a series of capitalist crises that have erupted over the past several centuries as capitalism developed and expanded from Europe to North America and elsewhere across the globe over this period. While the reference point for the current global capitalist crisis has been the Great Depression of the 1930s, and rightly so, given its intensity and duration which is continuing to persist beyond its fourth year onto the fifth—despite official proclamations to the contrary—there have been numerous such recessions during the course of the twentieth century that have disrupted the global economy and caused havoc on societies around the world, forcing states and economies into depressions and collapse from which few have been able to recover, as in the case of the decade-long depression in Japan and complete collapse of the East European economies in the aftermath of the transition to a capitalist economy in the 1990s and beyond, as well as massive defaults by states in the less-developed world under the threat of a banking crisis (as it happened in Argentina, Turkey, and elsewhere in the early 2000s). Now, merely a decade after the global economic chaos at the turn of the century, we are faced with massive disruptions and defaults by states through the sovereign debt crisis that has afflicted countries such as Greece, Ireland, Portugal, and others, including Spain, Italy, and several countries further East in Europe's periphery (e.g., Hungary, Ukraine, and other transitional economies).

The crisis that these and other countries have been experiencing under the close watch of the IMF and the World Bank as well as the key states in the E.U. like Germany, is clearly a product of not big-spending social welfare states that are on the verge of bankruptcy—though they certainly are accused of this due to their political character and responsiveness to mass pressures from organized elements within these states, e.g., socialist and communist parties in and out of the government at various times—but the result of their neoliberal capitalist policies that have led to their surrender to foreign capital and the likes of Goldman Sachs and other financial and corporate interests that profit from such crises. Greece is a prime example of this, as is Ireland, Portugal, and others, and the prescriptions provided by the IMF and other imperialist agencies to bail them out of their current predicament is indeed intended to relegate them to further indebtedness and enslavement that transforms them into appendages of the core capitalist states. Ironically, the very same process of neoliberal capitalist globalization that benefits a handful of large corporations and banks is affecting some of the most powerful imperial states, such as the United States—which is a clear sign of the decline and fall of the imperial state that represented the leading force of Western imperialism for so long. The stranglehold of the big banks and financial institutions over the imperial state forced by the very same interests to have a bankrupt state bailing them out of their toxic investments at public expense and forcing the state into further indebtedness to its arch (communist) rival China is another mystery of the workings of the capitalist system that gets resolved as soon as one discovers the divergence of the interests of global capital from that of the nation state (imperial or otherwise) whose responsibilities to its people are eschewed by the powers that be that rule over the global capitalist system—the global capitalist class (albeit still with national, as well as international, characteristics).

The complicated nature of the contemporary imperialist stage of global capitalist expansion in relation to the tasks and responsibilities of the imperial state in guiding the process through a fine line of its national obligations versus its total control by capital to serve capitalist interests through its assigned mission to protect the interests of the capitalist class as a capitalist state forces it to play this dual role, despite its character as an instrument of capital true to its class nature under conditions of global capitalism, or capitalist imperialism. It is this dilemma of the capitalist/imperial state that certainly will be the precipitating factor for the decline and fall of the Empire. Focusing on the leading imperial state today, the United States, its unwarranted military adventures abroad in the most recent period—first Afghanistan, then Iraq, and now Libya—at a time of severe economic crisis that has bankrupted the imperial state, clearly tells us that the adventures undertaken by the imperial state are not in the interests of the people in the Empire itself, but in the interests of the defense contractors and oil companies that profit from these wars while the cost of policing the Empire are borne by the people themselves. This is a sure formula for the enrichment of the biggest and most powerful capitalist corporations and their owners and the impoverishment of the people, while their nation goes to the gutter—a situation that widens the gap in incomes and wealth between capital and labor and relegates the capitalist Empire to the ranks of a third-rate nation destined to collapse.

The dynamics and contradictions of this process of rise and fall of the U.S. Empire and the recurrent crises of the capitalist system in the United States, as well as its global components leading to the crisis of global capitalism have been laid out very clearly and in great detail in this book, as well as the social and political responses provided against this process by those affected by the global capitalist system. Thus, as the current global capitalist crisis is a manifestation of capitalism and capitalist globalization at this stage of the globalization of capital and the capitalist/imperial state, to go beyond the crisis of global capitalism and imperialism we need to address a variety of issues that emanate from the system itself—issues that are directly linked to the very nature of neoliberal capitalist globalization in the age of imperialism. And this raises further questions as to the nature and sources of the changes that are necessary to take us beyond this predicament: who (which social class) shall lead the process of transformation, and in which direction? It is here that we benefit from analyses of capitalist imperialism that not only lay out the process at work that has taken us to the point where we are today, but help us move forward and go beyond the contradictions and crises of this exploitative and oppressive system.

In his *Imperialism: The Highest Stage of Capitalism*, Vladimir Lenin addressed this very question precisely and showed the way forward by identifying not only the source of the crisis (capitalist imperialism), but the class agents that will bring about its final downfall and transformation. Thus he wrote: "Imperialism is the eve of the social revolution of the proletariat ... on a world wide scale" (Lenin [1917] 1975: 640). And Karl Marx and Frederick Engels had similarly eulogized capitalism when they referred to the workers as the "grave diggers" of capitalism and urged them to unite across the world (hence their slogan "Workers of the World, Unite!") to rise up and overthrow the global capitalist system. Clearly, exploited and oppressed under capitalism, the working class is the only class that is destined to lead humanity in transforming society toward a new social order that is devoid of capitalism and capitalist wage-slavery—a society and social order that provides true liberty through collective social expression that is democratic, egalitarian, and socially responsible—an economic, political, and social system that can only be achieved under socialism—i.e., a state and society ruled by the working class in alliance with all other oppressed groups in society. Indeed, this is the way forward, as Walda Katz-Fishman and Jerome Scott contend in their essay, for the true liberation of humanity and end exploitation, oppression, war, and subjugation in all its varied forms, and help shape a future that holds the great promise of equality and prosperity for humanity across the entire global community. And to accomplish this, workers need to take charge of their own destiny by waging concrete political action supported by collective organization and mass mobilization as working people and the labor movement have always done in expressing their will throughout much of modern history, as they are doing today across the globe.

Hence, as once proclaimed by two well-known champions of the working class, Marx and Engels, "the history of all hitherto existing society is the history of class struggles," and such struggles are the engines of social change and transformation that working people have effected through the historic path that they have taken and will continue to take in bringing us to our present situation and move us forward to the future. In the closing lines of an earlier book that I published a few years ago, titled *Globalization of Capital and the Nation-State: Imperialism, Class Struggle, and the State in the Age of Global Capitalism* (Berberoglu 2003: 137), I wrote: "What the future holds for the dominant forces of modern-day conquest and plunder that have imposed their class agenda onto the rest of the world, history and the working classes of the world will ultimately determine" and added "And thus, it is not unreasonable to expect that, like everything else in history, the globalization of capital and the capitalist state may in fact one day be a thing of the past!" And that continues to be the case, but the question still remains: Where do we go from here in order to secure for us—and for future generations—a society and a social order that is beyond global economic crises and serves the interests of all of humanity? The answer to this question will undoubtedly come from those who are most severely affected by the current global capitalist crisis—the global working class, allied with other exploited and oppresses classes and groups around the world—who are conscious of their predicament and are able to organize to take the lead to change the course of history and society which we are bound to witness in the coming period.

Select Bibliography

Abdelal, Rawi. 2009. *Capital Rules: The Construction of Global Finance.* Cambridge, MA: Harvard University Press.

Aldcroft, Derek H. 1993. *The European Economy, 1914–1990*, 3rd ed. London: Routledge.

Amin, Samir. 2003. *Obsolescent Capitalism: Contemporary Politics and Global Disorder.* New York: Zed Books.

Amoroso, Bruno. 2001. *On Globalization: Capitalism in the 21st Century.* New York: St. Martin's.

Batra, Ravi. 1988. *The Great Depression of 1990.* New York: Dell.

——. 2005. *Greenspan's Fraud: How Two Decades of His Policies Have Undermined the Global Economy.* New York: Palgrave Macmillan.

Baylis, John, Steve Smith, and Patricia Owens. 2008. *The Globalization of World Politics*, 4th ed. New York: Oxford University Press.

Bello, Walden. 2005. *Deglobalization: Ideas for a New World Economy.* Revised edition. London: Zed Books.

Bello, Walden, Shea Cunningham, and Bill Rau. 1994. *Dark Victory: The United States, Structural Adjustment, and Global Poverty.* Oakland: California, Institute for Food and Development Policy.

Berberoglu, Berch. 1992. *The Legacy of Empire: Economic Decline and Class Polarization in the United States.* New York: Praeger.

——. (ed.). 2002. *Labor and Capital in the Age of Globalization.* Lanham, MD: Rowman and Littlefield.

——. 2003. *Globalization of Capital and the Nation-State.* Lanham, MD: Rowman and Littlefield.

——. 2005. *Globalization and Change: The Transformation of Global Capitalism.* Lanham, MD: Lexington Books.

——. 2009. *Class and Class Conflict in the Age of Globalization.* Lanham, MD: Lexington Books.

——. (ed.). 2010. *Globalization in the 21st Century.* New York: Palgrave Macmillan.

Bergman, Gregory. 1986. "The 1920s and the 1980s: A Comparison." *Monthly Review*, 38, no. 5 (October).

Blau, Judith and Marina Karides (eds). 2009. *The World and U.S. Social Forums.* Lanham, MD: Rowman & Littlefield Publishers, Inc.

Bluestone, Barry and Bennett Harrison. 1982. *The Deindustrialization of America.* New York: Basic.

Blum, William. 2001. *Rogue State: A Guide to the World's Only Superpower.* London: Zed.

Bonacich, Edna, Lucie Cheng, Norma Chinchilla, Nora Hamilton, and Paul Ong (eds). 1994. *Global Production: The Apparel Industry in the Pacific Rim.* Philadelphia: Temple University Press.

Bottelier, Peter. 2010. "China: Is the Recovery Too Strong?" *International Economic Bulletin* (March).

Braby, Don. 2008. *The Greatest Depression of All Time.* CreateSpace.

Braun, Denny. 1991. *The Rich Get Richer: The Rise of Income Inequality in the United States and the World.* Chicago: Nelson-Hall.

Brecher, Jeremy, Tim Costello, and Brendan Smith. 2000. *Globalization From Below: The Power of Solidarity.* Cambridge, MA: South End.

Brenner, Robert. 2000. *The Economics of Global Turbulence.* London: Verso.

———. 2003. *The Boom and the Bubble: The U.S. in the World Economy.* London: Verso.

Bureau of Economic Analysis (BEA). U.S. Department of Commerce. www.bea.gov.

Burns, John F. 2010. "Thousands in Dublin Protest Irish Austerity Plan." *The New York Times*, November 28: A13.

Campbell, Colin. 2004. *The Coming Oil Crisis.* Brentwood, UK: Multi-Science Publishing Company, Ltd.

Chossudovsky, Michel and Andrew Gavin Marshall. 2010. *The Global Economic Crisis: The Great Depression of the XXI Century.* Global Research Publishers.

Chu, Kathy. 2010. "China Posed to Replace Japan as World's No. 2 Economy." *USA Today.* August 16, 2010. Access at http://www.usatoday.com/money/world/2010-08-16-china-japan-gdp_N.htm on November 2, 2010.

Cohen, Daniel. 2007. *Globalization and Its Enemies.* Cambridge, MA: The MIT Press.

Correa Leite, Jose. 2005. *The World Social Forum: Strategies of Resistance.* Chicago: Haymarket Books.

Danaher, Kevin and Roger Burbach (eds). 2000. *Globalize This! The Battle Against the World Trade Organization and Corporate Rule.* Monroe, ME: Common Courage.

De la Barra, Ximena and Richard A. Dello Buono. 2008. *Latin America After the Neoliberal Debacle.* Lanham, MD: Rowman and Littlefield.

Devine, Jim. 1982. "The Structural Crisis of U.S. Capitalism." *Southwest Economy and Society* 6, no. 1 (Fall).

Dickenson, Torry D. and Robert K. Schaeffer. 2001. *Fast Forward: Work, Gender, and Protest in a Changing World.* Lanham, MD: Rowman and Littlefield.

Duboff, Richard B. 1989. *Accumulation and Power: An Economic History of the United States.* Armonk: M.E. Sharpe.

Duménil, Gérard and Dominique Lévy. 2011. *The Crisis of Neoliberalism.* Cambridge, MA: Harvard University Press.

Eichengreen, Barry. 2008. *Globalizing Capital: A History of the International Monetary System*. Second Edition. Princeton, NJ: Princeton University Press.

——. 2011. *Exorbitant Privilege: The Rise and Fall of the Dollar and the Future of the International Monetary System*. New York: Oxford University Press.

Engdahl, F. William. 2004. *A Century of War: Anglo-American Oil Politics and the New World Order* London: Pluto Press.

Epitropoulos, Mike-Frank. 2010. "Greece as a Demonstration Project: Will the BlackSheep Bite Back? Will the PIIGS? What about US?" *Dollars&Sense*, May/June 2010, pp. 9–11.

Evans, Ben. 2010. "O'Donnell said China Plotting to take over U.S." *The Associated Press* October 4, 2010.

Falk, Richard. 1999. *Predatory Globalization: A Critique*. Malden, MA: Blackwell.

Faux, Geoffrey P. 2006. *The Global Class War*. Hoboken, NJ: Wiley.

Foran, John (ed.). 2002. *The Future of Revolutions: Rethinking Political and Social Change in the Age of Globalization*. London: Zed.

——. 2005. *Taking Power: On the Origins of Third World Revolutions*. Cambridge: Cambridge University Press.

Foster, John Bellamy. 2006. "The Household Debt Bubble." *Monthly Review*, 58(1): 1–11.

Foster, John Bellamy and Fred Magdoff. 2009. *The Great Financial Crisis: Causes and Consequences*. New York: Monthly Review Press.

Friedman, Gerald, Fred Moseley, and Chris Sturr (eds). 2009. *The Economic Crisis Reader*. Boston, MA: Dollars and Sense.

Friedman, Jonathan (ed.). 2002. *Globalization, the State, and Violence*. Lanham, MD: Rowman and Littlefield.

Galbraith, John Kenneth. 1988. *The Great Crash, 1929*. New York: Houghton-Mifflin.

Gavin, Francis J. 2003. *Gold, Dollars, and Power – The Politics of International Monetary Relations, 1958–1971*. Charlotte: The University of North Carolina Press.

Glasner, David. 1997. "Crisis of 1873". In Glasner, David; Cooley, Thomas F., (eds). *Business Cycles and Depressions: An Encyclopedia*. New York: Garland Publishing.

Goldman, Michael. 2005. *Imperial Nature: The World Bank and Struggles for Social Justicein the Age of Globalization.* New Haven, CT: Yale University Press.

Gordon, Greg. 2010. "How Goldman secretly bet on the U.S. housing crash." *McClatchy*. Retrieved December 27, 2010 (http://www.mcclatchydc.com/2009/11/01/77791/how-goldman-secretly-bet-on-the.html).

Gosh, B.N. and Halil M. Guven (eds). 2006. *Globalization and the Third World: A Study of Negative Consequences*. New York: Palgrave Macmillan.

Gowan, Peter. 1999. *The Global Gamble: Washington's Faustian Bid for World Dominance*. New York: Verso.

——. 2010. *A Calculus of Power: Grand Strategy in the Twenty-First Century*. London: Verso.

Guthrie, Doug. 2006. *China and Globalization: The Social, Economic and Political Transformation of Chinese Society.* New York: Routledge.

Halliday, Fred. 2001. *The World at 2000.* New York: St. Martin's Press.

Harman, Chris. 2010. *Zombie Capitalism: Global Crisis and the Relevance of Marx.* Reprint Edition. Chicago: Haymarket Books.

Harris, Jerry. 2003. "Transnational Competition and the End of U.S. Hegemony." *Science and Society* 67, no. 1.

Hart, Jeffrey A. 1992. *Rival Capitalists: International Competitiveness in the United States, Japan, and Western Europe.* Ithaca, NY: Cornell University Press.

Hart-Landsberg, Martin. 2010. "The U.S. Economy and China: Capitalism, Class, and Crisis." *Monthly Review* 61 (#9): 14–31.

Harvey, David. 2003. *The New Imperialism.* New York: Oxford University Press.

——. 2005. *A Brief History of Neoliberalism.* New York: Oxford University Press.

——. 2010a. *The Enigma of Capital and the Crises of Capitalism.* New York: Oxford University Press.

——. 2010b. "Organizing for the Anti-capitalist Transition." *Radical Perspectives on the Crisis.* Aug 30, 2010.

Hedley, R. Alan. 2002. *Running Out of Control: Dilemmas of Globalization.* West Hartford: Kumarian.

Held, David and Anthony McGrew. 2002. *Governing Globalization: Power, Authority and Global Governance.* Cambridge, UK: Polity.

Held, David and Ayse Kaya (eds). 2007. *Global Inequality: Patterns and Explanations.* Cambridge, UK: Polity.

Hertz, Noreena. 2002. *Silent Takeover: Global Capitalism and the Death of Democracy.* New York: The Free Press.

Hook, Glenn D., and Hasegawa Harukiyo (eds). 2001. *Political Economy of Japanese Globalization.* New York: Routledge.

Hooks, Gregory. 1991. *Forging the Military-Industrial Complex. World War II's Battle of the Potomac.* Urbana-Champaign, IL: University of Illinois Press.

Houtart, Francois and Francois Polet (eds). 2001. *The Other Davos Summit: The Globalization of Resistance to the World Economic System.* London: Zed Books.

Hudson, Michael. 2003. *Super Imperialism: The Origin and Fundamentals of U.S. World Dominance.* Rev. ed. Herndon, VA: Pluto.

Hudson, Michael. 2010. "'Drop Dead Economics': The Financial Crisis in Greece and the European Union: The Wealthy Won't Pay Their Taxes, So Labor Must Do So." *GlobalResearch.ca: Center for Research on Globalization.* Retrieved September 18, 2010 (http://www.globalresearch.ca/index.php?context=va&aid=19107).

Hung, Ho-Fung. 2009. "America's Head Servant? The PRC's Dilemma in the Global Crisis." *New Left Review* 60: 5–25.

Hytrek, Gary and Kristine M. Zentgraf. 2008. *America Transformed: Globalization, Inequality and Power.* New York: Oxford University Press.

James, Harold. 2009. *The Creation and Destruction of Value: The Globalization Cycle* Cambridge, MA: Harvard University Press.

James, Harold. 2002. *The End of Globalization: Lessons from the Great Depression.* Cambridge, MA: Harvard University Press.

Jenkins, Holman W., Jr. 2008. "How to Shake Off the Mortgage Mess." *Wall Street Journal.* July 30. http://online.wsj.com/article/SB121737434767195077. html?mod=todays_columnists

Jessen, Corinna. 2010. "Entering a Death Spiral?: Tensions Rise in Greece as Austerity Measures Backfire." *Der Spiegel.* Retrieved September 2, 2010 (http://www.spiegel.de/international/europe/0,1518,712511,00.html).

Klein, Naomi. 2008. *Shock Doctrine: The Rise of Disaster Capitalism.* New York, NY: Metropolitan Books.

Kagarlitsky, Boris. 2000. *The Twilight of Globalization: Property, State, and Capitalism.* Herndon, VA: Pluto.

Katsiaficas, George and Eddie Yuen (eds). 2002. *The Battle of Seattle: Debating Capitalist Globalization and the WTO.* New York: Soft Skull.

Kennedy, Paul. 1987. *The Rise and Fall of the Great Powers.* New York: Random House.

Keynes, John Maynard. 1965. *The General Theory of Employment, Interest, and Money.* New York: Harcourt, Brace, and World.

Klak, Thomas (ed.). 1997. *Globalization and Neoliberalism.* Lanham, MD: Rowman and Littlefield .

Klare, Michael T. 2001. *Resource Wars: The New Landscape of Global Conflict.* New York: Henry Holt and Company.

Kozul-Wright, Richard and Robert Rowthorn (eds). 1998. *Transnational Corporations and the Global Economy.* New York: St. Martins.

Krippner, Greta R. 2011. *Capitalizing on Crisis: The Political Origins of the Rise of Finance.* Cambridge, MA: Harvard University Press.

Krugman, Paul. 2009. *The Return of Depression Economics and the Crisis of 2008.* New York: W.W. Norton and Company.

Kuroda, Haruhiko. 2009 "China's Policy Response to the Global Financial Crisis." *China Development Forum.* March 22, 2010.

Kushlis, Patricia. 2010. "The Greek Financial Crisis through a Political Lens Darkly." *Whirled View.* Retrieved September 10, 2010 (http://whirledview. typepad.com/whirledview/2010/03/the-greek-financial-crisis-through-a-political-lens-darkly.html).

Lechner, Frank J. and John Boli (eds). 2007. *The Globalization Reader.* 3rd ed. Oxford: Wiley-Blackwell.

Lewis, Michael. 2010. "Beware of Greeks Bearing Bonds." *Vanity Fair.* Retrieved October 10, 2010 (http://www.vanityfair.com/business/features/2010/10/greeks-bearing-bonds-201010).

Lenin, V. I. [1917] 1975. *Imperialism: The Highest Stage of Capitalism. Selected Works.* Vol. 1. Moscow: Foreign Languages Publishing House.

Leonhardt, David. 2009. "A Bold Plan Sweeps Away Reagan Ideas." *New York Times,* February 26. www.nytimes.com/2009/02/27/business/economy/27policy.html.

Levitt, Theodore. 1983. "Globalization of Markets." *Harvard Business Review.*

Magdoff, Harry and Paul M. Sweezy. 1981. *The Deepening Crisis of U.S. Capitalism.* New York: Monthly Review.

Magdoff, Fred and Michael Yates. 2009. *The ABCs of the Economic Crisis: What Working People Need to Know.* New York: Monthly Review Press.

Maltase, Michael (ed.). 1999. *Globalization and Its Victims As Seen by Its Victims.* Delhi, India: Vidyajyoti Education and Welfare Society.

Marquand, Robert. 2010. "Crisis in Ireland tests Eurozone Vision of Common Currency, Common Interests." *The Christian Science Monitor*, November 23: 1.

Marx, Karl and Frederick Engels. 1972. "Manifesto of the Communist Party." In K. Marx and F. Engels, *Selected Works*. New York: International Publishers.

Mason, Edward, S. Asher, Robert E. 1973. *The World Bank Since Bretton Woods.* Washington, DC: The Brookings Institution.

Massey, Douglas S. 1996. "The Age of Extremes: Concentrated Affluence and Poverty in the Twenty-First Century," *Demography*, 33 (November).

Mavroudeas, Stavros. 2010. "The Greek External Debt and Imperialist Rivalries: 'One Thief Stealing from Another.'" *MRZine, A Project of the Monthly Review Foundation.* Retrieved December 20, 2010 (http://mrzine.monthlyreview. org/2010/mavroudeas200210.html).

McDonough, Terrence, Michael Reich, and David M. Kotz (eds). 2010. *Contemporary Capitalism and Its Crises.* New York: Cambridge University Press.

McNally, David. 2010. *Global Slump: The Economics and Politics of Crisis and Resistance.* Oakland, CA: P.M. Press.

Melander, Ingrid. 2010. "Greek parliament passes austerity bill." *Reuters.* Retrieved April 23, 2010 (http://in.reuters.com/article/idININdia-46690820100305).

Mitchell, Wesley C. 1951. *What Happens During Business Cycles: A Progress Report.* New York: National Bureau of Economic Research.

Moghadam, Valentine. 1993. *Democratic Reform and the Position of Women in Transitional Economies.* Oxford: Clarendon Press.

Morrison, Wayne M. 2009. "China and the Global Financial Crisis: Implications for the United States." Congressional Research Service: CRS Report for Congress.

National Bureau of Economic Research, available at http://www.nber.org/cycles/ cyclesmain.html.

National Bureau of Economic Research (NBER). 2008. "Determination of the 2007Peak in Economic Activity." Business Cycle Dating Committee. December 11.

Nonini, Donald M. 2008. "Is China becoming NeoLiberal?" *Critique of Anthropology* 28 (2): 145–176.

Odekon, Mehmet (ed.). 2010. *Booms and Busts: An Encyclopedia of Economic History from the First Stock Market Crash of 1792 to the Current Global Economic Crisis*. Armonk, NY: M E Sharpe Reference.

Omadeon Worldpress. 2010. "Max Keiser on the Greek Debt Crisis – Video 1." *Al-Jazeera news segment translation and subtitle (English)*. Retrieved May 5, 2010 (http://www.youtube.com/watch?v=AbH1JsOTInk).

Panitch, Leo and Colin Leys (eds). 2003. *The New Imperial Challenge*. New York: Monthly Review Press.

Panitch, Leo, Greg Albo, and Vivek Chibber (eds). 2010. *The Crisis This Time: Socialist Register 2011*. New York: Monthly Review Press.

Perlo, Victor. 1988. *Super Profits and Crises: Modern U.S. Capitalism*. New York: International.

Perrucci, Robert and Carolyn C. Perrucci. 2007. *The Transformation of Work in the New Economy: Sociological Readings*. Los Angeles: Roxbury.

Petras, James. 2007. *Rulers and Ruled in the U.S. Empire*. Atlanta: Clarity Press.

———. 2009. *Global Depression and Regional Wars*. Atlanta, GA: Clarity Press.

Petras, James and Henry Veltmeyer. 2001. *Globalization Unmasked: Imperialism in the 21st Century*. London: Zed Books.

———. 2003. *System in Crisis: The Dynamics of Free Market Capitalism*. London: Zed Books.

———. 2007. *Multinationals on Trial: Foreign Investment Matters*. London: Ashgate.

———. 2011. *Social Movements in Latin America: Neoliberalism and Popular Resistance*. New York: Palgrave Macmillan.

Phillips, Brian. 1998. *Global Production and Domestic Decay: Plant Closings in the U.S.* New York: Garland.

Pieterse, Jan Nederveen. 2007. *Globalization or Empire?* London: Taylor and Francis.

Polet, Francois (ed.). 2007. *The State of Resistance: Popular Struggles in the Global South*. London: Zed.

Pollin, Robert. 2003. *Contours of Descent: U.S. Economic Fractures and the Landscape of Global Austerity*. London: Verso.

———. 2008. "How to End the Recession." *The Nation* (November 24).

Prasch, Robert E. 2010. "'Disaster Capitalism' Comes to Ireland." *CommonDreams. org.* Retrieved December 3, 2010 (http://www.zcommunications.org/disaster-capitalism-comes-to-ireland-by-robert-e-prasch).

Prashad, Vijay and Teo Ballve (eds). 2006. *Dispatches from Latin America: On the Frontlines Against Neoliberalism*. Boston: South End Press.

Quinn, Ben. 2010a. "Amid Greek debt crisis, Iceland still recovering from its own collapse." *The Christian Science Monitor.* Retrieved September 18, 2010 (http://www.csmonitor.com/World/Europe/2010/0217/Amid-Greek-debt-crisis-Iceland-still-recovering-from-its-own-collapse).

———. 2010b. "Iceland financial crisis: Voters reject debt repayment plan." *The Christian Science Monitor.* Retrieved September 18, 2010 (http://www.

csmonitor.com/World/Europe/2010/0307/Iceland-financial-crisis-Voters-reject-debt-repayment-plan).

Rajan, Raghuram G. 2010. *Fault Lines: How Hidden Fractures Still Threaten the World Economy.* Princeton, NJ: Princeton University Press.

Reifer, Thomas E. (ed.). 2002. *Hegemony, Globalization and Anti-systemic Movements.* Westport, CT: Greenwood.

Ritholtz, Barry and Aaron Task. 2009. *Bailout Nation: How Greed and Easy Money Corrupted Wall Street and Shook the World Economy.* Hoboken, NJ: John Wiley & Sons, Inc.

Robinson, William I. 2004. *A Theory of Global Capitalism: Production, Class, and State in a Transnational World.* Baltimore, MD: The Johns Hopkins University Press.

Rosen, Ellen Israel. 2002. *Making Sweatshops: The Globalization of the U.S. Apparel Industry.* Los Angeles: University of California Press.

Ross, Robert J.S.,1995. "The Theory of Global Capitalism: State Theory and Variants of Capitalism on a World Scale." In *A New World Order? Global Transformations in the Late Twentieth Century* (eds), David Smith and Jozsef Borocz. Westport, CT: Praeger.

Ross, Robert J. S., and Kent C. Trachte. 1990. *Global Capitalism: The New Leviathan.* Albany: SUNY Press.

Roubini, Nouriel and Stephen Mihm. 2010. *Crisis Economics: A Crash Course in the Future of Finance.* New York: Penguin.

Rowbotham, Sheila and Stephanie Linkogle (eds). 2001. *Women Resist Globalization.* London: Zed.

Santos, Bonaventura de Sousa. 2006. *The Rising of the Global Left: The World Social Forum and Beyond.* New York: Zed Books.

Sassen, Saskia. 2009. "Too Big To Save: The End of Financial Capitalism." *Open DemocracyNews Analysis*, April 2.

Schwartz, Nelson. 2009. "Asia's Recovery Highlights China's Ascendance." *The New York Times,* August 23, 2009.

Shambaugh, David. 2009. "Is China ready to be a global power?" *Global Times* (November 11).

Sherman, Howard. 1991. *The Business Cycle: Growth and Crisis Under Capitalism.* Princeton, NJ: Princeton University Press.

——. 2003. "Institutions and the Business Cycle." *Journal of Economic Issues* (3): 621–642.

Sklair, Leslie. 2002. *Globalization: Capitalism and Its Alternatives.* New York: Oxford University Press.

Sklar, Holly. 2010. "Wall Street Has Already Voted." *Common Dreams* (October 26, 2010) (http://www.commondreams.org/view/2010/10/26-6).

Smith, Jackie G. and Hank Johnston (eds). 2002. *Globalization and Resistance: Transnational Dimensions of Social Movements.* New York: Routledge.

Smith, Jackie and Marina Karides, et al. 2008. *Global Democracy and the World Social Forums.* Boulder, CO: Paradigm Publishers.

So, Alvin Y. 2003. "The Making of a Cadre-Capitalist Class in China." In *China's Challenges in the Twenty-First Century,* edited by Joseph Cheng. Hong Kong: City University of Hong Kong Press.

——. 2010. "Globalization and China: From Neoliberal Capitalism to State Developmentalism in East Asia." In *Globalization in the 21st Century*, edited by Berch Berberoglu. New York: Palgrave-Macmillan.

——. 2010a. "Post-Socialist State, Transnational Corporations, and the Battle for Labor Rights in China at the turn of the 21st Century." *Development and Society* 39: 97–118.

——. 2010b. "Globalization and China: From Neoliberal Capitalism to State Developmentalism in East Asia." pp. 133–154 in *Globalization in the 21st Century: Labor, Capital, and the State on a World Scale*, edited by Berch Berberoglu. Palgrave Macmillan.

Stephens, Philip. 2009. "A Summit Success That Reflects a Different Global Landscape." *Financial Times*, April 3, 9.

Stevis, Dimitris and Terry Boswell. 2008. *Globalization and Labor: Democratizing Global Governance.* Lanham, MD: Rowman and Littlefield.

Stiglitz, Joseph E. 2002. *Globalization and Its Discontents*. New York: W. W. Norton.

——. 2010. "A principled Europe would not leave Greece to bleed." *The Guardian*. Retrieved December 11, 2010 (http://www.guardian.co.uk/commentisfree/2010/jan/25/principled-europe-not-let-greece-bleed).

——. 2010. *Freefall: America, Free Markets, and the Sinking of the World Economy*. New York: W.W. Norton and Company.

Sweezy, Paul M. and Harry Magdoff. 1988. "The Stock Market Crash and Its Aftermath," *Monthly Review* 39, no. 10 (March).

Tanzer, Michael. 1974. *The Energy Crisis: World Struggle for Power and Wealth.* New York: Monthly Review.

——. 1991. "Oil and the Gulf Crisis." *Monthly Review* 42, no. 11.

Thomas, Janet. 2000. *The Battle in Seattle: The Story behind the WTO Demonstrations.* Golden, CO: Fulcrum.

Veltmeyer, Henry (ed.). 2008. *New Perspectives on Globalization and Antiglobalization: Prospects for a New World Order?* Burlington, VT: Ashgate.

Wagner, Helmut (ed.). 2000. *Globalization and Unemployment*. New York: Springer.

Wallerstein, Immanuel. 1974. "The Rise and Future Demise of the World Capitalist System." *Comparative Studies in Society and History* 16, no. 4 (September).

——. 2002. "The United States in Decline?" In *Hegemony, Globalization, and Anti-Systemic Movements,* ed. Thomas E. Reifer. Westport, CT: Greenwood.

——. 2003. *The Decline of American Power: The United States in a Chaotic World*. New York: New Press.

——. 2010. "Structural Crises." *New Left Review* 62: 133–142.

Weinberg, Meyer. 2003. *A Short History of American Capitalism*. Chicago: New History Press.

Westbrook, David A. 2010. *Out of Crisis: Rethinking Our Financial Markets.* Boulder, CO: Paradigm Publishers.

Wolff, Richard. 2009. *Capitalism Hits the Fan: The Global Economic Meltdown and What to Do About It.* Olive Branch.

Yao Shujie and Dan Luo. 2010. "Chinese Economy 2009: Leading the World Economy out of Crisis." The University of Nottingham, China Policy Institute, *Briefing Series,* Issue 59.

Yuen, Eddie, George Katsiaficas, and Daniel Burton Rose (eds). 2002. *The Battle of Seattle: The New Challenge to Capitalist Globalization.* New York: Soft Skull.

Index

For Product Safety Concerns and Information please contact our
EU representative GPSR@taylorandfrancis.com Taylor & Francis
Verlag GmbH, Kaufingerstraße 24, 80331 München, Germany